# Public and Private Life of the Soviet People

# PUBLIC AND PRIVATE LIFE OF THE SOVIET PEOPLE

## Changing Values in Post-Stalin Russia

Vladimir Shlapentokh

New York Oxford
OXFORD UNIVERSITY PRESS
1989

Oxford University Press

Oxford New York Toronto
Delhi Bombay Calcutta Madras Karachi
Petaling Jaya Singapore Hong Kong Tokyo
Nairobi Dar es Salaam Cape Town
Melbourne Auckland
and associated companies in
Berlin Ibadan



Published by Oxford University Press, Inc.,
200 Madison Avenue, New York, New York 10016



Library of Congress Cataloging-in-Publication Data
Shlapentokh, Vladimir.
Public and private life of the Soviet people.
Bibliography: p. Includes index.
1. Soviet Union—Social conditions—1970—.
2. Privacy—Soviet Union.
3. Soviet Union—Moral conditions.
4. Quality of life—Soviet Union.
I. Title. HN523.5.S434 1989 306'.0947 87-34962
ISBN 0-19-504266-2

9 8 7 6 5 4 3 2 1
Printed in the United States of America
on acid-free paper

*I dedicate this book to Askold Kantorov, my best Moscow friend, who was in the center of my private and public life in the Soviet Union, to his wife, Victoria, and son, Dmitry, whom I love deeply, and to the memory of his mother, Valentina Ksenofontovna, whom I respected and admired immensely.*

# Acknowledgments

I want to express my gratitude to the Ford Foundation and the National Council for Soviet and East European Studies, who financed my project on Soviet values which helped me collect the material for this book.

I also want to express my gratitude to the Department of Community Health Science at Michigan State University for creating ideal conditions for my work.

My special thanks to my friends—Bernie Finifter, Aron Katsenelinboigen, Vladimir Kontorovich, Bob Solo—as well as to my wife, Luba, and my children, Dimitri and Sasha, with whom I regularly discussed various issues in this book. Thanks also to Ron Anderson for his diligent editing of my attempts to restructure the English language.

I also want to express my gratitude to Susan Rabiner and Valerie Aubry, editors at Oxford University Press, for their kind attitudes toward the manuscript, and to Marion Osmun and Linda Grossman for their numerous and always thoughtful queries which forced me to improve the text.

I also want to use this opportunity to convey my thanks to my Soviet colleagues—brilliant sociologists whom I would still risk, despite the fascinating developments in the Soviet Union, if I named, and to whom I am so obliged for their close cooperation in the 1960s and 1970s.

# Contents

# Public and Private Life of the Soviet People

# Introduction

This work studies the life of Soviet people in the first three decades (1955–85) after Stalin. Although I broadly used publications on Gorbachev's first two years in office, I did not include this period in my analysis. Instead, I describe Soviet society as it appeared by the mid-1980s before the era of Gorbachev's reforms, whose influence on the everyday life of the Soviet people is impossible to measure at this time.

In my opinion, the distinction between the public and private spheres is of crucial importance for understanding Soviet society and for predicting its evolution.

The term "public" is used here without any serious deviation from the dominant tradition (about the definition see, for instance, Benn and Gaus, 1983, pp. 7–11): it designates those activities and institutions that pursue social and national goals.[1]

Public figures are supposed to ensure the well-being of the nation or its segments, to personify social, and not individual, private interests, and in the performance of their role, to be minimally influenced (let us remember the Weberian concept of bureaucracy) by the particular features of their personality.

In Soviet society, which expects everybody to be preoccupied with societal goals, each individual is supposed to be, especially in the workplace, a public figure and to subordinate personal interests to those of the state (Andropov, 1983, p. 244).

Public activity is supposed to be directed or supervised by the bodies which represent society or some major segments of it. Because of this, "public activity" and "public institutions" have to be open to the public or at least to the people or organizations (mass media, for instance) that represent "public interests." Since in modern society the interests of the whole nation are presumably represented by the state, the term "public" is mostly related to the central government and its agencies, to such a degree that the term "official" is often used in the same sense as public. This identification of "public" and "official" is especially true with respect to authoritarian societies like the Soviet Union in which the state controls all major spheres of social life.

I use the term "private" as an antonym to "public" and as a reference to any activity of single individuals or organizations in pursuing goals. This activity is beyond systematic control by outside forces and presupposes both wide initiative on the part of its instigators and their right to communicate and cooperate with only those whom they like.

Since Soviet ideology is deeply hostile to the term "private," official Soviet documents usually operate with such terms as "individual" and "personal property" instead of "private property," and "individual labor activity" instead of "private labor activity" (see, for instance, the Soviet Constitution, *Konstitutsiia*, 1977). At the same time, Soviet people widely use the term "private" in everyday life, as do journalists, writers, and film directors. One of the best movies of the 1980s was Iulii Raizman's *Private Life.*

The modern usage of the term "private" greatly emphasizes inaccessibility to information about developments inside the private sphere (Gavison, 1983). Sometimes it is even used as a synonym of "secrecy." Goffman's ideas about public and private spaces, as well as about front and back regions of contacts (Goffman, 1959, pp. 106–40), focus also on the informational aspect of this paradigm. Psychologists study such issues as public self-image and private self-concept, public and private expectancies, and related questions from the same perspective, often in the framework of interactionism (see Baumeister et al., 1985; Fenigstein et al., 1975; Foddy and Finnigan, 1978; Tunnell, 1984). However "public" and "private" are defined, it is the actual intrusion of the state or other organizations into the activity of groups and individuals that makes the real distinction between these two spheres of activity.

The concept of private autonomy emerged in Western Europe during the Middle Ages in direct connection with the immunity a ruler could bestow on individuals or collectives, exempting cities, for instance, from various state duties and granting them some self-rule.

The concept of the public-private paradigm does not contain a value judgment about the role of either the public or private sector in society, or whether each one's respective role should be expanded or diminished. Such a judgment depends on the value system of a particular individual defining what should be regarded as a "normal" or "pathological" level of privacy or publicness. Whereas the critics of American society see in individualism and privatism one of the main threats to the United States, the majority of Soviet intellectuals are sure that only the increasing role of the private sector can help Soviet society find its way out of stagnation.

Of course, the attitudes toward the role of the public and private sectors in society depends on a constellation of historical circumstances. In some cases people with the same ideological and political orientations can, at different stages in the historical development of their society, praise or condemn the growth (or decline) of the public sector. Even the antagonism between public and private is sometimes relative. For example, some people may be induced by societal influences to engage in a particular activity only privately, under the threat of sanctions if they do not. Thus, the distinction between public and private is not absolute, and the concept of a continuum is more appropriate in the application of this paradigm to social analysis.

Following the Hobbesian or especially the individualistic (in the spirit of J. S. Mill or Benjamin Constant) concept of the state as the protector of the interests of the general society as well as individuals, one can regard even the state as a special private organization (see Berlin, 1964, pp. 126–27). It is also possible, however, to move in the opposite direction, adhering to the Hegelian idea of the state as an executor of a special goal—relgious, social, or patriotic, for example—and to treat an individual as merely a servant of the state and the family as a unit which must implement state tasks. This Stalinist concept of the state has far from disappeared from Soviet ideology. In the past, this idea was supported by extremist Russophiles, using it as an apologia for the monarchy and the messianic role of Russia (see, for instance, Kuzmin, 1985; Melentiev, 1986; Nesterov, 1984).

The two approaches to the public-private paradigm reflect the difference between democratic and nondemocratic societies. The public-private paradigm is very helpful for analyzing the social life in any country. Western authors discuss various aspects related to this paradigm (see, for instance, among the most recent publications, Bellah et al., 1985; Benn and Gaus, 1983; Habermass, 1975; Moor, 1984 and 1985; Rubin, 1983; Sennett, 1977; Slater, 1970; Young, 1978).

The public-private paradigm has special significance for societies with a strong state, because in essence the distinction between both spheres lies in the degree of individual autonomy from government interference.

Broadly, the public-private paradigm postulates society as hierarchically organized, and containing at least four levels, with higher levels controlling lower ones. It is the scope of this control, and consequently the autonomy of each level and its influence on the activity of the higher level, which determines to a very great extent the nature of social and political order.

The individual can be regarded as the lowest level of this hierarchy; primary groups consisting of immediate family members, relatives, friends, neighbors, and lovers can be considered as the second; private, voluntary organizations (secondary groups not controlled by the state) and the human interactions based on them can be considered the third, and the state, with its agencies and apparatus of coercion, as the last level.

The terms "primary group" and "secondary group" are used here according to the existing tradition. A primary group is made up of a small number of people who interact with each other directly in relationships that involve many aspects of their personalities, whereas a secondary group is made up of people who have few emotional ties and who interact in order to achieve specified goals. If primary groups are small, secondary groups can be very large (see Smelser, 1981, p. 109).

If the state is taken as the point of reference it will be possible, albeit difficult, to include all of the first three levels in the private sphere as opposed to the public sphere represented by the government and its institutions.

However, the third level cannot be regarded as private as family or friendship. Privately owned businesses, religious congregations, or political parties have clear public overtones and claim to serve public interests. Genuinely private or voluntary organizations perhaps belong more to the second sphere. But this third level plays an intermediary role between the purely private and purely official domains.

The closeness of this level to the public one is also manifest in the institutionalization of many forms of human interactions. In a state that purportedly represents the whole society, various rules are established for private organizations to follow. But at the same time private activity based on these organizations emerges without state interference, due to the expectations of those involved. An example of this is seen in the Soviet "second (or illegal) economy." To use an Enlightenment term, "civil society" can refer to this third level. Class struggle and civil war are elements of civil society, which explains why the concept of civil society is so popular among scientists with a Marxist orientation.[2]

The concept of civil society as such emerged in the late Middle Ages when people gradually began to release themselves from the grip of absolute monarchy. Later the public-private paradigm became crucial for social philosophers such as Hobbes, Locke, Rousseau, and others.[3] The thinkers of the Enlightenment used these terms in their reflections on the relationship between the absolute monarchy and the individual. The civil society was a domain where the individual was free to pursue his own interests and not to serve goals alien to him. What is more, it is civil society which must delegate its authority to a democratic state, "remaining at the same time an alternate source of power and maintaining its relative autonomy" (Markus, 1982, p. 83). Hegel was among those of this period who in particular devoted much attention to the analysis of the difference between state and civil society (Hegel, 1945, [1821], p. 124). Karl Marx, Max Weber, and Jurgen Habermass took an active part in debates on the relationship between state and civil society, debates which are far from being concluded (see Keane, 1984; Alford and Friedland, 1985).

The degree of privatization in society (Peter Drucker claims to have introduced this term in 1969; Drucker, 1985, p. 145) is one of its most important characteristics and will be used here as a leading indicator of dynamics in democratic and nondemocratic societies.[4] This dynamism is endemic not only to the third level but also to the first and second. With an aggressive state like Stalin's or Mao's, private life in a society can be reduced to almost zero, with family and other small groups almost completely exposed to the regular intervention of state agencies, usually the political police.

To present society in terms of public and private demands the introduction of a dimension attributed by this paradigm to the state—the quality of legality. This attribute reflects the fact that state and society interfere in all forms of private life. Laws and rules attempt to regulate the most intimate human relations, which explains why the borders between public and private are so often relative, and why institutions such as marriage or friendship, and even the most intimate relations between lovers, have not only private but also public aspects (see Jones, 1984; Moor, 1985; see also Elshtain, 1981; Siltanen and Stanworth, 1984).

It is possible for a state to regard the same activity as legal, semilegal, and as completely illegal in different periods, with appropriate consequences for those engaged in behavior frowned upon or castigated by official ideology and law. In fact, human activity at each level can take legal or illegal forms.

Certainly, the definition of what is legal or not is anything but stable, especially in a dynamic society. Post-Stalin Soviet officialdom has experienced significant changes and oscillations in its attitudes toward many forms of human activity. Many deeds that were illegal in the 1950s became tolerable for the authorities in the 1960s, while actions which were severely punished in Breshnev's period were later praised in the era of *glasnost*. Vladimir Voinovich, a famous Soviet satirical writer, in observing the evolution of the official image of "the true Soviet citizen," could even publish a collection of essays with the title, *The Anti-Soviet Soviet Union* (1985).

It is especially interesting to note how much the official position toward many forms of private economic activity has changed in Soviet history, and in some ways the changes have been almost cyclical, as in, for example, the official stance toward private plots in agriculture or to free-lance building teams. The fluid nature of the legal status of many kinds of behavior in the Soviet Union in no way undermines the importance of the legal-illegal dimension because at each moment it has a tremendous impact on human life.

Combining two dimensions—the area of activity and the state attitudes toward concrete behavior—and avoiding for the sake of simplicity various types of semilegal activity, we can single out eight various domains of human life in society. Referring to Table 1, let me describe each sector, mostly with respect to Soviet society. The first one represents the activity of people inside state-controlled organizations which pursue official goals. Ideally, according to Soviet public ideology, the whole Soviet population must work and study in this sphere. I will describe later the normative Soviet perception of the behavior of the ideal as well as the "good" Soviet citizen.

The second sector reflects the legal activity of people beyond their small primary groups. In this sphere people interact with each other in the political process and as producers and consumers of goods and services outside the state.

The activity of citizens in a "civil society" demands, as was mentioned before, the creation of various organizations to satisfy human needs and interests without involving the state. The strength of these organizations in a civil society and their independence from the state determines the degree of influence people have on their government, the scope of the citizens' political freedoms, and the protection people

**Table 1.** The Major Types of Human Activity

| The Sphere and Subject of Human Activity | The Degree of Legality | |
|---|---|---|
| | Legal | Illegal |
| State | First | Fifth |
| Civil society | Second | Sixth |
| Primary groups | Third | Seventh |
| The individual | Fourth | Eighth |

have from state intervention in their private lives. Legal civil society constitutes the fulcrum of political pluralism. Self-government and community activity, insofar as they are close to direct democracy, are also a part of civil society.[5]

Public opinion, strictly speaking, is a phenomenon belonging to civil society, a circumstance which became clear in the Soviet Union in the 1960s when Soviet sociologists started to conduct their first polls. Boris Grushin, in his fundamental book *The World of Opinion and the Opinion of the World*, clearly defined public opinion as the unofficial views held by ordinary people as opposed to the views of the government (Grushin, 1967).

According to Western traditions tracing back to ancient republican Athens and Rome, the good citizen is one who is active in the performance of public duties on a voluntary basis, without special material reward, and as a servant of the people—not the state—is on guard against any encroachment of democratic principles. Of various issues related to the public-private paradigm, the decline of civic culture and civil society in the West is one of the most salient in Western literature, especially in recent decades (Almond and Verba, 1965; Giner, 1985; Janowitz, 1978; Sullivan, 1982; Turkel, 1980).

A Soviet-type society has a very weak legal civil society. Such Soviet organizations as the party, the trade unions, the young Communist League, and others could be regarded as pertaining to civil society, but in fact they are parts of the state apparatus. The same is true of "collectives," the contingents of people working in the same factories or offices or living together in the same blocks. These collectives have been formally assigned the autonomous role of being representatives of workers' interests. However, the state could never relinquish exploiting the collectives as a means of controlling their members.

It is remarkable that official Soviet documents such as the constitution and the program of the party cannot present a logically consistent scheme of the Soviet political structure. On the one hand, the Soviet elite wants to describe Soviet society as democratic, ruled by the people through the elected state bodies (Soviets, i.e., councils), and therefore based on civil society. But on the other hand, the same elite wants to legalize its political monopoly, using "the leading role of the Communist Party" as a label for it. By putting the party over the state (see the introduction and articles 6 and 51 of the Constitution, *Konstitutsiia*, 1977, pp. 3–5, 7, 22) and promising increased participation of the masses in government, the elite actually demonstrates the absence of a legal civil society through which the democratic process can more or less control the state apparatus.[6]

At the same time, the activity of Soviet people who grow vegetables in their private plots and sell them on the free market is a real element in Soviet legal civil society, as is the tutoring of teenagers for entry exams to universities if this activity is officially registered.

The third sector embraces all forms of legal activity in primary groups, especially in the family, a primary group strongly supported by the Soviet state. In the post-Stalin period the state interferes relatively rarely in the choice of partners, the relationships between spouses, family budgeting, entertainment inside the family, and so on.

The fourth sector contains all human activities not controlled either by the state or primary or secondary groups, but at the same time is not at odds with them. In post-Stalinist society the choice of an occupation, place of work, place of residence to some degree, marriage partner, forms of entertainment, as well as the selection of goods and services available in state stores and legal markets are mostly left to the individual.

The term "privacy," unlike "private," which deals more with primary groups, is mostly related to the right of the individual to protect himself not only against the state but even against the primary groups to which he belongs (Wilbur Moor often uses "privacy" in this sense; see Moor, 1984, 1985, as well as I. Altman in his studies of the social environment, 1975).

It is interesting that the notion of privacy is almost unknown to people living in nondemocratic societies, especially in totalitarian, Orwellian ones where the state extends its control over all spheres of human life. The individual, in order not to be suspected of any dissent, has to be "on public" all the time. The exploitation by the socialist state of the traditions of absolute monarchy as well as the idea of collectivism makes the concept of privacy even more alien to the mentality of its subjects. Only with liberalization and a growing standard of living does the notion of privacy begin to penetrate and influence the minds of people living in a socialist society.

So far I have discussed various forms of legal behavior. Now let me address the sectors which describe activities the state regards as conflicting with its interests.

All forms of corruption inside the state apparatus compose the fifth sector. The exploitation of official position for personal interests at the expense of the state is a phenomenon of special importance for an authoritarian society where the state exercises control over all sectors of social life. The actions of people here mean that they try to maximize the utility function—income, privileges, prestige—not through conscientiously serving the state and fulfilling the directives of the political elite, but through the abuse of power against the interests of the state as formulated by its leaders.

Of no less importance is another form of illegal activity inside the state sector—the imitation of real work, the ritualistic fulfillment of duties in economic, political, or cultural domains. The Soviet people have elaborated highly sophisticated procedures to imitate useful activity, deftly using the technology described by Erving Goffman (who had bourgeois society in mind, however) (Goffman, 1959) in order to impress others in everyday life. They are inspired in this activity by the Soviet state, which expends tremendous resources in order to create the "second reality" for domestic and international consumption (for more about this, see Shlapentokh, 1986).

The illegal civil society (or second society) is represented by the sixth sector. This sector comprises all unofficial individual activities in the economic, cultural, educational, political, entertainment, and other spheres. This illegal civil society is the most dynamic part of the larger society, especially in a Soviet-type society with its hostility toward any activity not controlled by the state, paving the way for intermittent periods of almost complete stagnation.

Recognizing the family as a positive institution, the state considers some activities inside it as illegal and punishes those responsible for them. For instance, the Soviet state protects children and women against abuse, sometimes takes measures against adultery, and prohibits the religious education of children as well as other deeds which it is felt can damage their political loyalty to the Soviet system. The Soviet state also persecutes the illegal family business, as well as other activities in culture, education, sex, and so on not approved by the state.

Most individual illegal activity is found in the primary and secondary groups, particularly in politics and the economy. However, there is a large area of illegal activity pertaining strictly to the individual as such. This would include giving bribes, buying illegal goods or services, being a member of a criminal organization or an underground political circle, contacting foreigners, and reading (but not disseminating) underground literature. These examples exclude "ordinary" criminal behavior such as burglary, rape, hooliganism, and others.

Societies differ from each other as well as from themselves at different stages of evolution not only by the degree of autonomy of each level in the hierarchy described above (the morphology of society) but also by the mechanism of interaction between various types of public and private activity (the physiology of society). Of special importance are the ways individuals as well as primary and secondary groups are stimulated to make a contribution to the public good or to implement the goals of the state.

Ultimately, the profile of any society reflects the distribution of human energy, time, and emotion among the various types of activity described above. The ideal Soviet individual, for instance, must concentrate his or her major efforts in the legal public sphere, whereas American society, based on the Protestant ethic, supposes that the legal civil society *is* the main field of human activity.

In the end, any activity performed by the average individual, as the theory of exchange suggests, is for his or her own perceived benefit, material or moral, and only a very small minority of people are moved by altruistic motives, even if the role of this minority in social processes is enormous (about the motivation of people to contribute to the public good, see Cook, 1984; Olson, 1965).

The success of public or private organizations or primary and secondary groups depends on their ability to compel people to regard the achievement of nonindividual goals as beneficial for them. Throughout history humankind has elaborated various methods of incentives, ranging from the fear of physical repression to the pure desire to acquire as many consumer goods as possible. Without an effective system of stimulation, no one type of public or private activity can prosper. Any system of stimulation can be efficient, but only on the condition that the evaluation of human performance is objective in the sense that the evaluation really serves the goals of the state or groups and not the interests of officials who represent organizations.

One of the major concepts of this book is that the decline of the legal public sector is the most prominent process of Soviet society in the post-Stalin period, and this process to a very considerable extent is the result of the failure of the Soviet system to evaluate and reward the performance of its people. The market mechanism, with consumers as the evaluators of the quality of all goods and services, turned out to be—with all its flaws—a much better judge of human performance (Alec Nove is close to this idea; see Nove, 1980). Since the late 1950s the Soviet people have gradually but unswervingly diverted their interests from the state to their primary groups (family, friends, and lovers) and to semilegal and illegal civil society as well as to illegal activity inside the public sector.

More and more people in the Soviet Union have found that diligent and conscientious work for official goals is not rewarded as much as the abuse of their position in public sectors for their personal interests or their activity in the second economy and other spheres of illegal civil society, and it does not provide the rewards of devotion to family, friends, and loved ones. The withdrawal of human energy and emotion from work for the state and the absorption of people in their private interests and the desire to improve their life by illegal means has led to the stagnation of the Soviet economy, the decline of its growth rate, and—what is especially ominous for the Soviet state with its international claims—to the slackening of technological progress and the deterioration of the quality of goods and services.

At the same time, having failed to effectively exploit the energy of its people for its economic goals, the Soviet state, possessing a monopoly on political power and a tremendous apparatus of coercion, has been able to prevent the development of illegal political life (a very important part of civil society) in the country and to elicit from a majority of Soviet citizens the manifestation of political loyalty. Certainly the Soviet people evince this loyalty mostly through ritualistic deeds which have little in common with their real thoughts and feelings. However, this ritualism is itself enough to maintain the current political order.

With the strong deviation of real Soviet life from the official model, the Soviet people have developed a mentality that allows them to ignore public interests and to absorb themselves in private or illegal activity in their workplace while preserving a surface allegiance to the Soviet system. This mentality operates on a mythological level, which helps ordinary people deal with public figures, and on a pragmatic level, which determines their private behavior (about the two-level concept of Soviet mentality, see Shlapentokh, 1985c).

The process I have described can be named as the privatization,[7] or even more properly as the destatization, of Soviet society, a process quite similar to the evolution Western European absolute monarchies underwent in the seventeenth and eighteenth centuries. This process, which increases the role of various activities based on the family as well as of small businesses and the natural nonmoney forms of exchange of goods and services, is somewhat opposed to the process assumed by the advocates of modernization theory, which presupposes a weakening of the family and personal relationships due to technological progress and urbanization (Inkeles and Smith, 1974; Lerner, 1968; about the conflict between the modernization theory and the public-private dichotomy with respect to the Third World, see Tiano, 1984).

The process of privatization is, in my opinion, one of the most important social developments in Soviet society, as well as in China, Poland, and Hungary, since the mid-1950s and comes up as an independent variable with respect to many trends in this society. Certainly this process must be seen in a broader international perspective because some trends in the West as well as in other countries attest to the growing indifference of people toward societal goals, civil society, and civic duties.

The goal of this book is to analyze the changing relationship between public and private spheres in Soviet society and to use this perspective to describe the life of the Soviet people in the post-Stalin period of the 1960s, 1970s, and early 1980s, especially during Brezhnev's regime when privatization spread across society with great rapidity.

Having formulated the major official requirements of the Soviet individual, I will devote the first part of the book to analyzing Soviet behavior in the legal economy and political life, and the second part to activity in the private domains of Soviet society.

I am well aware of the importance of a comparative approach to any significant social issue, especially in the relationship between public and private spheres of human life. The commonality and differences between Soviet society and others were always in mind when any generalization is made in the book. In many cases comparisons of Soviet and other societies are explicitly made. However, aware of the difficulties involved in analyzing Soviet society, where I lived for fifty years, I was cautious about giving a detailed comparative analysis, given the inadequacy of my knowledge about America and other countries. This predicament—the difficulty of knowing two (or more) societies equally well—accounts for the fact that so few scholars have dared to undertake comparative sociological studies which embrace radically different societies.

The study of public and private life in a semiclosed society such as the Soviet Union demands a special methodology regarding sources. Since all Soviet publications are censored by the authorities and quite often contain deliberately distorted information about Soviet life, only the multisource approach can help a researcher avoid blunders in an investigation of Soviet life. Thus the systematic cross checking of data through comparing information from various sources is absolutely necessary for such a study (about the multisource approach, see Campbell and Fiske, 1959; see also Shlapentokh, 1986).

Along with Soviet sociological data (including those which I collected myself in the Soviet Union in dozens of surveys in the 1960s and 1970s), this book made use of the Soviet mass media (including Soviet TV which the author was able to begin watching in his office in 1987), Soviet literature and movies, memoirs, scholarly publications in philosophy and history, as well as various materials published in the West (Western mass media, emigrant periodicals, the memoirs of former Soviet citizens, the Western publications of samizdat, and others).

The supposed audience for each source allows one to assess its validity and reliability. This is of special importance for sources controlled by the state, which exerts an active policy aimed at the creation of a "second reality," i.e., of a reality which must exist in the minds of the people inside and outside the country and which is beneficial to the given political regime.

Soviet scholars, writers, film directors, journalists—the authors of the sources of information on Soviet society—differ greatly from one another in their devotion to truth, as they understand it, and to their conformity to the regime. Even in the 1970s when the pressure of the authorities on Soviet intellectuals was extremely high compared to the liberal 1960s, many authors continued to be honest in their work, whereas many of their colleagues obediently participated in the maintenance of the "second reality" as their superiors wished.

In sociology the distinction between professionals faithful to their vocation and ideologues ready to manipulate figures in order to please the authorities is extremely obvious. For this reason, unless one knows who is who in Soviet sociology, it is quite possible to make many mistakes in using data produced by Soviet social scientists. In the process of analysis, the very different quality of Soviet sociological publications was always taken into account.

The same differentiation holds true with all other Soviet sources. The reputation of a writer or film director is vitally important in a researcher's decision about how to use a novel or a movie to describe Soviet life and trends. Certainly, the political tendency of each author—whether a Westernizer, a nationalist, or an official ideologue—has to be taken into account. Thus the analysis of the validity, reliability, and representativeness of sources plays a considerable role in this book (about the quality of Soviet sociological publications, see Shlapentokh, 1985a and 1987).

With all due respect for nonsurvey sources of information, such as mass media, literature, movies, and so on, valid and reliable quantitative sociological data are still preferable for this project. However, not all parts of the book could be documented with the same amount of survey data. The character of Soviet society accounts for the fact that the chapters about the legal public behavior of Soviet people are much better documented with sociological data than the chapters about private life and especially illegal forms of Soviet behavior. The Soviet authorities encourage studies that attest to the obedient political activity of the people, such as their participation in elections or in official social work. They are relatively tolerant and in some cases even supportive about the studies of labor attitudes in the public sector and legal private life. At the same time, these authorities look with suspicion at the studies of illegal private life and allow little, if any, investigation of illegal civil society and especially of illegal activity inside the state and the party.

Such a position of the Soviet leadership toward the studies of various spheres of Soviet life explains why the first parts of the book are so much better equipped with sociological information, whereas the last parts are based much more on nonsurvey information, anecdotes, and impressionistic data.

Luckily for this project the writing of this book coincided with the first years of the post-Brezhnev era, when censorship was drastically weakened over legal publications. First Andropov and then, to a greater extent, Gorbachev, took the lead in divulging the real state of Soviet society. If this book had been published in the late 1970s or early 1980s when Brezhnev's regime was thriving, its conclusions could have aroused in some Western readers (but not inside the Soviet Union) suspicion of its being influenced by an emigrant's bias and as denigrating the Soviet reality which was presented so radically different in official materials. Now, after the revelations of *glasnost* ("openness") in 1985–87, such an accusation could hardly be possible.

However, despite the benefits of Gorbachev's regime, Soviet sociology in the stormy 1985–87 years was, as is usual in such periods, far behind literature, journalism, and movies in disclosing the truths about Soviet life, which were suppressed by Brezhnev's regime for over two decades (for Soviet sociology in Gorbachev's era, see Shlapentokh, 1987).

# CHAPTER 1

# The Ideal and Good Soviet Individual: The State's Expectations

Any society can reasonably expect certain standards of behavior from its citizens and elaborate such standards. However, in Soviet society, these standards are of special importance. They determine to a very great extent the public life of the Soviet people and to a lesser degree their private life as well.

Whereas the Soviet state tries to implement these standards with all the power at its disposal and considers them of vital importance to its functioning, the people spend a considerable amount of their energy and intelligence skirting many of them. This is quite different from American society, because it is virtually impossible to speak about official rules of behavior and thinking set by U.S. government bodies for its citizens.

The official Soviet standards for behavior are hammered into the brains of the Soviet people by the gigantic ideological apparatus, and through education, the arts, and literature. What is even more significant is that this process serves as the basis for reward and promotion. So, before discussing the everyday life of the Soviet people, it is necessary to be acquainted with the official standards which they face.

## Ideal Standards

The Soviet political elite operates with two types of standards—ideal and practical. The ideal Soviet individual completely identifies himself or herself with Soviet society and the current political regime and always regards social interests as much more important than individual ones. In case of conflict between individual and societal interests, the former are always sacrificed for the latter.

The party program describes the ideal Soviet individual as "the all-round developed, socially active personality which combines spiritual richness, moral purity, and physical perfection" (Programma Kommunisticheskoi Partii, 1986, p. 133). The standards of behavior set for the ideal citizen in all main spheres of Soviet life are:

1. In the economic sphere the individual must "respect work as the main basis of the communist personality, his social prestige" and observe "the collectivist moral" which is "incompatible with egotism, selfishness, and self-interest and combines national, collective and personal interests."
2. In the political sphere the individual must take "an active role in the life of the collective and the country, reject everything that contradicts the socialist style of life and the persistent struggle for communist ideals, follow the prescription of the communist morality as based on collectivism, humanism, and activity, and observe Soviet laws."
3. In the international sphere the individual must be patriotic, ready to defend the motherland, politically vigilant, proud of achieving the first socialist society, capable of evaluating social phenomena from a class point of view, able to demonstrate solidarity with those who struggle against imperialism, and quick to defend the ideas of socialism.
4. In the private sphere the individual must observe the communist morality, based on the moral values of all humankind, and the rules of behavior which emerged in the process of the struggle for socialism. It means that a person (a) must lend active support to the family as the agent responsible for "the health and education of new generations" as well as the place "where the character of the individual with his or her attitudes toward work, moral, ideological, and cultural values is molded"; (b) must assert "genuine human relations among people; comradeship, friendliness, honesty, and modesty in personal and social life"; and (c) "must follow high culture in the communication between different ethnic groups and nations, and be intolerant toward nationalism and chauvinism" (Programma Kommunisticheskoi Partii, 1986, pp. 125, 134).

After defining behavior for the Soviet individual in these four spheres, the Soviet political elite also wants to shape the mind of the individual according to the interest of the state. The ideal individual must master Marxist-Leninist teachings, systematically improve his political culture, and be an atheist. It is supposed that this individual sincerely supports the party policy, participates in its implementation, and being an optimist believes in the "radiant future" (Programma Kommunisticheskoi Partii, 1986, p. 133).

Official ideology in no way considers this ideal as achievable only in the distant future; the essential element of public Soviet ideology is that it considers this image as almost completely realized in the average citizen. Soviet leaders themselves are inclined, especially after the first years of their regime, to portray the majority of the people as following the model established for them. Brezhnev was especially renowned for his bombastic encomiums on the honor of the Soviet individual. Evaluating the results of the tenth five-year plan (1976–80), a period later denounced by Andropov and Gorbachev as one of stagnation, Brezhnev said, "Soviet people worked well as shock workers. Closely attached to the party of Lenin, considering its prescriptions as their personal business, the toilers in cities and villages did not spare their efforts for the increase of the economic potential of the motherland" (Brezhnev, 1981, p. 44; see also Brezhnev, 1976, pp. 46–47).

Soviet leaders, one after another, have demanded that writers portray this official image in their characters, following the requirements of socialist realism, and present the Soviet citizen positively in novels, plays, and movies (see, for instance, Brezhnev's exhortations on this subject, Brezhnev, 1981, pp. 83–84).

All Soviet textbooks portray the average Soviet individual as already close to the ideal, with a possible exception being made for the "all-round developed personality," which most feel will be realized in the future (see, for instance, Fedoseev, 1985, pp. 389–91; Klementiev, 1984, p. 28; Pazenok, 1983; Rumiantsev, 1983). Only a few authors (see, for instance, Dontsov, 1984; Kon, 1983, p. 193; Krutova, 1985) write about the average Soviet individual as in the process of approaching the model described by Soviet ideology.

## Real Image of the Soviet Individual

However, when Soviet leaders leave the terrain of ideology and propaganda and engage in the solution of practical problems, they forget about the ideal model of the Soviet individual and often describe him in realistic terms, especially in the first years of a new regime when it is possible to shift the responsibility for various flaws in the country to the predecessor.

In this connection the speeches of Andropov and Gorbachev in the first period of their rule are especially noteworthy. Both of them, when they spoke about the economy, portrayed Soviet workers in highly unflattering terms. They accused the Soviet people of absenteeism, botching, pilfering, alcoholism, lying, and many other flaws (Andropov, 1983, pp. 212, 225, 234–35; Gorbachev, 1986). This gloomy image appears in all decrees which were adopted by Gorbachev, particularly on alcoholism and underground income (see *Pravda*, May 17, 1985; *Pravda*, May 28, 1986).

In referring to Gorbachev's critical report to the Central Committee in April 1985, Vadim Semenov, the editor-in-chief of the prestigious philosophical journal *Questions of Philosophy*, describes his image of the Soviet people, one which was undoubtedly endorsed by the censors from the Central Committee:

> A certain portion of the people, including the young, seriously deviate from the principles and moral norms [of socialist society] and are involved in behavior which has been termed "negative phenomena." The significant fractures, the reorientation of values, and consequently of behavior, have taken place for various reasons in the spiritual life of a certain part of the population, with the ensuing retreat from social collectivist ideals and interests and with a concentration on only individualistic, egotistic inclinations. The life based on high spiritual values is being replaced by the hunt for consumer goods and for wealth, and the principles of decency, conscience, nobility, and honesty with egotism, cynicism, and often cruelty. Such a lack of ideals, the spiritual devastation of a part of the people entails an increase in drunkenness, while the spiritual flaws endanger the physical health of many people, which forces us to consider the spiritual and physical health of the nation to be a very serious problem. (Semenov, V., 1985, p. 33)

The same issue of *Question of Philosophy* contains another article, "The Problems of Communist Education and the Development of the Personality of the Present Time," which summarizes a discussion on moral issues. The discussion participants, particularly M. Piskotin, the editor of *Soviet State and Law*, provided a gloomy picture of the Soviet people (*Voprosy Filosofii*, 1985, No. 5, pp. 60–77).

While it is possible to gain some understanding of the images of the Soviet population held by the leadership through various written materials and public speeches, we can also glean some sense of this through the behavior of the authorities toward the people. Restrictions on travel abroad are important in this respect. If the leadership considered the Soviet population to be as devoted to the motherland as ideological publications suggest, it is unlikely that the restrictions on travel abroad would be so extensive. In fact, there exists an enormous apparatus designed to check the political loyalty of those applying to travel outside the country, and only a minority are apparently considered sufficiently trustworthy to be allowed to visit other countries.

During the honeymoon period of *glasnost*, some Soviet newspapers even dared to unearth the once taboo question of restrictions on travel abroad. They demanded the abrogation of the humiliating procedures inflicted on anyone wanting to go abroad, especially to the West, and the no less insulting rules requiring that Soviet citizens in foreign countries go everywhere only in groups (see *Moskovskiie Novosti*, July 12, 1987; *Literaturnaia Gazeta*, August 26, 1987; *Sovietskaia Kul'tura*, October 13, 1987).

Emigration and defections began almost immediately after the 1917 Revolution, and those who left included not only members of the old dominant class, but many from other strata of the population, especially intellectuals. During World War II, Stalin obtained evidence to justify his suspicion about the loyalty of the people; millions used the vicissitudes of the war to leave the Soviet Union. Certainly these included some who had cooperated with the Nazis and therefore feared punishment. But there were many others who found themselves outside the reach of the state and took the opportunity to leave (Inkeles and Bauer, 1968).

During the liberalization of the 1960s with increased contact with the West, the number of defections rose again, as the leadership had predicted would happen with more Western contact. The 1970s and early 1980s saw more cases of defection of both ordinary and prominent people, including successful writers, artists, dancers, and musicians.

Jewish emigration, which the regime consented to in the 1970s, provided further evidence for the leadership that not all citizens were patriotic, even if official propaganda continued to assert the opposite. While the emigration of Jews may be explained by anti-Semitism, this does not account for the departure of so many other Russians as well as those belonging to other ethnic groups. The experience of other socialist countries with emigration is similar.

The ideal Soviet citizen belongs, of course, to mythology, and is used by the elite only for ideological purposes. In fact, the Soviet leaders hold quite a realistic image of the Soviet individual.

## The Good Soviet Citizen

Soviet leaders, having a rather gloomy perception of the average Soviet individual, are far from capitulation, however. Having a monopoly of power, commanding the gigantic apparatuses of coercion and ideology, being the main distributor of wealth and prestige, the Soviet state is able to strongly influence the behavior, and to some degree even the mentality, of its people.

At the same time, with the sober image of the real Soviet individual and not desiring to use mass repressions, the political elite knows the limit of the demands it can make even with those who are most devoted to the actual system. These people, who make up a minority, are regarded by the Soviet state as the realistic model for the masses. Unlike the mythical ideal, which is used for its propaganda value, "the good or genuine Soviet individual" (the terms "genuine" and "authentic" are widely used in the Soviet mass media when it lauds Soviet persons for positive deeds) is considered by the political elite as a realistic model for the rest of the population.

The major distinction between the ideal and good Soviet citizen lies in the role of individual interests. The Soviet state now recognizes that there must be some reconciliation between the personal interests of the individual and the interests of society. The good Soviet citizen who yearns for material comfort and prestige achieves these goals through conscientious work for the state and not through semilegal or illegal activities. Although not expecting a high degree of personal sacrifice from this citizen in normal times, the leadership does expect that official ideology and the current goals of the state will exert some influence on behavior.

The Soviet state has elaborated detailed requirements for behavior which the good Soviet citizen must meet.

## The Standards in Economic Behavior

In the early 1930s Stalin devised a system to stimulate work that consisted of two elements—ideology and fear of sanctions as a primary motivation and material incentive as a secondary influence (see *Bol'shaia Sovietskaia Entsiklopediia*, 1947, vol. 40, p. 787; vol. 55, pp. 76, 78). After 1953 the system of stimulation changed significantly, mostly because the noneconomic sanctions for the violation of labor discipline, such as publicly condemning certain workers for mistakes or inefficiency, were virtually removed from the arsenal of means used by the elite to achieve their economic goals.

Having emphasized material incentives, however, the post-Stalin leaders could not remove ideology and, to some degree, fear (mostly for people holding high positions) as important factors in the system of stimulation. These two elements must be used when the material stimulus does not work, which happens often in the Soviet economy with its rigid system of prices and salaries as well as the stifling of private initiative. The role of ideology in invoking patriotic duty is especially useful in calling for more and better work performance in those occupations where it is difficult to assess the quality of results, as well as in encouraging people to choose an occupation or residence, since Soviet people are relatively free to do what they want in this regard (about the role of ideological factors as stimuli of economic behavior, see Gvozdev's *Stimuli of Socialist Economy*, 1985, pp. 35–37). The ideological factor, coupled with moral considerations and the fear of criminal prosecution, is regarded by the elite as a major impediment to pilfering and the abuse of power for personal enrichment.

## *Productivity of Work: Discipline and Quality*

Without expecting average individuals to regard their work primarily as a patriotic duty—this is left for propaganda—the Soviet political elite wants them to be conscientious workers for the sake of a good reputation and on moral grounds. Workers are supposed to be strongly interested in material rewards, but at the same time it is assumed that they will not exploit every chance to be idle or to use work time for their personal needs (without even discussing drinking on the job). It is presumed that the average worker has professional pride and is concerned with the quality of his work. The worker should also be responsive to various forms of moral rewards such as commendation for his or her success in socialist emulation, i.e., official competition among workers in making high achievements in their work. In cases where personal interests and the interests of the enterprise are in conflict, the worker should be ready to sacrifice personal interests. Again, patriotism is a factor in productivity. The state expects workers to think about their jobs as an activity important for the country. In cases of conflict between local and national interests the workers will always try to secure the interest of the whole society.

## *The Choice of Occupation and Location of Job and Residence*

Considering their exhortations about patriotic duty when deciding about a job and residence as pure ideological exercises, the political elite realizes that people actually make these decisions based on material incentives (wages, housing, quality of services, climate, and so on) as well as on prestige. But the state still expects that the interests of society should have some influence on the choices people make in the economic sphere. Four issues are of special importance for the Soviet economy: (1) the readiness of young people to become workers, especially in industry and agriculture; (2) their willingness to work in nonprestigious and poorly paid branches of the economy; (3) their determination to stay at the same job location and not move to another even if it provides better material conditions; and (4) their readiness to relocate permanently to the eastern and northern parts of the Soviet Union. It is supposed that people will respond to the special appeals of the leadership to go to construction areas of national importance or to take part in emergency and even dangerous work, such as that related to the Chernobyl accident.

## *The Preservation of Socialist Property*

Soviet people, as any other, deal each day at their place of work with things of great material value—equipment, raw materials, and parts or finished products. The leadership again relegates to mythology the assertions that people have to treat these state assets as their personal goods. However, they assume that social instincts, the understanding of the importance of public wealth for the well-being of everyone, can persuade workers to consider themselves, if only partially, as the masters of their enterprises and offices. The political elite also relies on elementary moral feelings, as well as shame, if a person is accused of wasting resources or, even more, of being a thief.

## *Allegiance to the Collective*

The professional life of the Soviet people is closely connected with the so-called collective—a contingent of colleagues in industry, offices, or the university. Soviet ideology regards devotion to the collective in which the individual works as one of the major virtues in Soviet society. The praise of collectivism in Soviet propaganda is second only to the commendation of allegiance to the country.

The political leadership regards collectivism not only as an ideal, but also as a highly pragmatic means to control the individual and to induce him or her to submit personal interests to the interest of the state. Collectivism thus plays an important role in Soviet civil society. For example, the good Soviet individual is supposed to be ready, for the sake of the collective, to work long hours or on weekends if necessary, or to move from an efficient production unit to another which needs help, even if this incurs a loss of income. The same individual must attentively watch the behavior of the members of the collective and react immediately to any violation of morals or laws in public as well as in private life. A good member of the collective is active in all "self-management" bodies and takes an active part in various meetings, including those which are devoted to personal issues, and will participate in publicly criticizing "wrong" people.

## *Political Standards*

Although behavior in the work sphere is critical to the regime, political behavior is much more important to the ruling elite. If the state does not regard the conflict between society and the individual in the economic domain as very dramatic, the same conflict in the realm of politics is considered quite differently by the authorities, and its solution in favor of the state is, in their eyes, the only option for a genuine Soviet individual. The good Soviet citizen must volunteer for any political enterprise undertaken by the state and must be ready in extreme cases even to die fulfilling his or her assignments (see Akhlibininskii and Surin, 1980; Bikkenin, 1983; Bueiva, 1983; Titarenko, 1980).

As a matter of fact, the KGB actively operates with such a model of behavior in assessing the political loyalty of citizens. KGB members try to persuade individuals to become informers, and if they refuse, put the same sacramental question to them—are they a "genuine Soviet individual or not" (see Ashkenazy, 1985; Golyakhovsky, 1984; Voinovich, 1985). Even in prisons and camps political police, using the same terminology, force inmates to cooperate with them (see Plushch, 1979; Vail, 1980).

### PARTICIPATION IN GOVERNMENT

The legitimization of the existing political order is one of the primary tasks of the political elite and the first goal of ideological work. Since the Revolution this elite has tried to persuade the Soviet population as well as international public opinion that Soviet society operates on a democratic basis and that enterprises are controlled by workers. The Soviet leadership expends a lot of effort on activities to buttress this view, which is in direct conflict with the evidently authoritarian and deeply antidemocratic nature of the Soviet political order. Therefore they expect from the good Soviet citizen active participation in all undertakings which claim to bear out the democratic nature of the Soviet system. It means that the Soviet individual must take part in all phony elections, local and national (which occur once every one or two years), as well as in the ritualistic campaign which usually precedes each election. The good citizen should also be politically active and work toward getting elected to one of the governmental bodies. He or she must participate enthusiastically in various public discussions about the projects advanced by the government, respond to the questions of officially sponsored polls, and react with letters to the editor concerning issues in the Soviet mass media.

### THE NECESSITY TO STAY OUT OF CONTACT WITH POLITICALLY DUBIOUS ACTIVITIES AND PEOPLE

In order to demonstrate support for the current official policy, the good Soviet individual not only refuses any contact with dissidents, but even with liberal elements, as well as with any activity not completely endorsed by the administration. So a good Soviet citizen must not attend any unofficial exhibition, a private concert, or unofficial seminars and parties, even if their subject is politically innocuous, such as theoretical physics.

For the same reason, the good Soviet individual is not connected to and does not attend any church or synagogue and would never mark any event in his or her family by religious ceremonials, even the birth of a child or death of a parent.

Good Soviet individuals would not have among their close friends and visitors those who engage in illicit political activity, would not marry a person with a bad political reputation, and would do everything possible to prevent the marriage of a child to such a person. The good Soviet man or woman would not commend novels or movies which have been criticized in the mass media for their ideological errors or even display public interest in books regarded askance by the regime, even if these novels or films for some reason (perhaps pressure from some members of the political elite, or international considerations) were given the state's permission to reach the public. This means that in the late 1950s Dudintsev's *Not Only Bread Alone*, the first post-Stalin novel (now a classic in Soviet literature) to offer a scathing attack against Soviet bureaucracy, received no praise. In the early 1960s the good citizen would refrain from public applause for Soviet poet Yevgeny Evtushenko, who was regularly spurned at that time by the authorities but is now regarded as a leading poet. Of course, the good citizen would not be among public admirers of Solzhenitsyn when his stories began to be deprecated in the Soviet press.

What is more, he or she would not express interest in novels or movies that have received acclaim from liberals or the West. In the 1960s he or she would not even subscribe to *Novy Mir* ("New World"), a magazine which regularly featured liberal novels and articles. (At that time, this magazine was banned from army libraries.)[1]

### MEMBERSHIP IN OFFICIAL ORGANIZATIONS

Good Soviet citizens are members of various official organizations. During youth, they are expected to join the Young Communist League (Komsomol) and then in the early twenties become a member of the Communist Party. Even if for some reason, such as a policy of recruiting party members from workers instead of from professional ranks, it becomes difficult to join the party at a given moment, good citizens should demonstrate their wish to be in the party.

Besides Komsomol, the party and of course, the trade union, the good citizen belongs to other official organizations, such as DOSAAF (a paramilitary organization) or the Society of Sobriety.[2]

### PARTICIPATION IN SOCIAL ACTIVITY

The good Soviet individual takes part in any social activity sponsored and organized by the party and the state. This involves attending meetings convened by Soviet organizations, the party, trade unions, Komsomol, plant managers, the office, and so on. Not only is attendance desirable but active support should be voiced at these functions of official views. During the meeting those who express views which, in one way or another, are directed against the policy adopted by superiors, should be rebuffed. In party or trade union committee elections, the good Soviet individual should support resolutions and people endorsed by superiors. Even if one has doubts about something proposed by a superior, it is expedient to back the official stance and express reservations to the superior later, so as not to endanger the authority and prestige of superiors and official policy.

The good Soviet citizen has permanent political assignments, which he or she is expected to carry out conscientiously and enthusiastically. The model individual is usually a member of various governing bodies, from the enterprise (or shop) trade union committee up to the regional party committee. Besides this, a person may have the additional political duty to act as a "volunteer" agitator during election campaigns, assist the police in the maintenance of order in a village or city, and a multitude of other tasks.

#### COOPERATION WITH THE KGB

But the peak of political loyalty is reached when the individual agrees—without much pressure and even with some joy—to collaborate with the KGB as an informer or in other capacities (as an expert, for instance).

This cooperation with the political police means that the Soviet citizen has crossed the most important political border, much more important than joining the party, and has linked himself or herself with the fate of the Soviet system.

Once one is a secret employee of the KGB, the only way open to engage in opposition movements is in the capacity of an agent provocateur. It is necessary to conceal cooperation with this organization for two reasons—the KGB demands it and this activity remains ignoble in the eyes of a majority of Soviet people. It also engenders fear among acquaintances and colleagues, as they know that the recruited individual is open to any manipulation on the part of the political police and the party.

### *Standards for International Behavior*

The behavior of the Soviet people with respect to foreign countries is second in importance only to internal political behavior, and in fact is part of it, because the opposition of the Soviet system to Western society is the cardinal element of Soviet ideology and serves especially as a legitimation of the political order.

### PATRIOTISM AS A LEADING VALUE

As important as patriotism is in judging people's behavior in the workplace, it is even more important in judging them with respect to foreign policy. As with all countries, the leadership in the Soviet Union expects the average Soviet individual to sacrifice everything for the defense of the motherland. Volunteering for a war conducted by the Soviet state (including the war in Afghanistan) would be only slightly above the standard for the good Soviet citizen.

It is assumed that the Soviet people will hate enemies of the state. "Imperialist" is the code word for any adversary of the political leadership. This hatred is especially cultivated in works addressed to the youth and the army (Sobolev, 1984; see also Kon, 1983, pp. 210–11).

### REJECTION OF THE WEST IN PUBLIC BEHAVIOR

The good Soviet individual takes a hostile public stand toward the West, its policy, ideology, and style of life, and rejects Western views on the Soviet Union and other socialist countries. If someone did listen to Western radio or have access to other sources of Western information, they would certainly never speak of it to friends and colleagues. As Yuri Zhukov, a leading Soviet journalist, said during his appearance on Soviet TV in the early 1980s, "a decent Soviet person does not denigrate himself by listening to all these voices."

A Soviet citizen should not display any special interest in Western movies, exhibitions, or cultural events. A citizen should reveal no desire to make contact with Western tourists or businesspeople, and if contact is made, it should be at the request of the authorities and always in the presence of other Soviet people. Of course, it is out of the question to invite Western people to one's home unless it is suggested by those responsible for the foreigners.

Upon returning from a trip to the West, the good Soviet citizen brings back only negative perceptions of Western lifestyle. During such a trip the citizen never tries to separate from his (or her) Soviet colleagues in order to initiate individual contacts with Westerners or goes to places not officially recommended.

The good Soviet individual is supposed to condemn publicly those who want to emigrate as traitors and would in no way maintain any relationship with such people. Contacts with friends cease as soon as it is learned about their decision to apply for an exit visa. Not even attendance at a farewell party or accompanying departing friends to an airport would be acceptable. All correspondence with emigrants, even close relatives, is excluded from permissible behavior, although real sanctions against it were relatively rare in the 1970s.

As the good Soviet citizen should promote a positive image of the society, he or she would never draw the attention of foreigners to deficiencies in Soviet life and would always find ways, as a true patriot, to explain the nature of flaws in the Soviet lifestyle which foreigners may come across.[3]

#### THE PRESERVATION OF SECRETS

Another highly valued feature of the good citizen is discretion, so that no state or party secrets are communicated to others. One is extremely reserved in contacts with foreigners, whether they take place abroad or within the country, so as to minimize the amount of information given to them.

## *Standards in Ideology*

Soviet public ideology is as aggressive about the control over human mentality as it was in the first decades after the Revolution, and it still insists that the average Soviet individual should perceive the world through its glasses. But after 1953 the leadership, for reasons of practicality, softened its requirements regarding human emotions and thoughts.

Of course, Soviet leaders would be delighted with the individual who can sincerely change his or her mind with each new regime and new turn in politics. But since Stalin's time they have given up the hope of having as a practical model a Soviet individual who follows commands not only in deeds but also in thoughts. Today the Soviet elite, realistically assessing its potential to control the mentality of even its best citizens, does not make many demands in this area.

Thus the speech of Boris El'tsin, the first Moscow Party Secretary, at the twenty-seventh party congress (1986) is interesting. After lashing out against the Brezhnev regime—under which he played a significant role and was among the speakers at the previous Brezhnev congress—he included a rhetorical question in his speech: Why did he not speak out on all these flaws at the twenty-sixth party congress? Answering his own question, he bluntly said that he was scared and did not have enough political experience (*Pravda*, February 27, 1986).

Since the late 1950s, the state has become more tolerant of the dual thinking not only among the ordinary people but among apparatchiks and even, as we see in El'tsin's case, among the highest officials. Though no longer attempting to control intimate thoughts, the political elite still strives to control the political behavior of the Soviet people.

### PUBLIC SUPPORT OF CURRENT OFFICIAL POLICY

Of course, good Soviet citizens, whatever their personal feelings, always support current state policy. This quality is revealed especially well during such political junctures where the political elite significantly changes its domestic or foreign policy and new slogans are in brazen contradiction with previous ones. A Soviet joke from Stalin's time very well formulates this demand of the Soviet authorities from their citizens. Answering a question on his political views, the hero of the anecdote said: "Oscillate with the general line of the party."

Thus Khrushchev's regime expected that the Soviet public would easily move from the cult of Stalin to his denigration. With Tito, however, Khrushchev had to do the opposite. After denouncing the Yugoslav leader as an agent of American imperialism and a collaborator with Hitler, he then had to exalt Tito as the president of a socialist country.

The Brezhnev leadership, in its turn, supposed that Soviets would accept the policy of détente with the same ease as they did the previous policy of confrontation with the United States and West Germany. Brezhnev also assumed that the Soviet citizenry would easily move from a hostile position against a privately owned plot of land in a farming collective to a positive one, considering it an important part of the Soviet economy.

In the same way, the Gorbachev team believed that the average Soviet would be able to switch from feeling that the Brezhnev period had been the time of greatest successes to blaming it for the country's technological and economic retardation. Gorbachev also expected popular support for centralized planning to shift to support of more industrial autonomy and even private initiative.

Emotional involvement is expected from the good citizen mostly in the case of confrontation with the West, as in the case of the Korean jetliner incident in 1983 or the Chernobyl nuclear plant accident in

1986. In the second case, the withholding of information was definitely damaging to the health of residents of the areas close to the nuclear plant. But people were expected to take sincerely the official versions of what had happened without speaking of it (see *Der Spiegel*, 1986 #22, pp. 125–27; *Pravda*, June 5, 6, 12, 1980; *Sovietskaia Kultura*, June 17, 1986, p. 6).

The good Soviet citizen must accept the major ideological postulates which legitimize the Soviet system. This includes belief in the superiority of socialism over capitalism, the advantages of a planned system and collectivized property over a market economy and private property, and the superiority of the Soviet lifestyle over its Western counterpart, accepting the images of the West as they appear in Soviet mass media.

At the same time the elite today does not require that the Soviet individual sincerely believe in many other postulates of the Soviet ideology, such as the leading role of the working class, in socialist democracy, or in the wisdom of each new leader and his policy, but any doubts should not be manifested in public behavior. Although a number of dogmas have been excluded as part of an obligatory menu for the conscience of the ideal Soviet citizen, the political elite continues to preserve all of them in the ideological arsenal, even if sometimes in less rigid forms, and expends significant effort disseminating them. This is done mostly because these postulates legitimize its power, and whatever their plausibility, symbolize the determination of the leadership to maintain the political status quo.

This dual attitude relieves people from the necessity of displaying loyalty to such outmoded ideas as the leading role of the working class or of internationalism as the basis of Soviet foreign policy before family and friends; however, they must demonstrate respect for them in public. Of course, the political elite continues to speak about the importance of all these dogmas, but mostly as code words signifying their determination to keep their power intact.

## *Moral Standards for Private Life*

The standards set by the ruling elite for private life overlap significantly with political requirements. However, in many respects the public statements disguise the real expectations of the authorities in this domain.

### FAMILY

There is no doubt that the political elite genuinely supports the family as an important social institution and demands that the good Soviet citizen also be a good family member. Here there is no divergence between public ideology and pragmatic requirements, such as raising the birthrate. The state is quite open in its concern for encouraging more people to have children—especially the Russians and other Slavs whose share in the Soviet population is rapidly declining in favor of Muslims—and is trying to reduce instances of divorce, family instability, and singles who do not want to marry.

The state views the family as the guardian of children's welfare and as responsible for instilling in them behavior acceptable to the existing social norms. The broken family is seen, logically, as a factor in juvenile delinquency.

However, this warm view of family life obscures more subtle political duties of the family. It is assumed that a good citizen will monitor the political conscience of family members, especially that of children. A person strongly attached to his or her family will be much less prone than a loner to engage in activities not endorsed by the state. Family, for instance, was among those reasons most often cited by the Soviet intellectuals who did not want to join the liberal movement in the 1960s, or by those in the 1970s who explained their collaboration with authorities, including their participation in persecuting colleagues and friends.

A strong family drastically diminishes the chances of defection during trips to the West or the possibility of someone working with the West in other ways, including being recruited for the intelligence service. Bylenko, the Soviet pilot who defected to the West in 1975 with his MiG, a new model of military plane, had many troubles with his family (see Barron, 1982), as have had a number of other defectors.

Besides political and demographic reasons, there are economic reasons why the state strongly supports good family ties. Devotion to the family is supposed to make someone be a diligent worker, try to earn more and get promoted, as well as avoid drunkenness or something more criminal.[4]

### HUMANISTIC VALUES

The current Soviet regime is not as openly hostile toward so-called universal, humanistic values as were the Soviet regimes up to the middle of the 1950s. Kindness, for instance, is mentioned, among other qualities, in the decree on the reform of secondary education adopted by the Soviet government in 1984 (Strizhov, 1984, p. 48). In *The Dictionary on Ethics* (1983) edited by Igor Kon, as well as in other Soviet publications (see, for instance, Zhuravkov, 1974), such qualities as altruism, tolerance, shame, and sincerity were mentioned positively, even if with serious reservations (about this trend in Soviet ideology, see Shlapentokh, 1982; 1984; 1986). But in spite of these new trends Soviet authorities still do not include many humanistic values in the norms for Soviet people, and the recent publications with guidelines for teachers and professors on how to educate almost ignore these values (see, for instance, Lebidinskii and Mal'kovskaia, 1984; Volkov and Novotnyi, 1984). The reference book, *Communist Education* (Ponomarev and Toshchenko, 1984), of which 300,000 copies were published, simply ignores entries such as kindness, altruism, magnanimity, nobility, tolerance, gratitude, pride, self-respect, or sincerity.

These and other humanistic qualities, once subject to attack, are tolerated today only if they do not bring the citizen into conflict with the current interests of the state. The old revolutionary term "class approach," even if it has lost almost all of its previous meaning, is still used as a code word to denote the superiority of the interests represented by the political elite over any moral requirements.

### THE AMBIGUOUS MORAL QUALITIES

If the Soviet political system unequivocally praises some human traits such as self-discipline and collectivism, and essentially dislikes others such as magnanimity or tolerance, it is ambivalent with regard to some other qualities. This ambivalence reveals itself during transition periods, when a new leader criticizes his predecessor, changes party ideology, and establishes new criteria for selecting and evaluating party cadres.

In general, honesty is highly lauded by the authorities when it concerns the relations between the citizen and the state party. However, as a regime gradually ossifies and the leader refuses to make changes, this quality, as well as its opposite—mendacity—gradually disappears even from the party lexicon. The publications on education and ethics prepared in Brezhnev's time almost completely ignored honesty as an important positive human trait (see, for instance, Bogdanova et al., 1983; Kharchev, 1976; Ponomarev and Toshchenko, 1984).

The new regime, under Gorbachev, determined to improve party morals after two decades of unbridled corruption, dramatically emphasized the role of honesty among the most desirable human features, and mention of this quality began to appear in numerous publications, especially in the mass media (see, for instance, Olga Chaikovskaia's "The word of honor," a rare direct attack on lying as a major phenomenon in Soviet mass media [*Literaturnaia Gazeta*, April 16, 1986]).

Two other qualities—initiative and having a critical attitude—have had widely fluctuating treatment under different regimes. They both were almost always included in the ideal image of the Soviet individual. But during a period of stagnation, as occurred under Brezhnev, these qualities were mentioned much less frequently than in more dynamic periods, and in those cases when they were used it was clear from the context that it was done more to pay lip service to these traits than to actually suppose they would be realized.

Kon (1983) was quite reserved about the quality of altruism, arguing that "it retains its importance mainly in the domain of personal relations. In the sphere of socially useful activity, in work, people, as Lenin showed, serve not those who are 'close' to them but those who are 'far' from them, i.e., the whole society" (p. 11). The authors also expressed some reservations about gratitude, which can "come into conflict with more lofty principles," particularly those connected with "service to society." The main danger of gratitude lies in the fact that "this quality pertains to the private sphere of social relations," whereas "communist morality gives superiority to social relations, not private ones" (p. 28).

# CHAPTER 2

# Soviet People in the Factory and Office

## The Official Picture of Soviet Work Life

Not only in the image of the ideal but also in the image of the good Soviet individual is work, based on the Marxist glorification of labor, presented as the crucial activity in a citizen's life. The beloved heroes of novels and movies made in the spirit of socialist realism are people who are completely absorbed with the fulfillment of production plans despite any obstacles. Such heroes were portrayed in Shaginian's *Hydro Power Station*, Leonov's *Sot'*, Il'in's *The Great Assembly Line*, Kataiev's *Time Forward*, Ehrenburg's *Second Day*, and others (see Metchenko and Petrov, 1983).

But by the early 1980s the average Soviet citizen was even further from upholding the ideals exemplified by such heroes than in the 1930s and 1940s. Contrary to the expectations of the founders of Soviet society, people do not feel the need to work for its own sake and regard occupational activity mostly as a necessity to achieve other things in life.

Of course, so closely have the Soviet people absorbed the mythological ideal, that they still appraise work as a vitally important value for society as well as for themselves personally. A survey conducted by Irina Changli in the mid-1970s elicited from 95 percent of the workers interviewed in various cities support for the following statement: "Labor is the source of well-being for the motherland and each citizen" (Changli, 1978).

With one of the most complacent quotations from Brezhnev about the Soviet working class on the title page of his book, Narimanov Aitov "bravely" generalized in 1981, only one year before the radical reappraisal of Brezhnev's economic performance, that "the majority of Soviet workers do not consider more work only as the means of subsistence or for promotion, but recognize work as one of the greatest values of their life. . . . Work is gradually becoming the first life need of the Soviet worker." He also suggested, referring to empirical data, that there had been a steady improvement in labor discipline in the 1970s (Aitov, 1981, pp. 51, 103).[1]

Along with data attesting to the great devotion of Soviet people to work, Soviet sociologists use four types of arguments to buttress this view. Two are openly ideological, and the other two are sophisticated and ambivalent in their interpretation.

## *Socialist Emulation*

Soviet politicians and social scientists cite the mass participation of Soviet people in socialist emulation, a competition among workers that is organized by an enterprise's administration and that rewards the winners both materially and morally. According to the data published by the Central Statistical Board in 1982, 85 percent of all employees in the economy took part in socialist emulation, 64 percent of them joined the movement for communist labor, and 30 percent had already gained the title of "shock workers" (TsSU, 1985, p. 408).

These figures were cited with innumerable variations by ideological sociologists such as Sdobnov (1985, p. 85), Sbytov (1983), Changli (1973, 1978, 1979), and even by more pragmatic sociologists such as Shkaratan (1978) and Klopov (1985, p. 231) as evidence of the great labor activism of a large majority of Soviet workers.

Ideological sociologists, conducting numerous studies, found the majority of employees, including scholars, greatly devoted to the goals of socialist emulation (see, for instance, Ianovskii, *The Issues of Socialist Emulation Among Scientific Collectives*, 1982; see also Emanuel, *Socialist Emulation and the Increase of Efficacy of Scientific Research*, 1982; Ianovskii, 1979a, pp. 236–51; Ianovskii, 1982). Changli's respondents unanimously praised this emulation as a means of educating people in the spirit of "collectivism," "honesty and fairness," and "initiative and innovation" (Changli, 1978, pp. 148, 182).

Many other sociologists who shared the viewpoint of Changli found a lot of other data to support the finding of the great involvement of Soviet workers in socialist emulation (see, for instance, Babosov et al., 1983, pp. 191–92; Blinov, 1979, p. 47).

## *Social Usefulness of Work*

As the second proof of the great dedication toward work of the Soviet people, social scientists refer to the significance of social motives in people's labor. This argument is based on the assumption that if people are conscious of the social importance of their work then they must work all that much harder. During the last two decades Soviet sociologists amassed a huge amount of data attesting to the great importance people placed on the social usefulness of work. No less than 40–50 percent of the respondents in various surveys, including those conducted by first-rank sociologists such as Vladimir Shubkin, declared the great significance of this element of work (Shubkin, 1984, p. 96; see also Blinov, 1979, p. 59; Plaksii, 1982, p. 70; Shkaratan, 1985, p. 33; Titma, 1973, p. 3).

## *Satisfaction with Work*

The third argument in favor of this high-toned picture of Soviet labor attitudes was rather modern, and like the content of work theory (to be discussed in the next section) with which it was closely connected, was initially spurned by ideologues. This argument forwarded the theory that there was a high correlation between productivity and satisfaction with work. In the beginning the new concept aroused the suspicion of ideological watchdogs because it focused attention on the individual and his feelings rather than on the collective. Soviet sociologists who introduced this concept had problems defending their right to use it (see Iadov et al., 1967).

The first surveys conducted by Soviet sociologists discovered, contrary to the fears of the authorities, that the majority of Soviet people (from 50 to 80 percent in various groups—practically the same as in the United States) are satisfied with their work (about workers, see Dmitrenko and Kornakovskii, 1984; Ivanova and Stoliarova, 1979; about the farm laborers see Kolbanovskii, 1970; Simush, 1965; about scholars see Kelle et al., 1978; Kugel and Nikandrov, 1971, p. 156; Mangutov, 1980, pp. 159, 161; Natalushko, 1981; Shanov and Kuznetsov, 1977; Sheinin, 1980; about the United States see Andrisani et al., 1977, p. 70; Campbell et al., 1976, p. 301; Yankelovich, 1974, p. 106).

In view of these data Soviet officials drastically changed their attitudes toward the "satisfaction" concept, finding in it a new, apparently modern proof that labor ethics in the country were at a high level.

## *Content of Work as the Main Motivating Force*

The fourth argument demonstrating the high labor ethics of the Soviet people was, like the third, individualistic and ambivalent. Out of all possible motives for worker satisfaction, ideologues focused on the content of the work.

According to the new theory advanced by Soviet sociologists in the late 1950s, it is the content of work (not material reward or even the awareness of the social utility of work) and more specifically, the amount of creativeness in it, which is the dominant variable in determining labor attitudes.[2]

The offensive by proponents of the content of labor theory started with the work of two Leningrad sociologists, Vladimir Iadov and Andrei Zdravomyslov. Their research examined the attitudes of a sample of more than 2,600 workers between the ages of eighteen and thirty. The results, presented in *Man and His Work* (1967 and 1970), were summed up:

> The verification of the first main hypothesis shows that under the given social conditions of the development of our society, the content of labor and the creative opportunities of work are the leading specific factors that determine the worker's attitudes toward labor, either primarily as a need of the personality, or primarily as a means of subsistence. (p. 285)

While admitting that material incentives were important, the authors insisted that "only if the content of labor itself is high is the (material) stimulation an effective means of forming an attitude of labor as a need of the personality" (p. 236). Among other data which supported this conclusion, Iadov and his colleagues cited the fact that only 3 percent of young, unskilled workers were greatly satisfied with their work, as opposed to 25 percent of those engaged in more complex work (p. 289). Other statistics demonstrated that the correlation between work satisfaction and job content was significantly higher than that between satisfaction and wages (pp. 138, 162).

The methodology of Iadov and his colleagues was rapidly adopted and employed in other studies around the country. The subsequent research, conducted mostly in the late 1960s and early 1970s, supported the idea that the content of work was a dominant factor in shaping job attitudes (see Dmitrenko and Kornakovskii, 1984; Ivanova and Stoliarova, 1979). The emphasis on creativity was found particularly in studies of professional workers, especially scholars (see Kelle et al., 1978; Kugel and Nikandrov, 1971, p. 156; Mangutov, 1980, pp. 159, 161; Natalushko, 1981; Shanov and Kuznetsov, 1977; Sheinin, 1980).

It is notable, however, that the same relationships were found among collective farmers; they too appeared to be more oriented toward work content than material incentives. The majority of collective farmers in the Orlov region clearly indicated a preference for an interesting job over higher wages (Kolbanovskii, 1970), as did those in the Stavropol region (Simush, 1965) and elsewhere.

At about the time that Iadov and his colleagues conducted their study, Vladimir Shubkin initiated a similar investigation of the attitudes of young people toward various occupations. The results were even more striking, for they demonstrated that students in the final year of secondary school strongly preferred to enter occupations that offered chances for the most creativity, generally the professional occupations (Chernovolenko et al., 1979; Kostiuk et al., 1980; Shubkin, 1970, 1984; Titma, 1973, 1977).

By the end of the 1970s the content theory gave rise to numerous books and articles that presented Soviet workers as becoming more absorbed with creative work. Irina Sizemskaia portrayed this society as moving, under the influence of the technological revolution, toward a universal "intellectualization of work and an economy in which people would have an 'independent mentality' and in which increasing numbers of workers would be more oriented to spiritual values and creative activity, leading to an increase in the level of culture and intellectual contacts." Society was seen to be moving toward "the limitless development of all essential forces of the human being, the transformation of the workers into the real subject of social production" (Sizemskaia, 1981, pp. 84–87).

The data describing the glorification of work by the people, their absorption with the social importance of their work, and their satisfaction with their job, mostly due to its creativity, created a false picture of real labor attitudes in the Soviet Union. This picture has been almost completely destroyed since Brezhnev's death, but even before, in the late 1970s, some sociologists cast doubt on the conclusions of those colleagues who participated in creating these myths on Soviet labor attitudes. The critics even used the very data produced by ideological sociologists against them.

## Loopholes in the Official Picture

However, as soon as the sociologists moved from the abstract level to a more concrete one and asked questions personally relevant to the workers, they found another picture, even if, under the pressure of the Brezhnev regime, they used loaded alternatives that prompted people to answer in an ideologically acceptable way.

Some data gathered by the same sociologists ideologically supportive of Brezhnev was strongly discordant with the bombastic optimism of these researchers regarding Soviet labor ethics. Changli included—rather uncautiously—a question about the role of work in personal life ("Will you continue to work if you get the same amount of money without working") in her survey, which was carried out in eight enterprises in different Russian cities (1975–76).

Among workers in Perm, 38 percent indicated that they would not work if they got the same amount of money without working. In Ivanovo this figure was 32 percent and Rostov on the Don 25 percent (in Erevan, which was not included in the main sample, the figure was 43 percent). The average for all the cities was 27 percent. The number of those who would prefer not to work was especially high among young people—members of the Young Communist League—and quite high even among the members of the party—35 and 20 percent, respectively (Changli, 1978, pp. 186–87; Kuregian, 1979, p. 90).[3]

The studies on values conducted by Soviet sociologists turned out to be even more remarkable. First of all, almost none of these studies, even those conducted by the ideological sociologists, could elicit data, whatever the formulation of the question or list of values, showing that work as such was an activity of vital importance for any group of respondents. As a rule, work was preceded by "personal life" and "material well-being" (Fainburg, 1969, p. 93; Kosolapov et al., 1982, p. 131), "family" (Arutiunian, 1972; Blinov, 1979), "health" (Iadov,

1979, p. 90), "friends" (Babosov et al., 1985, p. 144), "love" (Sokolov, 1981, p. 55), and "personal happiness" (Fainburg, 1982, p. 73).[4]

Although the respondents listed work behind other values, mostly personal, in order of importance, they did place work among the first five values. But this still does not reflect the real role of work in the lives of a majority of the Soviet people. In almost all these surveys, work was defined as "interesting" (Babosov et al., 1985; Blinov, 1979; Iadov, 1979; Sokolov, 1981), allowing those who hate their job to assert that the value of work is of great importance to them without any practical implications.

If a serious researcher of values probes deeper, using a somewhat sophisticated methodology of analysis, he discovers—as Iadov did—that work does not play such an important role. Only 9 percent of Leningrad engineers regard professional activity as the fulcrum of their lives, whereas 43 percent of all respondents felt work played a secondary role (for the rest, family and work can be regarded as equally important values) (Iadov, 1979, pp. 72–74).

## *The Importance of the Utility of Work*

In the early 1980s, especially after Brezhnev's death, professional sociologists could look more soberly at the data claiming the high devotion of the Soviet people to the social importance of work, data profusely used, as mentioned before, to present Soviet people as absorbed with production activity for the sake of the motherland. Some sociologists such as Zdravomyslov (1981) and Shkaratan (1985, p. 33) were not able to dismiss this myth completely, advancing the idea that the social importance of work as a source of gratification is closely interwoven with material reward because income from labor is an indicator of the individual's contribution to the well-being of society.

This interpretation of the data is at least more realistic than the previous ones. In fact, despite the general decline of ideological commitment and growing cynicism, only a minority of the Soviet people regard work as having no or minimal social significance. The majority still prefer to have work which they consider useful for the country and appreciate its social recognition (see, for instance, a collection of interviews with Soviet shock workers, Iakovlev, 1977).

But there is no evidence that any of these people would sacrifice anything personally for patriotic duty (except in extreme cases). The social importance of work remains a nice additional moral bonus that Soviet people are ready to accept.

There is another factor which should be taken into consideration when evaluating the role of commitment to society in the motivation of Soviet workers. As in any society, a significant number of people in the Soviet Union view their work as a means of self-fulfillment, whatever its specific content may be. They will set challenges for themselves and strive to meet them, regardless of the extrinsic rewards they receive. Of course, the desire to be a good team member only enhances such people's enthusiasm, even when their political orientation is unrelated to their job commitment. They are driven by what U.S. sociologist Thorstein Veblen called the "instinct for craftmanship." The desire to accomplish quality work and to do something useful can be found in many people, and under certain circumstances this inclination can be further promoted.

Solzhenitsyn illustrated this process in *One Day in the Life of Ivan Denisovich*, showing how even inmates in the Gulag could forget about their immediate environment and become dedicated, if only for a short period, to work assigned to them. Similarly, Viktor Proniakin, the hero of Vladimov's *Big Ore* (1984), who was quite removed from politics and ideology, got caught up in the desire to accomplish something important and prove his abilities. Thus a common personality trait can be exploited and presented as being directly derived from political commitment, when in fact it has little to do with politics or ideology. In the surveys, only 10 to 20 percent of the respondents claimed their occupational choices were shaped by the single factor of the social importance of the work (Aitov, 1983; Semenova, 1979).

## *The Real Role of Socialist Emulation*

The data on socialist emulation, which has been used on a large scale to suggest the great role of work in the life of the Soviet people, reveals after even a superficial scrutiny that it cannot serve this goal.

The work of Changli and other sociologists of the same viewpoint shows the deep indifference of people toward socialist emulation and especially to the surveys devoted to it.[5] Up to one quarter of all workers who are considered participants of emulation have no idea who and how their own "socialist obligations" were endorsed. Answering another question, 30 percent of workers said that they had no part in the elaboration of this obligation related to their team, and about 90 percent to the enterprise on the whole. What is more, only 39 percent of Moscow workers displayed interest in the results of emulation in which they presumably took part; in Minsk, only 22 percent (Changli, 1978, pp. 161, 163–64; see also Rotman, 1979).

It is significant that all popular Soviet novels and movies in the last decade either ignore social emulation (see, for instance, novels of such writers as Abramov, 1973, 1982; Astafiev, 1984a, 1984b, 1986; Bondarev, especially *Game* [1985]; Rasputin, 1980, 1985a, 1985b; Trifonov, 1983a, 1983b; or essays of journalists such as Agranovskii, 1982; Strelianyi, 1984) or derogate it (see, for instance, such movies as *Moscow Does not Believe in Tears* or *Fell in Love at Own Request*). Particularly interesting are those novels devoted to describing manufacturing life in the Soviet Union. They demonstrate the extent to which physical laborers hold socialist emulation in contempt (see, for instance, Voinovich's *I Want to be Honest* [1963] and Vladimov's *Great Ore* [1984], and especially two recent Shtemler novels: *Supermarket* [1984] and *Train* [1986]; see also the memoirs of Lysenko, a former Soviet captain, *The Last Cruise* [1982]).

At the same time, Soviet people are not indifferent to some aspects of socialist emulation. The authorities often reward emulation materially (bonuses), with official recognition, and with promotion to get people interested in "winning." Even in Changli's data we find that about one-third of the workers named as a stimulus for their participation in socialist emulation "the desire to improve their own material well-being" (Changli, 1978, p. 20). So it is not amazing that some people are delighted or frustrated by the results of socialist emulation when these results are announced by managers. Of course, it is often the "professional enthusiasts" who desire to be the official model workers in their factories and offices.

Some Soviet researchers try to approach socialist emulation more realistically than their ideologically motivated colleagues. Kharchev, Odintsov, and Simonian present socialist emulation as an activity where people can realize their desire for "self-assertion, for drawing the attention of others, to stand out from the crowd" (Kharchev and Odintsov, 1977, p. 10; see also Kapustin, 1984, pp. 32–47; Kozlov and Khlevniuk, 1985, pp. 55–64; Shlapentokh, 1985b, 1987; Simonian, 1986, pp. 63–70, 80–84, 86).

Since Gorbachev, it has even become fashionable to approach socialist emulation more critically. Journals of the mid-1980s contain data which deeply contrast with the ebullient pictures of socialist emulation presented in the 1970s (see, for instance, Fadeev, 1985).

### *Satisfaction with Work: The Real Role*

In the 1970s, with labor morals obviously deteriorating, Soviet sociologists (ignoring for the moment the questionable validity and reliability of data concerning satisfaction with work) gradually realized that high job satisfaction, even if correlated with productivity, for some people, is often determined by circumstances usually antagonistic to efficiency—lax discipline, ease of pilfering, social life in the workplace, and so on (see Iadov and Kissel', 1974; Ivanov and Patrushev, 1976, p. 69; Lobanov and Cherkasov, 1981). Changli, with stupefaction, noted that 75 percent of systematic violators of labor discipline declared that they liked their current job and 36 percent their occupation (Changli, 1973, p. 449). Vladimir Magun (1983a, 1983b) found that in his sample of 4,000 Leningrad workers one group showed a positive correlation between satisfaction and productivity, but there was a group within which the opposite occurred.

Under the influence of the new, critical approach to the earlier studies of labor attitudes, Klopov looked at the data showing the satisfaction of Taganrog workers with their jobs. Although he still noted as a positive sign the fact that 71 percent of the employees were happy with their work, he did not exult as did his colleagues ten years earlier, but added, "yet, less than two-thirds of those who are satisfied with work demonstrated high productivity. At the same time, half of those not satisfied with work are good workers" (Klopov, 1985, p. 255; see also similar reflections in Shkaratan, 1985, p. 28).

Thus by the early 1970s Soviet sociologists began to cast doubt on the role of content of work as a major factor determining labor attitudes.

## The First Sober Glimpses after Brezhnev: Zaslavskaia's Stratification

While many Soviet industrial sociologists helped create the Brezhnevian myth about the growing labor enthusiasm of the average individual, in reality social processes were moving in the opposite direction. In particular, a new stratification of Soviet workers was taking place.

Before 1983–85, classifying workers according to their production activity was often discussed among Soviet academics. Many authors, mostly ideological sociologists, classify workers according to their amount of participation in socialist emulation (see, for example, Changli, 1978). More realistic authors avoid the connection with socialist emulation and use such designations as shock workers, efficient workers, and nonefficient workers to classify. Some use the intensity of labor turnover as the basis of their classification, employing the terms "stable workers," "workers oriented to their profession" (those who often change enterprises but never occupations), "workers oriented to the given enterprise" (those who change occupations once inside an enterprise), and unstable workers who often change occupations as well as places of work (see Klopov, 1985, p. 170).

One of the few Soviet sociologists who showed independent opinion during the 1970s, Tatiana Zaslavskaia who had previously studied farmers in the countryside (1970), turned out to be the first Soviet scholar who recognized the emergence of the new class of Soviet workers with deeply ingrained negative attitudes to any work. She was also the first to dare publicize her views in the first months of Andropov's regime when the new leader began to take stock of the state of the country. She was followed by Narimanov Aitov with the book *Good and Bad Workers* (1983).

Certain social and historical patterns have led to the creation of large groups of unproductive, even disruptive, workers. The most productive, the "social" type of worker, is seen as shaped by "firmly acquired norms of behavior in the spheres of production, distribution, exchange, and consumption," resulting in the adoption of a series of desirable qualities, such as "conscientiousness, responsibility, reliability," and so on (Zarlavskaia, 1984, pp. 38–40). Yet not all workers are receptive to these norms of behavior despite the efforts of the society to develop them. Immediate social circumstances, Zarlavskaia argues, do not alone condition behavior, for they interact with long-term historical patterns. Hence, she refers to "the spiritual influence of older generations on the younger" regarding personal values and the "historical receptiveness" of specific character traits generally attributed to various nationality groups (i.e., Russians, Georgians, Estonians, Germans). Each trait "somehow bears the imprint of the path of the development of the corresponding peoples over the centuries." Such historical patterns have "great inertia and will not yield easily to the influence on the part of management organs."

The result is the creation of a large group of workers who, claims Zaslavskaia, "fails to answer not only the strategic goal of a developed socialist society, but the technological demands of contemporary production as well." This group of workers is characterized as follows:

> A low level of labor and production discipline, indifferent attitudes toward the work being done, low quality of work, social inertia, low importance of work as a means of self-realization, and a low level of morality are traits common to many workers, which have been shaped during recent five-year plans. It is enough to recall the broad scale of the activities of so-called "pilferers," the spread of all sorts of "shady" dealings at public expense, the development of illicit "enterprises" and figures-finagling, and the "worming out" of wages regardless of the results of work. (Zaslavskaia, 1984, p. 40; see also Zaslavskaia, 1986a, 1986b and her interview with *Izvestia*, June 1, 1985, p. 3.)

The importance of the influence of social milieu on work attitudes, as opposed to the focus on the intrinsic and extrinsic values of a current job, is a point strongly underscored by some Western scholars, particularly Melvin Kohn and his coauthors (Kohn, 1969, 1978, 1981, 1983; Kohn and Schooler, 1973, 1982). Zaslavskaia, in reaching similar conclusions, followed a number of Soviet sociologists who investigated various factors which shape the attitudes toward work before the individual acquires work experience.

In this respect the correlation between a person's grades in secondary school and labor discipline is of great interest. Aitov asked foremen in Ufa to evaluate labor discipline among their workers. It turned out that among those who usually got a C in school 44 percent were evaluated as good workers, among those who got B, 65 percent, and A, 100 percent (Aitov, 1983, p. 33). V. Popov got the same results from studies in Bashkiria, Magnitogorsk, and other cities (Popov, 1979, p. 106).

## Who Are "Good" and "Bad" Workers?

The classification of people according to work attitudes in some ways is as important for social analysis as that based on political and social factors. In fact, this stratification of workers exerts an enormous impact on all aspects of Soviet life.

The bottom category in the hierarchy—"greedy bunglers"—consists of people who try to extricate from the workplace as much material advantage as possible (high salary, advantageous connections, objects to be pilfered, etc.) while doing as little as possible on the job. Soviet novels, plays, and movies have depicted many examples of this group—Soviet wheeler-dealers in the service occupations and commerce as well as apparatchiks.

The second lowest category—"bungler careerists"—contains people oriented to promotion, not through socially useful work but through its imitation. The imitation of activity is a feature typical of the majority of bad workers, but members of this group are real virtuosi in it. They are especially found among those who want to make an administrative career in the party, state, or economic bureaucracy. As will be discussed later, these people make up the bulk of activitists in official public life and are great experts in political ritualistic games. El'dar Shengelaia, a Soviet film director, was probably the first to devote a movie (*Blue Mountains*, 1984) to them—the masters of imitation of activity.

The third category—"passive shirkers"—consists of people who, unlike the two previous categories, do not try to get everything they can from their place of work. They are satisfied with a modest salary and are concerned mostly with minimizing their efforts at the workplace. These people also avoid social "voluntary" work as much as possible and, depending on their education and cultural background, put their energy in alcoholism, illicit sex, sports, cultural activities, or in personal relationships.

The category of good workers can be divided into four groups, which are even more intertwined with each other than the divisions of the bad workers.

The highest group in this category—"conscientious workers"—considers good work as the sole decent source of income and, having a deeply internalized respect for hard work, will not perform badly on any project. They are closest to the Soviet image of the "good worker" and more than any other group are inclined to appreciate the social importance of their job. Many still believe in many ideas of Soviet ideology and regard themselves as patriots. Strongly influenced by material reward and highly sensitive to official praise, these people are sometimes motivated to work for reasons of social usefulness. Thus the content of work, its diversity, and creativity, are often of secondary importance to them.

This category of workers is ideal for Soviet managers. Shock or vanguard workers, for various innovations are usually recruited from it. But in a short time most of these people become corrupted by the prominent role, participation in various meetings, and travel, and gradually lose contact with professional work, joining the ranks of the second group of bad workers—the imitators of active work. Waida's movie *Man of Marble* describes the cycle of such a shock worker.

The second highest group—"professional enthusiasts"—is composed of people who consider their work to be of major importance in life. They make no distinction between working and nonworking hours. The majority of these workaholics are engaged in nonroutine jobs that demand a certain amount of creativity, such as hunters, geologists, highly trained mechanics, physicists, composers, and film directors.

These people enjoy their work anyway, viewing it as a means of self-fulfillment, but of course are happy if their profession is also well-paid, publicly praised, and has social importance.

Viewing content of work as an essential factor in determining the attitudes toward it, Soviet sociologists presented this group as almost the dominant one in the Soviet economy and as constantly expanding.

Such Soviet writers as Granin or Panova use these types of people as heroes because they could describe their characters' devotion to work without warping reality or conflicting with official ideology, even if they present their heroes as concerned more with self-fulfillment than with the social utility of their work.

The third group—"honest careerists"—consists of people who have no internalized respect for work but try to make their career through application and industry. However, they are practically indifferent to the content of their work, usually preferring administrative activity. People from this group provide the party apparatus and the corps of managers with the best workers.

The fourth group—"the unwilling good workers"—consists of people forced to perform well due to the nature of their work. The technology in many branches of the economy demands that people do their jobs relatively well, although even here there is a possibility for deterioration in the quality of work. For example, schoolteachers, unlike their friends in research institutes or offices, cannot shop during working hours simply because they have to be in class with the children. The same is true for bus drivers and people working on assembly lines.

The strength of administrative control is of crucial importance in determining how these people carry out their jobs, but this control is not the same in all sectors of Soviet society. Thus the quality of work in military industries is significantly higher because the consumer—the army—rejects products that do not meet its demands. The discipline in the party apparatus, the KGB, and the army, even if it is not ideal, is much higher than in civil service, the health service, or commerce. Many people who chose a career in these key institutions cannot afford to blatantly violate elementary rules of job performance as can be done elsewhere and so find themselves in this category.

Although various sources, for instance the memoirs of dissidents (see, for instance, Amalrik, 1982; Bukovskii, 1979; Grigorenko, 1982; Terts, 1984; see also Kaminskaia, 1984), described KGB prosecutors as conscientious and highly skilled professionals who could definitely be classified as professional enthusiasts, many apparatchiks, as soon as they find themselves in a key Soviet institution, for instance as a fellow in a research institute or a professor in the department of history of the party, immediately commence the style of the honest careerist.

If a person in this category feels that his or her job puts them at a disadvantage compared to others, at the first opportunity the individual will change this technology-bound work for something else, which usually allows them to reveal their real attitudes toward work. Thus it is not amazing that the turnover of operators in industry is extremely high.

Between the two classes of good and bad workers is an intermediate class of passive workers who fulfill their minimal obligations and in general do not violate labor discipline. The great majority of these people are married or single women with children, people in poor health, young people still living with their parents, and those who, while hating their job, need it too much to defy official requirements (about this group, see Zaslavskaia, 1986a, p. 8).

## Labor Ethics in Both Classes

Having inundated sociology publications with data about participation in socialist emulation, worker satisfaction, and the role of content of work in labor motivation, Soviet sociologists and economists have adduced almost no hard, objective data (such as the number of violations of labor discipline, the magnitude of absenteeism, the number of people appearing drunk at the workplace) on the real state of labor ethics in the country. The Central Statistical Board has been more than restrained on this issue.

Although censorship eased in Gorbachev's era, even books and articles published in 1985 and 1986 contained very few objective figures. The best publication on labor discipline, which stands out for its objectivity and honesty, is Mikhail Sonin's *Socialist Discipline of Labor* (1986), enabling readers to get an idea about the number of good and bad workers based on some concrete facts.

Sonin also managed to show that even if classified data on labor discipline in the country were available it would hardly reflect the real state of affairs. The magnitude of wasted time, as indicated in the official reports filed by enterprises, was only one-hundredth of the figures collected by researchers: .02–.05 percent compared to 4–5 percent. In many enterprises researchers calculated the loss of working time was as high as 20 percent. But managers often cover the absenteeism of their workers, presenting it in the record as legal days off (Sonin, 1986, pp. 68, 243; see also Gvozdev, 1985, p. 194).

Only a few publications show figures which can shed light on labor discipline in the country. In one, a survey of 30 thousand of the industrial workers in the Moscow metropolitan area established that in the early 1980s three-fourths of them regularly left the workplace during working hours. This number decline to 69 percent in 1983 as a direct result of Andropov's measures against violators of labor discipline. Three main causes of absenteeism were given by the respondents: the necessity of going to the hospital (41 percent in 1983), to the cafeteria (11), and to the police in connection with the internal passport (11) (Volgin and Sidiakin, 1985, p. 44).

The lack of objective data makes it necessary to rely on the subjective data gathered by Soviet sociologists, even those with strong ideological tendencies. The data mostly reflects the evaluation of labor discipline by foremen and other experts as well as the perceptions of labor ethics held by workers themselves. As a rule, Brezhnev sociologists applied various euphemisms to bad workers, such as "workers—nonparticipants in socialist emulation," "nonshock workers," "nonefficient workers," and so on, allowing them to make the figures compatible with claims about the successes of the working class.

If we throw away the ideological covering, we find that most social scientists who collected data on labor ethics converge on 30–40 percent as the number of workers whose discipline was very low, even by Brezhnev's standards. This figure was arrived at by Edward Klopov, a leading Soviet industrial sociologist, who bases it on a number of surveys conducted in Leningrad (of twelve enterprises in

1976), Moscow (of bus and truck drivers in 1981), and Armenia (industrial workers, 1979–1981) (Klopov, 1985, pp. 229–30, 234).

Klopov's figure is supported by such well-known industrial sociologists as Kesel'man, who also used the data from the Leningrad survey in 1976–77 (1981, p. 149), Reznik and Lipovskii, who studied labor discipline in the building industry in the 1970s (1981, p. 140), and others (see, for instance, Kuregian, 1983, pp. 129–30; Tukumtsev, 1979, p. 110). Even ideological sociologists serving the Academy of Social Science at the Central Committee of the Communist Party and the High School of the Young Communist League use nearly the same figure when speaking about workers who do not meet official requirements (Blinov, 1979, pp. 44–45; Sokolov, 1981, p. 112).

How many good workers are there compared to bad ones? On this issue Soviet sociologists in Brezhnev's time were not in complete agreement. In general, most of them gravitated toward 10–30 percent as the number who, by the standards of the time, could be regarded as "good workers" (Klopov, 1985, pp. 223–40; Plaksii, 1982, p. 53; Tukumtsev, 1979, p. 110). Zaslavskaia, in an article published under Gorbachev, feels at most one-third of all employees work "at full strength" (1986b, p. 63).

## *The Labor Ethics of Young Workers*

The majority of Soviet sociologists and economists contend that labor discipline is especially weak among young people. Such is the opinion of Vladimir Iadov, based on his serious study of Leningrad workers. According to this study the number of violators of labor discipline among workers below the age of thirty was twice that of older workers (Iadov, 1983, p. 56).

Among older workers another author found 41 percent could be classified as good while among the young only 21 percent. The number of those who did not regularly fulfill their assignments was three times more among workers in the 20–25 age group than among those in the 30–40 age group. The ratio between workers in both groups whose products are of poor quality is 2:3 (Plaksii, 1982, pp. 53, 56–57). According to Babosov and his colleagues, a survey of Byelorussian workers in the early 1980s found that only 44 percent of people under thirty fulfill their production norm, compared to 58 percent among older workers (Babosov et al., 1985, p. 113). Mikhail Sonin also found the young as leaders in violating labor ethics (Sonin, 1986, pp. 143–44).[6]

### *Labor Turnover*

Though the intensity of labor turnover as such cannot be formally regarded as an indicator of labor discipline, Soviet researchers are inclined to indicate that people prone to changing jobs trespass the norms more often than so-called stable workers.

According to reliable data (the computations of A. Kotliar, a prominent expert on labor turnover) based on state statistics, up to one-fifth of all workers change their place of work each year, including 10–12 percent who transfer to another job in the same city or village (*Pravda*, May 13, 1984). Soviet economists view this as harmful to the economy, regarding as "normal" a labor turnover of only 7 percent.

Young people change where they work as well as their occupation much more often than older workers. This can be attributed not only to the natural process of maturation and fitting into a new role in life, but to the high aspirations and self-evaluation of the young. The number of people who want to change jobs among Novosibirsk workers in the late 1960s was 43 percent for the 20–29 age group compared to 10 percent among those aged 40–49 (Antosenkov and Kalmyk, 1970, p. 70). The data collected in Orel (1976) as well as in other regions (Ukraine, Bashkiria, Kuibyshev, and others) in the 1970s confirms the conclusions of Novosibirsk sociologists: labor turnover among young people (below thirty-five) is 60 percent higher than that of older workers and makes up one-third of the total turnover (Kotliar 1982, p. 134; Kotliar and Trubin, 1978, pp. 41–42; Kurman, 1971, pp. 106–07; Sonin, 1986, pp. 77–78).

### *Perceptions of Labor Ethics*

In general, when Soviet people are asked about labor discipline, they often evaluate it as being rather poor.

A survey conducted by the Moscow Sociological Institute (1981) in five big cities found that only half of the population (55 percent) consider labor discipline good even using Brezhnev's standards. Muscovites were more pessimistic than the others—only 44 percent of them evaluated the discipline in the country positively ( Bozhkov and Golofast, 1981, p. 97). In a nationwide study of young people conducted in 1978–79, Alekseeva also found 44 percent said labor discipline was good (Alekseeva, 1983, p. 49). The Soviet people's perceptions of the moral atmosphere were revealed by the fact that 89 percent of the respondents in a survey of 7,000 people in 1981–83 supported the idea that the norms for labor behavior had to be more stringently enforced (Blinov and Titma, 1985, p. 16).

But although most people regard labor discipline in general as poor, they do not feel it is primarily responsible for economic failures, do not want to take part in improving it, and what is more, do not consider themselves as violators. In Novgorod (1981) 480 workers (18 percent of those polled) ranked labor discipline third among the causes responsible for the low quality of work. The major responsibility they shifted to managers—44 percent named bad organization of work and 20 percent the lack of concern about occupational conditions and everyday life. Workers surveyed in Erevan (1979–81) also relegated labor ethics to last place among causes for poor work quality (Bindiukov, 1983, pp. 134–35; Kuregian, 1983, pp. 129–30).

A survey of 30,000 workers in the Moscow region revealed that most did not feel they were to blame for great losses in working time. Only 5 percent attributed it to poor discipline, whereas 56 percent pointed to a faulty supply of raw materials and parts, 29 percent to the low quality of equipment, 26 percent to poor service in the cafeteria, and so on (Volgin and Sidiakin, 1985, p. 44).

A realistic assessment of the state of labor ethics indicates that violations are generally treated with indifference and few steps are ever taken to improve them. Only one-third of the respondents in a survey of 6,200 workers in twenty-eight enterprises condemned the violations of discipline by their colleagues, which means that most would not go on the record to disapprove of admittedly bad behavior (Plaksii, 1982, p. 53; see also Blinov, 1979, p. 44). In another survey, no more than 15–20 percent were inclined to resort to "institutionalized forms of control," as Soviet sociologists put it, in other words, to criticize comrades publicly, drawing the attention of superiors. About one-third of the workers in the survey did not promise to react at all to a violation of labor discipline, giving one pretext or another as an excuse (about 10–15 percent did not give any reason for refusing to act) (Norkin, 1982, pp. 90–91; Romashov, 1976, p. 70; Sokolov, 1978).

The majority of workers are also against strong measures being taken against violators of labor discipline. A survey conducted at a large enterprise in the Urals (1981) showed that only about one-tenth of all workers approved of administrative actions against them, with the rest preferring the use of moral persuasion (Kogan and Merenkov, 1983, p. 88).

But even these figures exaggerate the willingness of Soviet workers to help discipline their colleagues in the workplace, as participating in any measures would expose them to the same pressure from their coworkers. The same sociologist who glibly interprets his survey as presumably demonstrating the "active-rigorous position" of 71.9 percent of all workers (the decimal point suggests the "high accuracy" of the data) adds with some embarrassment that "40 percent of all violations of discipline occur in the presence of colleagues without arousing any reaction" (Norkin, 1982, p. 93).

## *The Dynamics of Labor Ethics*

The cries about the rapid deterioration of labor ethics had already begun in the early 1970s, mostly in the works of writers of the so-called "rural prose," that is, authors who wrote about life in the countryside. Fedor Abramov, Vasilii Shukshin, Vasilii Belov, Viktor Astafiev, and Valentin Rasputin raised the issue, mostly only in relation to the countryside. The same subject reached some prominence in samizdat through Sokirko's works (1981).

At the same time, the official ideologues, economists, and sociologists almost completely ignored the problem. A number of social scientists, and not only those who followed Changli's politics, kept silent on this issue and poured out on readers still respectful of "scientific data" a host of figures proving the steady progress in labor ethics (see Aitov, 1981; Shkaratan, 1978).

Only after Brezhnev's death and the change in regime did a consensus between the leadership and public opinion about the dangerous decline of labor ethics in the nation emerge.

In 1985–86 two prominent Soviet authors, Valentin Rasputin and Viktor Astafiev, published novels which, among other things, portrayed the frightening fall of work values in the country. As Rasputin said in *Fire* (1985b), work ceased to be a norm in the life of the people of the small city he described. The same picture is drawn by Astafiev in the novel *Sad Detective* (1986).

Iurii Chernichenko, a prominent Soviet journalist, describes the heroes of Rasputin's works as "arkharovtsy," forming a considerable part of the village, who "are deeply alien to the quality of work. . . . They will never work better and do not even understand the meaning of good work. The combine assembled by arkharovtsy will never thrash grain, the cars which they produced will at best keep silent and at worst blow up. No, dear readers, 'arkharovtsky'—it is very serious" (*Sovietskaia Kul'tura*, August 16, 1986).

By this time the Soviet mass media was presenting a gloomy picture of the evolution of labor discipline. Andropov, and especially Gorbachev, did not mince words when they touched on this issue (Andropov, 1983; Gorbachev, 1986).

However, this deterioration is extremely difficult to document empirically and statistically. Of course, some official data can be used as an indication of productivity dynamics. From 1966–70 the increase in productivity was 37 percent, from 1971–75 it was 25 percent, and from 1976–80, 17 percent. The amount of investment per worker grew twice as fast as productivity till the end of the 1970s (Bagdasarov and Pervushin, 1983, p. 16; Gvozdev 1985, p. 148; TsSU, 1971, p. 63; 1981, pp. 42–43).

However, it is impossible to attribute the entire decline to deteriorating labor ethics or even assert a correlation. More direct evidence is needed.

But Soviet social science could not provide the data, due not so much to the rarity of longitudinal studies carried out but to the failure of some sociologists to withstand the pressures of the Brezhnev regime to embellish the data on quality of life.

Using a type of longitudinal study (although usually not executed according to elementary methodological requirements, as in making sure questions are comparable), some sociologists asserted that the 1970s saw an increase in the number of people who cherished work as the most important value, in the participants in social emulation (see, for instance, Shkaratan et al., 1977, p. 42), in those satisfied with their work (Osipov et al., 1982, p. 21), and in those as concerned with the social usefulness of work as in its content (Osipov et al., 1982, p. 18). But this avoided more direct measures of labor attitudes.[7]

It is curious how Edward Klopov, caught between the data he had collected and described under Brezhnev and by the new regime with its realistic approach to the state of the national economy, managed to include in his book, *The Working Class of the USSR* (1985), some incompatible conclusions. On the one hand, Klopov writes about "the increase in labor activity of the working class of the USSR in the 60s and 70s" (p. 242). But only a few pages later he laments about the decrease in the rate of growth of productivity and "the tendency toward the deterioration of labor discipline" in the same period (p. 251). In the same way, he is quite enthusiastic about socialist emulation and especially the movement for communist labor, which "in a short period acquired real mass character" (p. 231). However, this did not prevent him from adding, reflecting the influence of the Gorbachev regime, that "almost half of the participants of socialist emulation knew nothing about the results of their activity or that of their partners in emulation" (p. 253).

In fact, there is only one longitudinal study that really pinpoints the major trends in Soviet labor ethics. This survey of young workers was done under the guidance of Vladimir Iadov in Leningrad in 1962 and 1976. Of course, Iadov and his colleagues could not avoid the influence of the Brezhnev atmosphere, and their publications about the changes that occurred between the two dates, which came out in the first half of the 1980s, bear its clear impact. But even so, these publications clearly reveal a lowering of labor ethics during the period spanned by the study.

For example, the data revealed that the number of workers reprimanded for violations of labor discipline doubled, from 10 to 20 percent, despite the policy to cover it up during Brezhnev's regime. The number of workers who failed to fulfill production quotas increased from 9 to 11 percent. The number of workers who surpassed their quotas fell from 63 to 43 percent (even the most efficient workers showed a decline in overproduction from 11 to 4 percent).[8]

By all accounts the deterioration of labor ethics affected all groups of "good workers," the sizes of which shrank considerably in Brezhnev's era, but probably the decline among professional enthusiasts was especially harmful to the country.[9]

## *The Decline of Professional Enthusiasm*

Developments in the post-Stalin period were conducive to the growth of the class of bad workers, but they also affected the composition of good workers. Perhaps the group of "conscientious workers" suffered more than others from the erosion of labor ethics. Having a special link to their profession and sustained in high labor morals by tradition and social duties, people belonging to this group could not withstand as much as others the process of labor demoralization going on around them. However, the most deleterious effect on labor morals was the declining number of professional enthusiasts, because they serve as models for new generations.

The group of professional enthusiasts could resist the demoralization somewhat better, but even those committed to their creative activity, such as writers or scholars, could not escape the impact of the general atmosphere in the country and many degenerated to the first class (bad workers). Various Soviet sources, including official media for instance, describe the significant, sometimes even drastic, decline in the quality of work among scientists, actors, and writers.

Soviet drama critics unanimously contend that professionalism in a majority of Soviet theaters is deteriorating. Discipline in even the best theaters, including the famous Bolshoi Theater or Vakhtangov's Theater, became more and more lax (see the discussion on the state of Soviet theaters in *Literaturnaia Gazeta*, December 25, 1985, and November 19, 1986; *Pravda*, February 14 and 21, 1986; *Sovietskaia Kul'tura*, January 16, August 5, and December 6, 1986). No less prevalent in the 1980s were the complaints about the poor quality of novels and poems, due perhaps not so much to a decline in good writers but an increase in the number of mediocre authors in the 1970s (see, for instance, gloomy estimates of the quality of literary works in *Literaturnaia Gazeta*, October 23, 1985, p. 3; December 18, 1985; January 15, 1986, p. 12; *Pravda*, March 26, 1986, p. 3).

This decline in labor values was also evident among scholars, which is one of the major factors responsible for the significant deterioration in Soviet science. This became public with the disclosures about the state of Soviet science in 1985–86 (see the materials of the twenty-seventh party congress, especially Gorbachev's report, as well as the speeches of Anatolii Alexandrov, President of the Academy of Science, and other delegates, *XXVII S'ezd* KPSS, 1986).

One of the most important ways this decline in scholarship was manifest was the refusal of academics to criticize each other or themselves. This lack of professional rigor in applying standards meant that scholars could work for years without producing any serious results. What is more, instances of "fudging" experiments, as well as the indifference of colleagues to such practices, became almost a norm in the Soviet scientific community. *Literaturnaia Gazeta* revealed in 1986 a scandal involving hundreds of scientists in one of the leading Soviet academic institutions, the Institute of High Pressure Physics, which had, from 1972 to the mid-1980s, conducted fraudulent studies on the "transformation of hydrogen into metal" (*Literaturnaia Gazeta*, June 25, 1986, p. 13). This blowing of scientific bubbles became a fixture in Soviet scientific institutions, particularly those related to economics (about the falsification of data in a leading Moscow design institute, see *Literaturnaia Gazeta*, December 16, 1987).

These developments seriously affected the prestige of science and other areas of academia in the country. By contrast, in the 1960s scientific activity had been a symbol of professional dedication and the quest for truth, a value which Robert Merton considered a generic feature of the ethics of scholars (Merton, 1957). The Soviet mass media, arts, and literature limned the image of a scholar, committed only to research, for example Agranovskii's article in *Izvestia* (Agranovskii, 1982, pp. 145–51) about Bogdan Voizekhovskii, the fanatic of science in the Novosibirsk academic city, the novels of I. Grekova; particularly, *Entrance Gate* (1983), or Mikhail Romm's movie *Nine Years of One Year*. Journalists, film directors, and writers reflected public attitudes toward science and its priests.

Shubkin's studies in the early 1960s revealed the extremely high prestige accorded scholarly occupations by young people. According to Shubkin's data, male graduates from secondary schools in Novosibirsk gave scholars an average score of 6.61 on a 10-point prestige scale. Engineers received an average score of 6.55, industrial laborers 4.01, and agricultural workers 2.50 (Shubkin, 1970).

But since then the prestige of scholarly occupations has significantly declined. Cherednichenko and Shubkin's investigations revealed that the attractiveness of the occupation of physicist for men dropped over a twenty-year period by more than one-fourth, by 10 percent for biologists and nearly as much for historians (Cherednichenko and Shubkin, 1985, p. 62).

The fall in prestige of the intellectual professions can be attributed not only to the sinking of labor ethics in these professions and the waning of their moral authority during the political reaction of the 1970s, when they proved subservient to the administration, but also to the "bourgeoisization" of Soviet society. This process has been well portrayed in Soviet movies in the early 1980s; examples include Zorin's *Good People* (1980) and *The Blond at the Corner* (1984). Bourgeoisization, which will be discussed in greater detail later, is being driven by the growing consumer aspirations of the Soviet people, primarily the youth, which encourages some people to use even semilegal ends to achieve a high material reward. This has been the case even in the scholarly occupations that demand exact, intensive work.

## What Hurt Labor Ethics: Weakening of the System

The deterioration of labor ethics in the country since the late 1950s is the product of the interaction of many factors. Among these factors are those related to the radical modification of the social environment, resulting in changes in the values of the Soviet population and their ways of making a living.

First of all, in the post-Stalin period, the role of two extrinsic stimuli for hard work—mass repressions, with the accompanying fear of being accused of being a wrecker, and the promotion of ideology—was drastically diminished.

Ideology, in the sense that one must support the system, is usually called upon only in critical cases, as was the case for some people in connection with the Chernobyl accident, but this has not been used for a long time.

But changes in the political system cannot be reduced only to these two factors no matter how important they are. The general relaxation of Soviet political life brought a number of other consequences that had a direct effect on labor ethics. One of them was the weakening of the whole mechanism of administrative control over work. This mechanism not only became more lenient toward violators of labor discipline but in many cases simply ignored them.

This development manifested itself in the 1970s when Brezhnev's regime created an atmosphere of general complacency. Managers at all levels covered up infractions of rules, negligence, sluggishness, and so on. One of the most striking facets of this period is the spread of drinking in the workplace without any serious resistance on the part of managers.

With the obvious laxity of the bureaucracy, the prestige of the Soviet manager fell sharply in the eyes of workers. This contributed to the decline of labor ethics, as it deprived workers of a model for behavior and deprived the manager of the moral authority necessary for directing people (see Rosenbaum, "Personal Example of a Manager," *Literaturnaia Gazeta*, July 20, 1983, p. 13).

The cadre policy of the Soviet political elite also had a big impact on labor ethics. In many cases ignoring professional records and skills when promoting people, the political elite, especially under Brezhnev, discouraged conscientious and talented workers in all branches of the economy, sometimes pushing them into other careers or so discouraging them that they gave up the thought of career advancement and became absorbed in their personal life.

The decline in the birthrate after the war and the low productivity of workers along with the continuing expansion of the Soviet economy exacerbated the labor shortage, which helped accelerate the decline of labor ethics. Practically every worker fired for alcoholism or other breaches of labor discipline could easily find a job someplace else. Of all those fired for a breach of discipline on the job, 30 percent not only immediately found a new job but also received an increase in salary of 30 percent (*Pravda*, May 13, 1984).

## *The Outburst of Envy and Aspirations*

In the post-Stalin period, with a significant growth in the standard of living, aspirations of the average Soviet individual underwent radical changes. In the last two decades particularly, Soviets have dramatically increased their demand for a comfortable lifestyle, greatly exceeding the material progress objective in Soviet society. The new aspirations created a sort of "mass culture"; people from all walks of life want to have the same clothes, apartments, furniture, books to read, leisure time, and vacation opportunities, as well as have their children study in the same prestigious schools.

This mass culture sharply magnified social envy among people and created a desire to "keep up with the Joneses." Envy became one of the most important factors in Soviet life in the 1970s and 1980s (see Shlapentokh, 1976). The case with housing is quite typical.

The dwelling space in cities increased by 2.6 times between 1960 and 1984 while the population increased by only 1.6 times (TsSU, 1985, pp. 5, 441). Improvement in housing conditions is reflected by sociologists in many surveys. In Taganrog, in 1967–68 only 16 percent of the workers lived in single apartments and 33 percent lived in communal apartments. In 1978 the figures were 41 and 12, respectively. In the 1960s only 13 percent of all families lived in apartments or houses with "all or almost all" of the main amenities; in the late 1970s this had risen to 46 percent (Klopov, 1985, p. 122).

However, despite the significant progress in housing conditions after 1953, the discontent of the people with them increased enormously. Before this, without any chance to better housing conditions and with everyone else in the same boat, people regarded their life in communal apartments as normal. According to a recent nationwide study of the adult population conducted by the Sociological Institute, only 52 percent are satisfied with their housing conditions. Among young people the degree of satisfaction is lower—36 percent (Levykin, 1984, p. 94). The number of lawsuits related to apartments has been growing steadily: from 62 per 100,000 residents in 1970 to 87 in 1984, a 40 percent increase (Iakovleva, 1986, p. 77). The number of people who leave their place of employment because of bad housing increased from 10 percent in 1964 to 17 percent in 1981 (Shishkina, 1985, p. 119).

### WHAT BROUGHT CHANGES IN SOVIET ASPIRATIONS?

These changes in aspirations can be attributed to a number of circumstances.

1. *The immense rise in educational level.* The average Soviet individual has earned at least a secondary education, whereas his or her parents studied no more than seven years in school and grandparents no more than four years. Since 1959 the number of people with a higher education rose from 36 to 69 percent (TsSU, 1985, p. 29).

With higher social mobility and an increase in the number of people in the intelligentsia (here defined as those with higher education) from 3.8 million in 1959 to 18.5 million in 1984, almost every Soviet family, urban or rural, has children or other close relatives who have graduated from a college or university (TsSU, 1985, p. 22).

Soviet social scientists, especially in connection with the content of the work concept, hailed the rise in educational level as an important factor positively influencing productivity.[10] But they disregarded the effect it would have on aspirations and that it would be at least partially responsible for the deterioration of labor ethics.

2. *Access to the mass media.* This period also saw a revolution in Soviet mass media. Each Soviet family has a TV set (about 20 percent have two), transistor radio, and subscribes to two or three newspapers and three or four magazines.

3. *Contact with the West.* The isolation of the Soviet people from the West under Stalin greatly affected their aspirations, and when contacts with the West became a part of Soviet life, even if the authorities try to curb them, it had a tremendous influence on Soviet behavior, a fact which I will discuss later. I will mention here only that the desire to imitate the Western style of life in one way or another turned Western goods into the most coveted objects in the Soviet Union, making them symbols of well-being and prestige for a majority of the population.

## *The Failure of Material Stimulation*

This growth of aspirations, coinciding with the weakening of state authority, became a factor in declining work ethics. This development was directly connected with the failure of the material incentives system introduced in the 1970s.

When the state no longer used the fear of mass repressions or the unusual efforts inspired by ideology to induce hard work, the managerial apparatus became well aware that material stimulation had to play a decisive role as an impetus. Since 1953 (and before) the Soviet government had been trying to create a system of material incentives which, backed by ideological indoctrination, could induce people to work efficiently. Over the last three decades Soviet managers and economists proposed and implemented hundreds of such schemes. With few exceptions, however, the Soviet economy entered the middle of the 1980s with an inefficacious system of material incentives.

For instance, a raise in bonus pay of 80 percent raised productivity by only 8 percent (*Pravda*, August 29, 1983). A survey conducted by the Sociological Institute in five large Soviet cities in 1981 revealed that only 28 percent of all respondents were satisfied with the material bonuses offered as rewards. In Moscow this figure was only 19 percent (Bozhkov and Golofast, 1985, p. 97).[11]

There are a number of reasons that explain this system's failure, and they will be discussed in the following sections. Each reason affected various groups of people differently, depending on objective factors (education, sex, age, social status, place of residence, and ethnic background) as well as subjective ones, such as work attitudes.

The flop of the Soviet system of material incentives affected professional enthusiasts as well as the honest career seekers and helped weaken the especially strong labor ethics of people who are consumer-oriented but who at the same time try to spare their effort (for more about the stimulation of work in the Soviet Union, see Kontorovich and Shlapentokh, 1986).

### THE DECLINE IN MARGINAL UTILITY OF THE RUBLE

The attitude of the Soviets toward their currency is one of the most important factors contributing to the failure of the material stimulation program.

There is much evidence that despite the growing role of nonmonetary factors to well-being in the Soviet Union (access to privileged stores and other facilities, pilfering, direct exchange of services, and so on), people are still very much absorbed with getting more money.

Dissatisfaction with salaries is a dominant feature of Soviet life. According to a study in five large cities in 1981, previously cited, only 10 percent of the employees are content with their legal income (Bozhkov and Golofast, 1985, p. 98; see also Klopov, 1985, p. 117).[12]

In most surveys no less than 10–20 percent of those polled indicate a low salary is one of the major factors inducing them to change employment and place of residence (see Antosenkov, 1969, 1974; Antosenkov and Kalmyk, 1970; Kupriianova and Pushkarev, 1982). There is good reason to suspect that the real number of people who change jobs and cities because of salary is much higher due to the "desirable values effect," which induces respondents to conceal their real motives and choose only those alternatives that are endorsed by dominant values, i.e., to respond in accordance with values perceived to be those that the state considers desirable. For this reason, many people do not name salary as the cause of their decision (see Shlapentokh, 1969c).

The growing interest in money changes attitudes toward many occupations. The majority of Soviet people feel they don't have enough money. According to a study in Leningrad in the early 1980s, no more than 11 percent of the respondents think they have enough money for their life, without considering the purchase of a car, which involves special strains (Protasenko, 1985, p. 105). In large cities no more than 34 percent of the people (38 percent in the nation as a whole) consider their "well-being as good" (Bozhkov and Golofast, 1985, p. 98; Levykin, 1984, p. 94). In a 1978–79 nationwide survey, young people named money, after time, as the reason for not being able to enjoy their leisure ( Alekseeva, 1983, p. 189). The respondents in a Latvian survey of the adult population (1978–79) view money as the main problem in everyday life ( Eglite, 1985, p. 64).

The eagerness of most Soviets to increase their income is combined with their propensity to save. Savings have risen steadily since the war and have now reached a level (221 billion rubles in 1985) equivalent to two-thirds of the value of all goods bought by the population in state and cooperative commerce (TsSU, 1986, pp. 448, 464).

However, with all their passionate desire to have as much money as possible, a majority of the Soviet people do not want to work hard for additional income.[13] Like everyone else, they weigh the effects of extra work on their physical and emotional well-being with the marginal utility of money (or the satisfaction "brought by an additional ruble"), they can earn in the factory and office. The average Soviet individual does not want to sacrifice too much to earn big money for four main reasons: (1) lack of consumer goods at moderate prices in state Stores; (2) limited investment possibilities; (3) state limits on high earnings; and (4) the existence of many semilegal and illegal means to get money with minimal effort.

#### THE SHORTAGE OF CONSUMER GOODS AT AFFORDABLE PRICES

In general, income in the Soviet Union is insufficient for purchasing goods people feel they need. With rising aspirations and a higher standard of living than before, most people do not want to buy many goods available in state stores because they are usually of poor quality. People often cannot find what they yearn to purchase in these stores—high quality, prestige goods, mostly of foreign origin.

Of course, all desirable goods can be found on the black market but at prices beyond the means of the average individual. For instance, according to the figures published in *Pravda* (July 23, 1984), over the years the price of a coveted pair of foreign-made jeans has risen higher (200 rubles in the early 1980s) than an average monthly salary (in 1983 the average salary was 182 rubles, TsSU, 1984b, p. 393). A sheepskin coat cost 1,500 rubles, a woman's fur coat cost 2,000 rubles, and a pair of women's shoes 100 rubles.

In recent years the official market raised the prices of many goods almost to the level of the black market, making many consumer goods even at official prices hardly accessible to the majority of the Soviet people. Thus, some brands of color TV sets cost up to 740 rubles (almost four average annual salaries), a woman's winter coat 323 rubles, telephones 90, women's boots 95, and so on (*Nedelia* 49, 1987). This serious inflation—prices of consumer goods rose in the last three decades by no less than two times—has also contributed to the decline in the marginal utility of the ruble (*Literaturnaia Gazeta*, September 16, 1987).

The poor supply of consumer goods is regarded by the majority of Soviets as the number one problem in their lives. Only 20 percent of the respondents in the five large cities (1981) indicated that they were satisfied with internal commerce. According to sociological studies, an average individual spends four to five hours a day in search of consumer goods and services (*Literaturnaia Gazeta*, October 19, 1983, p. 13). Even in Moscow, which is in a privileged position in comparison with other cities, no more than 18 percent evaluated positively the supply of goods. In the same study, 36 percent of those polled in these cities are satisfied with the clothes available and 52 percent with their food (respective figures for the nation as a whole are 40 and 53 percent). This correlates with the evaluation of Soviet commerce by the people (Bozhkov and Golofast, 1985, p. 980; Levykin, 1984, p. 94). Similar data were produced by other studies (see Aitov, 1985, p. 99; Klopov, 1985, p. 120; Zaslavskaia et al., 1986, p. 71).

The problem of supply is especially bad in the countryside, where residents do not even have the limited assortment of goods available to city dwellers. Ryvkina's data indicates that 71 percent of all rural residents went to the administrative center to buy goods unavailable in their village (Ryvkina, 1979, p. 227).

The lack of goods at prices that reasonably correspond to salaries significantly diminishes the incentive of a monetary bonus, as the people, with their relatively high savings (which could easily be spent on the black market), do not receive enough from their labor bonuses or wage increases to use on the black market and the money is of no use for state store purchases.

Pavel Bunich, a prominent Soviet economist, cites as an example of the inefficiency of the current program of material stimulation the statement of a woman worker who rejected a new bonus saying, "I prefer to do nothing for 200 rubles than to plod for 220 rubles" (*Literaturnaia Gazeta*, February 12, 1986, p. 10).

In many cases people straightforwardly asked superiors to give them not rubles but goods in kind as an incentive. This is particularly true in the countryside, where the supply of goods is very poor. *Pravda* cites a remarkable fact: rural residents often refuse to take a cash advance from state wholesalers for agricultural produce, preferring instead special rights to buy rare commodities in stores (*Pravda*, July 21, 1986). What is more, as Alexander Nikitin, one of the best Soviet economics journalists, found, rural residents want to have better access to particular foods (for instance, butter and sausage) instead of increase in salary (Nikitin, 1986, p. 10).

According to a study of Leningrad sociologists about the kind of remuneration they desired for effective work, about the same number—one third—wanted cash bonuses as wanted more vacation time (Pashkov, 1983, p. 128).

Valerii Vyzhutovich, a prominent Soviet journalist, reports on a gang of counterfeiters who were discovered in Ul'anovsk. The gang was involved not only in the printing of false money but also in the forgery of coupons necessary for obtaining butter and meat (products which are rationed in Ul'anovsk as well as in many other Soviet cities). The fact of coupon counterfeiting demonstrates the decline in the role of money in the Soviet economy (*Ogoniok* 43, 1987, p. 6).

The problem of housing is particularly relevant in analyzing the problem of the ruble. As was mentioned, the level of dissatisfaction with housing conditions is extremely high even though they have improved dramatically since 1953.

Official statistics show that by the beginning of the 1980s about four-fifths of the urban population lived in single apartments. However, these data conceal the fundamental fact that many of these apartments are occupied by two, three, and even four generations of relatives. According to Shkaratan's data, 46 percent of Leningrad workers think they do not have their own apartments. For engineers, this figure was 66 percent, and for managers 73 percent (Shkaratan, 1985, p. 238). The situation is especially bad for young people. According to the Taganrog study (1978) only 6 percent of single young workers, and only 33 percent of newlyweds, had their own apartment (respective figures were 4 and 5 percent in 1967–68) (Klopov, 1985, pp. 121–22).

In the campaign for truth launched by Gorbachev, the mass media revealed the real facts about the housing situation. *Pravda*, in an article on life in the Ul'ianovsk region, disclosed that workers may wait for an apartment and even one room for ten to fifteen years (*Pravda*, July 11, 1986, p. 2). So-called *limitchiki* (young workers from the provinces who are allowed to live in Moscow's or Leningrad's hostels on the condition that they take the worst work at the enterprise to which they are assigned) can hope (if they are not sent home for some offense) to get their own rooms only in twenty to twenty-five years—when they will have reached their forties (*Ogoniok* 41, 1987, p. 7; *Sovietskaia Kul'tura*, September 24, 1987).

Those who regard their housing conditions as bad—and these, as it was mentioned, make up half of the population—cannot improve their situation through money alone in most cases. The majority of apartments, new and old, are distributed by the authorities, and only a small fraction of the new ones that are condominiums can be bought by the public. However, even the limited number of condominiums are under the strict control of the authorities, and the availability of money does not mean that the apartment can be purchased if the claimant is not qualified for it. As Abel Aganbegian, a leading Soviet economist, contends, no less than one million people are in line to purchase an apartment in a condominium (Aganbegian, 1987, p. 12).

But of no less importance is that for many people, especially young ones who do not have any savings, the price of an apartment is extremely high. A down payment often takes four to seven years of an average annual salary. Therefore, the majority of people cannot necessarily improve their housing situation through a higher salary.

#### THE LIMITED INVESTMENT POSSIBILITIES

Even if we disregard the lack of quality consumer goods in state stores, another factor influences the lack of interest in earning higher salaries. This is the very limited possibility for people to invest their savings. The interest rate in Soviet banks is extremely low—2 or 3 percent. Only in 1987 did the government decide to offer the population a certificate with a five-year maturity and 4 percent interest. A Soviet journalist, describing the material goals of the people, could point to only four objects: an apartment, a country house, a color TV, and a car (*Sovietskaia Kul'tura*, November 22, 1986, p. 8). And with restrictions on travel abroad, the Soviets cannot use their money for trips or invest in foreign businesses.

#### THE LIMITS ON EARNINGS

The system of material incentives created by the Soviet government exerts different influences on different people. Along with people who minimize their work as soon as basic needs are satisfied, are a considerable number of people who are oriented toward maximizing their income. In the latter group are overachievers and a high proportion of talented and energetic people.

With all their support of material incentives for work, the Soviet leaders have always been afraid of allowing people a high income, even if it was a fair reward for good work. It is especially characteristic that Gorbachev, proclaiming his devotion to "the radical reform" of the Soviet economy and to the overhaul of the whole system of management, simultaneously passed the decree (May 1986) directed not only against nonlabor income (speculators, bribers, and so forth), but also against high income in general. The decree demanded documentation of sources of savings from anyone who purchased anything worth more than 10,000 rubles.

Two circumstances account for the reluctance of the Soviet political elite to allow people to earn large amounts of money—fear of inflation and fear of uncontrolled social differentiation. The fear of inflation and all its implications (including the weakening of material stimulation) is directly related to the incapacity of the Soviet economy to provide an adequate supply of consumer goods.

Since 1953 elements of egalitarianism have been manifest in various ways, such as in the establishment of minimal salary and pension levels, in the increase of salaries for poorly paid workers, and so on (see Rogovin, 1980, 1984). But this egalitarianism is also responsible to some extent for the unwillingness of Soviet leaders to permit high incomes for considerable numbers of workers. Such a policy, of course, discourages a number of energetic and ambitious people, and was the main cause of the failures of a number of organizational innovations in the Soviet economy, in particular the famous experiment of Ivan Khudenko in agriculture (where people in organized teams earned "too much" for the approval of Soviet officials).

## *Corruption of Society—the Main Cause of Labor Demoralization*

Whatever the importance of the other factors, labor ethics would never have declined as they did without the corruption in other parts of society. Corruption in the Soviet context means the use of one's official position to obtain material advantages for self, family, and friends.

The full impact of corruption on labor attitudes can be formulated in the following way: corruption divorces an individual from social goals, with the individual putting his or her well-being above concern for the national well-being.

Soviet corruption, which increased radically in the 1970s, made it impossible for the honest, hardworking citizen to reach the same level of material comfort as colleagues or neighbors who plunged into various forms of illegal activity, either inside or outside the public sector. Thus the image of the conscientious worker carried no prestige in the eyes of the majority of the Soviet population. The managerial class was also discredited by corruption, no longer maintaining a reputation for fairness and honesty.

The main ways to illegally boost income were through bribery of officials, under-the-counter commerce, and exchange of illegal services. Many other ways to beat the system were tried.

In the 1970s whole areas of Soviet life fell into the control of the "second economy" (or illegal economy) and its "wheeler-dealers." For instance, the repair of privately owned cars was a function that almost completely moved into the second economy. As Anatolii Rubinov, a famous Soviet journalist, convincingly demonstrated, nearly all car owners in the Soviet Union participate in this illegal business—particularly to obtain spare parts—in order to keep their cars operating (*Literaturnaia Gazeta*, May 9, 1984; see also *Literaturnaia Gazeta*, June 29, 1983; *Nedelia* 20, 1984, p. 7). The same was true about the distribution of almost all hard to get consumer goods, especially of foreign origin.

Not only some branches of the economy, but whole regions of the country fell into the zone of the dominant second economy. This was the case, according to the revelations of Gorbachev (1986) (see also El'tsin's speech at the twenty-seventh congress, *Pravda*, February 27, 1986), with practically the whole of central Asia, with a population of 45 million, and to a considerable extent with the Caucasian republics (14 million). Moscow, under the direct benevolence of Brezhnev himself, was almost turned into a reservation for corruption. Gorbachev and his lieutenants spoke frankly in 1985 and 1986 about "whole zones of the country" which "were excluded from criticism."

With this laxness in official morality, first party secretaries could fearlessly run their own domains so that their personal interests and those of their underlings, rather than the interests of the state, determined to a great extent the rules of behavior for a majority of the population. Again, as in many other cases, it was not the social scientists, but only a few writers who managed to document this, even if they had to leave out any connection of the phenomenon with Moscow (see Guseinov's novels *Family Secrets* [1985] and *Mahomed*, Mamed, Mamish [1977]; see also Ibragimbekov, 1984; Kurchatkin, 1986).

## Choice of Occupation

### *The Disregard of Social Interests*

In making decisions concerning their future occupations, Soviet people in general, and the youth in particular, almost completely ignore societal interests if they do not coincide with their personal interests. This was first shown by Vladimir Shubkin, who presented the results of his studies with two pyramids, laid one on another, with their peaks in opposite directions; the first pyramid symbolized societal demands on certain occupations, and the other the occupational plans of young people. This presented a clear picture of the antagonism between social and individual interests (Shubkin, 1970).

The most striking illustration of this antagonism was and still is the attitude toward the occupation of industrial workers. Soviet youth are reluctant to join the working class, which the ideology regards as the leading social force in the Soviet Union. Numerous surveys conducted in the Soviet Union over the last two decades show unanimously the low attraction laboring occupations have for young people. One showed that male youth ranked workers' occupations 25–35 out of a possible 80 occupations. The occupation of agricultural worker ranked even lower (Shubkin, 1970, pp. 280–86; 1984, p. 80). The index of prestige ascribed by graduates from Kiev secondary schools on a scale ranging from +1 to −1 was +0.78 for scholars, between +0.24 and +0.58 for engineers, and between +0.14 and −0.35 for workers (Chernovolenko et al., 1979, pp. 139, 205; Nikitenko and Ossovskii, 1981, p. 42). Data describing the attitudes of Estonian youth were roughly the same (Titma, 1973, p. 308; 1982, p. 126).

As education is a prerequisite for avoiding the occupation of worker or farmer and for achieving a modest social status (party membership is another), Soviet youth usually want to get a higher or at least a special college education and regard working at a plant as at best a temporary occupation.

This stress on higher education, even if it has declined recently, is such that a considerable number of Soviet youth are ready to attend any kind of a higher level school (Anufriev, 1984, p. 214). This accounts to a great extent for the fact that only one-third of the people with a higher education like their occupation, and about one-third of the population has a job commensurate with their college degree (Klopov, 1985; Shubkin, 1984, p. 98).

The determination to get a higher education for one's children, even if they do not have the capacity for it, was revealed in a Moscow study (1973). Parents were asked about their expectations concerning the future of their children after secondary school, while at the same time the teachers of these children were asked about their recommendations. Only 2 percent of the parents wanted their children to go to work after secondary school, which usually means manual, physical labor, whereas the teachers suggested that 31 percent of the children go to work. The personal plans of the children themselves were, of course, close to the parents' expectations—only 3 percent of them were willing to start work after secondary school (Kozyrev et al., 1975, p. 46).

In the 1960s and 1970s no more than 15 percent of the young wanted to become industrial workers, though workers made up about

62 percent of all employees in the country, and collective farmers made up another 10 percent (Konstantinovskii, 1977, p. 127). At the same time, no less than 70–90 percent of young people in the 1960s, 1970s, and early 1980s wanted an occupation based on higher or a special college education (Konchanin, 1975; Shubkin, 1984, pp. 61, 145; Shubkin and Babushkina, 1986, p. 38).[14]

Most young people who find themselves as factory workers want to leave their job and hope to do so through additional education (adult workers usually abandon this idea as unrealistic). According to Shubkin's data, such plans are nurtured by 75 percent of unskilled young workers, 65 percent of semiskilled, and 66 percent of skilled workers (Shubkin, 1984, p. 123).

Soviet youth are not the only ones who do not like workers' occupations. It is true even for adults who are workers themselves and who are inclined, as is everyone, to assess their occupation higher than the rest of the population. According to the studies of A. Baranov, only 3 percent of Leningrad workers and 18 percent of those at Al'metievsk (Tataria) wanted their children to become workers (Baranov, 1981, p. 103; also see Faisulin, 1978, p. 39).[15]

It is practically impossible for these people to change their actual social status (one study shows that only 2 percent of workers have a chance to become engineers, but other studies indicate 4–5 percent; see Kotliar, 1982, p. 100; Shkaratan, 1985, pp. 249–50; about the low mobility of workers see also Reznik, 1982, p. 111; Rossels, 1979, p. 33). In the same Shubkin study, significantly less than 50 percent of skilled workers said they would choose their occupation over again (among unskilled, only 25 percent) (Shubkin, 1984, p. 100).[16]

Although desirous of escaping the occupation of worker as much as possible, children of workers and workers themselves (the latter have their children in mind) are not as oriented toward higher education as professionals and their children; the difference, however, is not significant. Shubkin discovered in the early 1960s that 60 percent of workers' children were oriented to higher education as compared to 70 percent of professionals' children (Shubkin, 1970, p. 180; see also Samoilova, 1978, p. 115). More recent data only confirmed this finding (Shubkin, 1984, p. 139).

However, these differences should be ascribed not so much to the different value systems of workers and intelligentsia (as some authors suggest), but more to the realistic evaluations of each group of the chances of getting such an education. Despite an "affirmative action" policy in their favor, the children of workers and farmers pass college admittance exams much less frequently than professionals' children. According to one study among the applicants to Moscow schools of higher education, 36 percent had fathers with a low educational background. They made up only 28 percent of those admitted, whereas the respective figures for youth with parents having higher education were 41 and 62 percent (Samoilova, 1978, p. 102).

Realistic about their chances of getting into a university, the children of workers and farmers set getting into a technical college as their goal more often than professionals' children. A technical college degree will also help the recipient avoid having to do manual labor (see Alekseeva, 1983, p. 110; Filippov, 1976, p. 201).

Oddly enough, it was not official exhortations but rampant consumerism that helped improve attitudes toward some kinds of manual work. With large shortages of workers leading to higher wages on one hand, and with growing material aspirations on another, a considerable number of professionals, engineers in particular, began to change jobs and join the worker class. In some branches up to 20 percent of the engineers claimed they preferred the position of worker (*Pravda*, May 20, 1985).

## *Motives in the Choice of an Occupation*

An acquaintance with life in the Soviet Union clearly shows that an individual in no way chooses an occupation based on the desire to be useful to society or to respond to appeals from the leadership. As was mentioned, most people are glad if their work is important for the country, but if certain occupations, such as cosmonaut or writer, are declared by the authorities as socially important, while at the same time giving those who pursue these occupations a high standard of living, people can satisfy their material as well as social obligations. This should be taken into account when interpreting data claiming that up to 40 percent of Soviet youth indicate that social usefulness influences their attitudes toward an occupation (Semenova, 1979; Shubkin, 1984; Sokolov, 1981; Staroverov, 1979). However, in those cases, as with industrial or agricultural workers, where young people see no personal advantages, no ideological campaign can persuade them to like occupations regarded by the state as important.

The motives behind job choice are generally intangible. Among the most prominent are material reward, prestige, the content of work, and the degree of challenge and autonomy.

Unfortunately, sociological data can give only an approximate idea about the importance of each of these variables in shaping the attitudes toward various occupations. Numerous studies of job attitudes conducted in the Soviet Union in the last three decades could not neutralize the influence of "desirable values," or the impact of dominant values in social surroundings (see Popova, 1984; see also Jackman, 1978). They also cannot separate genuine motives from collateral ones used by individuals to rationalize a choice made for other reasons.

Studies of labor motivation were also impaired for a long time by the desire of leading Soviet sociologists to present the content of work, or more precisely, the degree of diversity and creativity, as the main variable determining attitudes toward work.[17] Only by comparing various sources and data accumulated by various scholars is it possible to get some picture about the structure of motivation behind job choice. Of these sources, the studies of labor turnover and migration—not surveys with direct questions about the motives for choosing a job—and to some extent the studies about the cause of dissatisfaction with work are of special value. But the information about why people change their occupation, place of work, and residence is also "infected" by socially desirable values (see, for instance, Shlapentokh, 1969c). However, this information is much more likely to reflect real behavior than the other studies and enables researchers to grasp the true labor motives of people.

Let us start with the bulk of the Soviet population—the masses, the industrial workers and farm laborers, who make up about two-thirds of all employees in the country.

The data on job turnover and migration (even in the period when the concept of content of work was in favor) suggests that material factors (salary, housing conditions, facilities for children, etc.) play a dominant role in decision making about work and the place of residence. In almost all studies material rewards and living conditions account for from one-half to two-thirds of all such decisions. The next most important factor influencing the decisions of workers and farmers is the difficulty of the job itself (the degree of physical tension, cleanliness, working hours, and so on). This accounts for 10 to 20 percent of the decisions. Other factors—like content of work or its usefulness and its prestige—are of minor importance. No more than 10 to 15 percent of all who leave their job cite dissatisfaction with its character as a reason for leaving (see Novosibirsk's studies in turnover—they are the best in the country—Antosenkov and Kalmyk, 1970, pp. 40–41; Kupriianova and Pushkarev, 1982, pp. 166, 168, 216; Shishkina, 1985, p. 118; see also Kononiuk, 1977, pp. 24, 38, 86; Pruts et al., 1980).

But the comparison of labor turnover rates in various industries supports the view that material factors influence job selection. The industries with the highest rates of turnover are those with the lowest salaries, such as light and food industries (25 percent and 29 percent, respectively, leave these jobs each year compared with 15 percent in machine building and chemical industries) (for further data of the 1982 Novosibirsk study, see Shishkina, 1985, p. 97).

Results from one of the most representative studies of the 1970s of 125,000 young workers who were employed in 181 enterprises in 73 cities of the Russian republic are of great interest in this respect. Sociologists asked young people about the reasons they were not satisfied with their job. Respondents could choose several alternatives from a limited number of options. Data show that "egotistical," self-oriented motives, mostly connected with the standard of living, prevailed over other motives. Thirty percent of all respondents indicated "bad or inconvenient working hours" as a reason for dissatisfaction, 27 percent bad housing conditions, 25 percent low salary, 23 percent poor work organization, and 18 percent bad working conditions. Motives which with some stretching could be regarded as having social meaning, such as dissatisfaction with the profession itself, no chance to improve job skills, or the impossibility of combining work with further study, were chosen by significantly fewer respondents—12, 7, and 6 percent respectively (Kotliar and Trubin, 1978, p. 154).

When discussing motivation in choosing an occupation, analyzing the role of the content of work is particularly significant in view of the myth created by Soviet sociologists in the 1960s regarding its importance.

## *The Role of Content of Work as a Motive*

Skepticism about how important the content of work really was as a stimulus for work was expressed by some sociologists as early as the 1960s, when this idealized concept, which pleased both Marxist liberals and the authorities, gained most popularity. However, their criticism was practically ignored until the late 1970s, when it became obvious that sociologists in the Soviet Union (as well as some in the United States) had fallen prey to two fatal methodological errors: (1) disregarding the high correlation between the content of work and extrinsic reward, and (2) disregarding the influence of socially acceptable values on the responses of their respondents.

For example, complex and diversified (or creative) work tends to be higher paid in the Soviet Union just as it is in the West. It also carries more prestige than routine work. Thus, when people profess their devotion to "creative work," it may not be because of its content but because it is better rewarded and gives them a higher status.

In a socialist society, where the marginal utility of money is low, prestige takes on a special significance. Research conducted by Vodzinskaia (1967) on the attitudes of Soviet youth found that prestige was one of the principal factors determining the attractiveness of occupations seen by the respondents as creative.

Since then other studies have investigated the role of prestige in a variety of areas of social life. Balandin (1979), for example, studied a sample of workers in Perm and found a high correlation between work satisfaction and the prestige of the job (see also Loiberg, 1982). Prestige was found to be of special significance for intellectuals, scholars, writers, and painters (Kelle et al., 1978).

Various data also show that there is a high correlation between salary level and the number of people who declare that the content of work is their primary motive in choosing a profession. According to Shkaratan's research, among engineers with a salary of less than 200 rubles per month, only about 49 percent are "oriented toward the content of work," but among those with a salary of more than 200 rubles 65 percent are concerned with work content. For managers the corresponding figures are 21 and 74 percent (Shkaratan, 1985, p. 163).

Another error committed by many who explore labor attitudes is the neglect of the "desirable values effect." Creative, complex work is praised in the mass media, literature, and schools. Those who like money are poorly regarded. It is only natural, therefore, that many respondents, when asked to give their motives for job choice, present those which are socially approved.

In the early 1980s the first decisive blow to the romantic concept of labor motivation was delivered by Irina Popova in two articles (one coauthored with Viktor Moin) demonstrating how shaky the empirical basis of this concept was. The core of their work was a comparison of respondents' answers to questions about their motives with the motivation they ascribe to others. For example, when asked their reasons for leaving a place of employment, only 34 percent indicated low wages as their principal motivation. However, when asked why other people left their jobs, 86 percent cited dissatisfaction with salary. When asked why they left the countryside to move to the city, a mere 4 percent explained their migration by a desire to increase their income; yet the same motive was attributed to others by 29 percent of the respondents (Popova and Moin, 1982, p. 29). Thus it was concluded that the limited significance attributed to wages when questions directly refer to the respondents can be traced to socially approved values and the desire not to appear too concerned with money (see Popova, "Images of Values and the Paradoxes of Self-Consciousness," 1984). After these ground-breaking articles, other Soviet sociologists began to distance themselves from the work content concept (see, for instance, Golofast et al., 1983; Klopov, 1985; Shkaratan, 1985; see also Zdravomyslov, 1981).

There is no doubt that the content of work is an important factor influencing popular attitudes, including choice of occupation. However, the real number of people for whom work content is crucial is much lower than was suggested in the past by Iadov and his followers. Recent Soviet studies now find that no more than one-fourth of those polled find this factor pivotal in their job decisions. Sociologists studying the Urals recognize that about 25 percent of workers evaluate their job only by its content, whereas 60 percent attributed a key role to salary along with content of work (Fainburg, 1982, p. 52).

Labor motivation among the intelligentsia, engineers in particular, is not radically different from that of the workers. Material conditions play a leading role in the decision of professionals to change their place of work and residence as well as their narrow occupations (Mozyreva, 1982, p. 190).[18]

Yet the importance of work content, along with self-fulfillment and prestige, is somewhat higher for professionals than for the general population, a fact which is especially notable in the studies of young peoples' attitudes toward occupations. According to Shubkin's studies in Kostroma in the late 1970s, young people with higher education felt that first, work should be "interesting," second, it "should be adequate to personal abilities and inclinations," third, "useful for society," fourth, of "social importance," fifth, "should allow the acquirement of new knowledge," and sixth, it should be "well rewarded." Those with a low education assigned less importance to almost all those requirements (except the first) that related to self-fulfillment and professional progress (Shubkin, 1984, p. 96).

The same conclusions were drawn by sociologists studying graduates of secondary schools in Kiev. Those who planned to go to a university placed self-fulfillment in second place and prestige fourth in enumerating factors in choosing a job, whereas those who planned to go to work straight from high school indicated sixth and fifth, respectively (Chernovolenko et al., 1979, p. 154; see also Titma, 1973, p. 305).

These data, as any other about attitudes toward work, should be regarded with many caveats. However, they can be used, along with other evidence, to show that people who have an orientation toward higher education appreciate more diversified and creative work, although perhaps not to the degree suggested by Soviet sociologists in the 1960s.

## Trends in Attitudes toward Work in the 1970s and 1980s

### *The Influence of Consumerism and Corruption*

The increasing role of consumerism in Soviet life has dramatically increased the popularity of occupations that pay well by Soviet standards.

As a result, a number of occupations that were regarded in the late 1960s as nonprestigious, such as bus or truck driver, where the salary exceeded that of scholars and professors in many cases, are becoming more attractive. According to the unique longitudinal studies conducted under Shubkin's guidance in Novosibirsk, in 1982 the occupation of driver was about 40 percent more popular among male youth than twenty years earlier (Cherednichenko and Shubkin, 1985, p. 62).

At the same time, another development—corruption—spread and infiltrated all spheres of Soviet life. Corruption, along with an inefficient system of material incentives, has enhanced the status of many occupations in which one can obtain semilegal or even illegal access to consumer goods and services. This forms a network in the second economy where it is possible to exchange one scarce good or service for another.

This has led to a dramatic rise in the attractiveness of occupations in commerce and services. After being openly disdained by youth in the early 1960s (these occupations were rated lowest in popularity, even behind that of agricultural work), these occupations have made a miraculous leap in appeal.

One explanation for this shift can be found in Tatiana Protasenko's data about the standard of living of people employed in the commerce and services sector compared to other groups in the general population. The average salary of employees in commerce and services was practically the same as that of teachers and engineers (about 150 rubles a month) but much less than that of workers (200). However, 40 percent of those employed in commerce and services have a color TV set as compared with 32 percent among engineers, 27 for teachers, and 26 for workers. The same figures roughly apply for ownership of other prestige items—stereos, expensive suits, rugs, jewels, crystalware, etc. Fourteen percent of the people employed in commerce and services said they have sufficient money for their needs, including durable goods (except a car), whereas this figure was only 8 percent among workers and engineers (Protasenko, 1985, p. 107).

As Shubkin's data (confirmed in other studies; see Babosov, 1985, p. 135) shows, the attractiveness of sales-related occupations rose by 70–75 percent; for women it rose by 81 percent. The attraction of being a waiter rose to 23 percent for men. This change of popular attitudes toward people in commerce has been recently documented in Soviet novels and movies, such as Shtemler's *Supermarket* (1984) and the film, *The Blond Around the Corner* (1984).

At the same time most occupations in industry and agriculture (some counter-tendencies were mentioned earlier) have declined in prestige. The attractiveness of industrial work, such as that of lathe operator, decreased between 1962 and 1982 by as much as 20 percent, a worker in the building industry by 29 percent, and a weaver by 20 percent. But the prestige of some agricultural occupations has increased, the appeal of tractor driving is up 44 percent, and work in cattle breeding is up 46 percent (Cherednichenko and Shubkin, 1985, p. 62; Shubkin and Babushkina, 1986, p. 36).

A recent survey of teenagers, carried out by *Literaturnaia Gazeta* and the journal *Sotsiologicheskiie Issledovaniia* (*Sociological Research*) in Moscow, Leningrad, Ashkhabad, and Erevan in 1987, casts light on the perceptions of Soviet young people about occupations. These teenagers were asked which professions bring the highest income in Soviet society. They listed black marketeering first; military jobs second; automobile servicing; bottle recycling, and jobs in remote areas of the country (Siberia and others) third. Pilots, actors, and college professors were last on the list, preceeded by hairdressers, salesgirls, prostitutes, and taxi drivers (Shchekochikhin, 1987, p. 13).

## *The Decline of Educational Prestige and Changes in Attitudes toward Engineering*

This shift in popularity of some occupations has led to a decline of prestige of higher education, a process accelerated by the egalitarian policy of the government which eliminated differences between workers' and engineers' salaries, as well as between many other occupations no matter what educational level was required. The ratio of salary difference between an engineer and a worker went from 2.15 in 1940, to 1.51 in 1960, to 1.15 in 1980, and to 1.11 in 1984. In the building industry this ratio changed from 2.42 down to 0.98, and in agriculture (state farms) from 2.43 to 1.34 (TsSU, 1985, pp. 417–18). Scientists, who earned the highest salary compared with ten fields in 1940–50, earned fourth highest in 1975–83; art figures earned the second highest salaries in 1940, whereas in 1975–83 they ranked ninth in earnings (Gvozdev, 1985, p. 184).

According to a survey in Latvia, the difference in wages between people of the highest and lowest educational levels is no more than 22 percent. Furthermore, the difference in wages between people with the same education is higher than that between differently educated groups (Eglite et al., 1984, p. 194; see also Shkaratan, 1982, p. 47; 1985, p. 84).

As the professions no longer command the high salaries they once did in comparison to other fields, particularly in science, significant modifications in attitudes toward those occupations requiring university or college degrees have occurred. Engineering, mathematics, and physics have all lost in popularity. Occupations in these fields demand much more intellectual tension and responsibility than many people wish to assume. So-called "easy" occupations in the humanities, which provide practically the same salary and the same if not greater prestige, are now more popular than in the 1960s (see Shubkin, 1984, pp. 80–81). Accordingly, the number of students in colleges and universities who want to major in engineering and natural science has declined drastically whereas the competition for vacancies in the humanities has increased significantly (*Pravda*, June 24, 1986, p. 3).

## *The Quest for Easy and Comfortable Work*

The number of people concerned not so much with maximizing their well-being as with minimizing their effort has been growing rapidly in the last decade and exerts a highly visible impact on the Soviet labor market, and indeed on the mentality of the entire adult population. This manifests itself in the increasing importance which people now attach to working conditions.

The significance of working conditions—such as cleanliness, lack of noise, flexible regime, regular hours—attests not so much to an interest in the work itself as to the desire to have it easy. In the last decade Soviet scholars have found that conditions in the workplace are often more important than salary and content of work. The most authoritative statement about this new trend belongs to Vladimir Iadov, who, in analyzing the data from his longitudinal study of Leningrad workers, found that the number who paid significant attention to working conditions rose from 40 percent in 1962 to 60 percent in 1976 (Iadov, 1983, p. 60; see also Iadov, 1982).

A 1981 survey found that only 34 percent of the adult population in big cities are satisfied with occupational conditions. For Moscow this figure was 31 percent and for Leningrad, 24 (Bozhkov and Golofast, 1985, p. 97; see also Shkaratan, 1985, p. 256). Shishkina and other Novosibirsk sociologists found that the number of people who quit their job because of working conditions increased from 1971 to 1981 by 60 percent, whereas the number of those who changed place of employment because of work content declined by 17 percent, or because of salary by 5 percent. The sociologists noted with amazement the emergence of a new motive for labor turnover: "conditions not good enough [for a worker] to put himself or herself in order after the working day" (Shishkina, 1985, pp. 117–19).

A number of researchers recently found that workers rank job conditions first among all the factors influencing their attitudes toward work. For instance in one survey, 89 percent of the Byelorussian industrial workers questioned evaluated "comfortable conditions on the job" as "very important" compared to 23 percent who said the same about "diversity of work" (Babosov, 1985, p. 109; Sokolova, 1984, p. 71). Aitov indicates that "we observe more and more cases where people prefer lower-paid work to better-paid, but it is usually more difficult and highly unattractive. This tendency is revealed especially strongly among young people" (1983, p. 71). Farm workers also give importance to their job conditions, rating them at −0.44 on a scale of −1.0 to +1.0, whereas the diversity of work was rated at −0.11, and wages at +0.22 (Khaikin, 1979, p. 68). A number of other sociologists have collected data in support of these findings (see, for instance, Kamaieva, 1977; Kolodizh, 1978, pp. 113–14; and Loiberg, 1982, pp. 32–33).

## *The Increasing Role of Externalities*

With the general yearning for an easy life, the Soviet people have significantly increased their aspirations for better living conditions, or for "externalities" connected with their place of work. Thus the importance attributed to the distance between job and home is remarkable, directly resulting from people's dissatisfaction with mass transit. Only 30 percent of the residents of big cities find public transport acceptable; even in Moscow, with its super subway, the figure is 15 percent. Big city residents rate only the supply of goods worse than public transportation.

A study of workers newly arrived in Moscow (1979) from the provinces found that 45 percent considered the distance between home and place of work as the main factor determining positive work attitudes. Twenty-eight percent felt that the psychological climate at the job was most important, and 11 percent felt content of work was the main factor (Moiseenko, 1983, p. 20).

In Orel, for example, 20 to 25 percent attributed closeness to (or great distance from) home as a factor in choosing or quitting a job (Kotliar, 1982, pp. 139, 175). In another survey, specialists (party functionaries, personnel departments, managers, and others) and construction workers at a nuclear power station were asked what could prevent people from leaving the construction site. Both groups pointed to public transportation as one of the most important factors; it was ranked fourth among twenty alternatives, more than content of work, opportunity to raise qualifications, and so on (Alekseeva, 1983, pp. 175–79).

## *Accommodation to Demographic Trends*

So far I have discussed changes in work attitudes brought about by the evolution of human aspirations. Also of significance are the changes in the labor market which took place in the Soviet Union in the 1970s.

These changes are mostly due to the combination of two factors—trends in the birthrate and an increase in the number of teenagers finishing secondary school. The 1960s experienced a shortage of students as a result of the decline in the birthrate in the 1940s. In the 1970s the number of graduates from secondary schools rose dramatically. Therefore, in the 1960s young people had a strong chance of getting a higher education, but in the 1970s this chance significantly decreased. Again, the declining birthrate of the 1960s greatly affected the labor market in the 1980s (see Cherednichenko and Shubkin, 1985, pp. 80–124).

The ratio of high school graduates to newly admitted university students was 1.57 in 1965 and 3.77 in 1980. Thus, in the mid-1960s two out of three high school graduates had a chance to be admitted to the university immediately, whereas by the end of the next decade only two out of seven had the same chance. According to one estimate, no more than 10 to 20 percent of teenagers in the early 1980s will go directly from secondary schools into the university (Dobrynina, 1978; Konstantinovskii and Shubkin, 1977, pp. 82–83; *New York Times*, July 20, 1986, p. E3).

Even in Moscow, where for various reasons (such as the number of colleges, the higher educational level of the parents, the high quality of Moscow secondary schools, and connections) it is easier to get a higher education than in the provinces, teenagers became workers seven times more often than they planned, and clerks thirteen times.[19] In the early 1980s only 57 percent of Muscovites were satisfied with educational opportunities for their children (Bozhkov and Golofast, 1985, p. 98).

The school reform of 1984 (see Strizhov, 1984) had as one of its openly declared purposes the channeling of at least 30 to 40 percent of children after the middle school (eighth or ninth grade) to vocational schools or directly to industry and agriculture as workers. The reform also intended to intensify vocational training in secondary schools (Prokofiev, 1985, pp. 107–18, 157–74).

Soviet youth, reacting to the new circumstances and weighing their chances of entering a university, began to set lower goals and planned to get a less prestigious education. One study in Novosibirsk revealed that, while in 1966 89 percent of new graduates applied for admission to higher schooling, the figure dropped to 80 percent in 1970, and 60 percent in 1975 (Solovykh, 1977). This reorientation toward education by teenagers was so drastic that some colleges had difficulty in recruiting sufficient students, particularly in engineering (Karpukhin and Kutsenko, 1983, p. 46; *Pravda*, June 15, 1986).

All this led to some decline in the value attached to higher education (the magnitude of this decline has not been exaggerated), as people, once they must resign themselves to lower aspirations, tend not to like what they cannot get (otherwise known as the sour grapes effect).

It is strange that the rise of consumerism, with its focus on money, and the difficulties in getting a higher education even for children from the intelligentsia (22 percent of young people whose parents were professionals had to leave the intelligentsia, even if only temporarily [Shubkin, 1984, p. 169]), led to some democratization in the public mind, diminishing the differences in prestige of occupations.

## *New Attitudes toward Children and Work*

The rise in consumerism and interest in money also started to change attitudes toward teenagers getting paid for their work.

Pre-Revolutionary feudal traditions, coupled with the Marxist rejection of any form of mercantilism, accounts for the contempt of money which was dominant in Soviet society until the 1970s. This attitude in many cases was not genuine and only reflected the accepted rules of social behavior.

It was felt that paying children for their work would have a pernicious impact on their moral education and foster greedy instincts. The attitudes toward paid work for high school and college students was less restrictive but it was still regarded as indecent for them to work "only for money," for instance as waiters, waitresses, and salespersons.

Since the late 1950s popular attitudes have begun to change, although slowly. College students first got public approval to work during summers, and then gradually approval was extended to teenagers. These developments were supported by the state as a means of reducing labor shortages (Alekseeva, 1983, pp. 96–122).

A survey in Moscow (1984) showed that the majority of Soviet people now consider the work of their high school children as a positive thing. It is peculiar, however, that among the laboring class the support of this idea was not nearly as strong as among the intelligentsia—60 percent compared to 74 (Kinsburskii, 1985, p. 103).

A survey conducted by the Institute of Sociology in various regions of the country in 1984 also showed that 64 percent of the respondents preferred to lower the minimum age for work in various occupations (Voinova and Korabeinikov, 1984, p. 100; for articles in support of teenagers' work, see *Pravda*, August 7, 1983, and *Literaturnaia Gazeta*, April 6, 1983). Furthermore, the evolution of public opinion about the participation of children in work went so far that high-school students were permitted to work for the private cooperatives that emerged in 1986–87 (*Nedelia* 46, 1987, p. 2).

## Choice of Residence

As with jobs, the Soviet people choose their place of residence solely on the basis of personal interests. They virtually ignore the recommendations of the authorities unless the suggestions are buttressed by adequate rewards.

In general, the place of residence in the Soviet Union plays a much more prominent role in life than in the West, even in a country as large and diverse as the United States. This is because the disparities in living conditions between different parts of the Soviet Union are so tremendous. Among other things, climate, the supply of food and consumer goods, the price of food, housing conditions, and the quality of services vary immensely across the country.

A unique calculation made by Aitov, who determined eighteen indicators of the quality of life, shows that even within the same republic—Bashkiria—the quality of life in Ufa, the center, is 1.52 times higher than in Kumertau, an industrial city. It is easy to imagine that this figure would increase enormously if we compared Moscow or Leningrad with a remote village in the Far East (Aitov, 1985, p. 105).

In general, the quality of life is best in the big cities, especially in administrative centers, although it has deteriorated in recent decades.[20] The quality decreases with the diminution of the size and administrative status of the city. The countryside, on the whole, experiences a lower quality of life than the cities. At the same time, life in the west (the European part of the country) and in the south (Central Asia and the Caucasian republics) is much better than in the east (Siberia and the Far East) and the north (the northern part of the European section as well as the Asian parts of the Soviet Union).

The population movement follows these differences, and people try to transfer from a village to a city, from a small city to a large one, and from a regional center to Moscow or Leningrad. People leave the east for the west, and the north for the south. People can move to other areas with better living conditions only if they can find a job there.

Kozhevnikova compared two types of regions—those with a positive balance of migration and those with a negative one. It turned out that salaries in the first region are 1.24 times higher than in the second, the availability of kindergarten is 1.34 times greater, the number of physicians per 10,000 people is 1.64 times greater, the value of sales of goods per person is 1.35 times greater, and dwelling space per person is 1.10 times greater than in the second region (Kozhevnikova, 1985, p. 86).

In the period of industrialization (the late 1920s and the 1930s) the government favored some migration from the countryside to the cities and from small cities to larger ones. It did not even oppose the influx of people into Moscow, Leningrad, or other big industrial cities. But by the late 1950s the official policy about rural migration as well as the migration from small cities changed, and since that time Soviet authorities have been at odds with the population in respect to the different kinds of population movement across the country. They try to prevent rural people and inhabitants of small cities from leaving their place of residence, they closed Moscow and dozens of other big cities in the country, and they try to encourage people to move to the east and north and from Central Asia with its labor surplus (the birthrate here is three to four times higher than in other parts of the Soviet Union) to other parts of the country that suffer from labor shortages.

On the whole, over the last three decades, using direct administrative measures, the government has been more or less successful only with closing the big cities. They did this by requiring the "propiska," a stamp in the internal passport (it is issued by local police) indicating the approved address of a permanent resident, thus regulating the number of new residents.

In all other aspects the migration policy failed and was not accepted by the population. Soviet economists compete with each other in computing economic losses due to migration. According to some, the increase in migration between 1970 and 1979 led to the loss of 3 million full-time workers (Aitov, 1985, p. 10). Other scholars insist that only migration caused by dissatisfaction with facilities and housing conditions brought a loss of 1.5 billion rubles (Kocherga and Mazaraki, 1981, p. 64).

The last two decades have witnessed the growing role of the place of residence in the life planning of the Soviet people. Along with the increasing attention to occupational conditions and externalities within the same city, this trend reflects their determination to make life as comfortable as possible.

The growing role of location of the workplace in the choice of a job has attracted the attention of sociologists since the late 1970s. Vladimir Iadov singles out this trend as one of the most significant, noting that the difference in labor motivation of people with the same job living in cities with a different quality of life is greater than that between people with different occupations living in the same city (Iadov, 1982, p. 34). Boris Kononiuk came to the same conclusion (1977, p. 38).

People searching for a place of residence where they can best satisfy their needs accounts for why the "city-city" migration (which brings only losses to the national economy) became so prominent in Soviet society. In the early 1970s, 5.3 million people moved from city to city compared to 4.4 million who moved from a village to a city, and 1.7 million from a city to a village. Today 4–5 percent of the whole population change their place of residence each year, a high figure for Soviet society (Moiseenko, 1985, p. 254).

This tendency to move is another important sign of the prevalence of individual over social interests. According to the census of 1979, the number of those who lived at a given place of residence for less than two years increased by almost half. They made up 16 percent of the population, and together with those who lived between two and five years at the same address formed one-third of the population (TsSU, 1984b, p. 361).

## *Readiness to Live in Siberia and the Far East*

Since the twenties the ruling elite has considered the economic and demographic development of the eastern part of the country to be an extremely important part of the Soviet economic program. Persuading people to move to the east took a significant toll on ideological work before the war (let us remember, for instance, Valentina Khetagurov's famous movement, the voluntary recruitment of young women for settlement in the Far East), and this effort has been continued since.

However, the government has not created living conditions there which could reconcile people with the climate and the remoteness of these regions. What is more, in most cases housing conditions in Siberia and the Far East are much worse (almost twice as bad according to Perevedentsev's calculation) than in the European part of the country. No less than 50 percent of the Siberian population in 1984 were strongly dissatisfied with their housing conditions and regarded them as an eventual impetus to migration. Even though people in these regions receive a higher salary than in the western part of the country (although salaries were significantly increased only recently), this was not enough to compensate for the hardship of life in north Siberia or the Far East[21] (Perevedentsev, 1975, pp. 157–72; Zaslavskaia et al., 1986, p. 41).

Of all the people who come to the Far East, only one-third remain (Khorev, 1981, p. 268; Morozova, 1985, p. 28; Zaionchkovskaia, 1972, pp. 66–70). As a result, the relative number of people living in the eastern part of the country has steadily declined since the late 1950s from 17.6 percent of the total population in 1959 to 11.4 percent in 1984. This trend has been slightly reversed since additional material incentives were added at the end of the 1970s to induce people to remain (Riabushkin and Rybakovskii, 1981, p. 258; TsSU, 1985, pp. 14–16).

Not only has the government failed to diminish this economically harmful migration, but it has also failed to stimulate the migration of Moslem residents from Central Asia where they suffer massive hidden unemployment. All attempts to induce large emigration from this region have so far been unsuccessful (Breev, 1977, p. 85; Perevedentsev, 1979, pp. 19, 23–25; Tarasova, 1985, pp. 50, 58; Zaionchkovskaia, 1985, p. 93).

The inability of the government to assimilate the Central Asian peoples can be seen in the construction of the BAM ( Baikal Railroad), which was proclaimed as a national construction project. All republics were called on to take part in it. Only 7–9 percent of the workers were from the Central Asian region and Kazakhstan, which comprise 15 percent of the total Soviet population. And of the people who did come from these regions, only 11 percent were of the dominant ethnic group that makes up 50–60 percent of the total population of Kazakhstan and the republics of Central Asia (Belkin and Sheregi, 1985, p. 41; TsSU, 1985; Zhelezko, 1980, p. 107).

## Attitudes toward Socialist Property

Socialist, or collectivized, property is considered one of the most fundamental features of Soviet society and economy. The concept of socialist property (i.e., that the means of production belong not to single individuals but to all the people) occurs in the Soviet mind in both highly abstract and concrete forms, strongly complicating the study of popular attitudes regarding this value that is so important for an understanding of Soviet economic behavior. Also, popular attitudes toward socialist property have been undergoing great changes since the post-Stalin period, which does not make an exploration of the issue any easier.

An absolute majority of the Soviet people, in the most abstract sense, accept the existence of socialist property and agree with the official position about the importance of guarding this property against those who want to exploit it for their own personal interests or who would handle it indifferently, allowing the waste of resources belonging to the state.

However, I do not believe, for reasons stated below, that most people of the Soviet Union feel any emotional involvement with this issue. As soon as they move from the abstract concept of property to a more concrete level, their attitudes become more specific and even verbally they do not feel themselves committed to the total support of socialist property. Many people believe it may be necessary to change the existing property relations in the country, especially with respect to agriculture, services, and commerce. In this case, the abstract concept of property evolves into more definite objects, such as raw materials, tools, equipment, and finished products.

There are a number of official myths regarding socialist property that the average Soviet citizen does not even subconsciously believe in because everyday experience shows otherwise. First of all, people reject the official dogma that every worker, together with his or her colleagues, is the master of the factory, business, or collective farm where he works. Second, workers observe that their superiors do not manifest real concern about the preservation and efficient use of material resources under their command. Third, they observe every day the regular waste of raw materials, semiproducts, and finished products not only at the workplace but everywhere.

Respect for socialist property eroded rapidly in the 1970s. One indicator of popular attitudes toward concrete public property is judgments about theft in the workplace. Moscow sociologist Alexander Grechin explored attitudes of Moscow workers to various work violations. Asked about pilfering at work, only 17 percent (despite the highly loaded character of the questions) felt violators should be punished. The vast majority—79 percent—openly refused to condemn this act, and 3 percent even approved of theft. At the same time, contrary to Marxist-Leninist belief, crime against individuals is condemned much more strongly than crime against socialist property. Thus 85 percent of the respondents approved punishing those who hurt a woman; 77 percent felt sales clerks who cheated customers should be punished (Grechin, 1983, p. 124). Another Moscow sociologist interviewed 425 young workers in Moscow, Leningrad, and Minsk in the 1970s. Among other questions, he asked his respondents whether it was acceptable to steal parts from a plant—40 percent said "yes" (Shalenko, 1977, p. 74).

In the study conducted by Babosov and his colleagues in Byelorussia and Estonia (1981–84), only 53 percent of the young people declared that they are worried about embezzlement in their enterprises. Many more expressed their concern about toadyism (68) and hooliganism (68) (Babosov et al., 1985, p. 141).

According to Soviet studies, 30 percent of all cases of pilfering are performed in the presence of colleagues. The same studies show that only 4–5 percent of all people detained for theft in enterprises were turned in by their colleagues (see Norkin, 1982, p. 93).

The Soviet people see the main remedy against pilfering at the workplace as improving control over material resources and not in raising the morals of the workers. In a study in Chuvashiia in the 1970s, 40 percent of the workers pointed to bad supervision as the main cause of theft within enterprises. All other causes were ranked substantially lower (Mus'ko, 1979, p. 113).

While supporting socialist property as a general concept, and being rather indifferent to it in observing the behavior of others, the Soviet individual definitely does not feel any respect for this property if it concerns his or her own interests. Four phenomena can be used to study the attitudes of the Soviet people toward socialist property at this personal level: (1) the waste of raw materials and products; (2) the exploitation of equipment for personal use; (3) their attitudes toward their own personal property; (4) their participation in pilfering (which will also be discussed in the second part of the book).

## *The Waste of Resources*

The spoilage of resources is a phenomenon known in any society, and in a capitalist one in particular. Soviet textbooks on political economy (until the 1980s) as well as monographs on capitalist economies never forgot to recall specific cases, as those that occurred during the Great Depression and in other economic crises in capitalism (see, for instance, Volkov, 1979, pp. 140, 449–50). However, socialist societies have positively outrun capitalist ones in the waste of resources.

The negligence of people in the Soviet Union toward material resources—raw materials, parts, semi- and finished products—has been ongoing since the Revolution. As late as 1961 Krushchev complained about this in his report to the twenty-second congress (Khrushchev, 1961).

But in the early 1980s, with the depletion of natural resources such as oil and coal, which had seemed inexhaustible, Soviet society suddenly ran into a shortage of raw materials. This new phenomenon finally brought to a halt one of the greatest infirmities of the Soviet economy—the gigantic waste of resources by the Soviet population.

This went on in practically all spheres of the economy. However, some areas played a leading role and in some ways served as the "model" for others. By all accounts, agriculture had long set the pattern in this domain. According to various sources, Soviet farmers are basically indifferent to what they produce at the collective, or state, farms. Even official data, which evidently underestimate the scope of waste, show that losses of grain were calculated at 20–25 percent, vegetables and fruit at 30 percent, and milk and meat at 10–15 percent (Gvozdev, 1985, p. 88).

Many sources, including official ones, indicate that at least one-third of the entire harvest does not reach the consumer. This waste is a result not only of the sloppy work of Soviet farm laborers and those city residents coming to their help, as well as of workers in stores and food processing industries (see *Nedelia*, 1985, #10, p. 6; 1985, #26, pp. 6–7; *Pravda*, November 13, 1984), but also of other deficiencies, particularly the shortage of stores.

Agriculture has served as a gigantic school for educating people in contempt for socialist property. The majority of city residents—from teenagers in secondary schools to senior fellows in Soviet academia—are required to work for a few weeks each year either in the countryside or in a vegetable store in the city. Here they face the waste of valuable food products, the scope of which usually exceeds what they had imagined. The mass media and the speeches of Soviet leaders describing this waste as spoilage of agricultural products only increases their anger and cynicism. City dwellers quickly learn to follow rural residents in their disregard for the harvest (see, for instance,

Gorbachev's speech in Murmansk, *Pravda*, October 2, 1987; see also *Pravda*, November 13, 1984; *Nedelia*, 1985, #26, *Pravda*, February 2, 1983).

Agriculture is also renowned for the abuse of such resources as water, pesticides, and especially fertilizers. The timber industry vies with agriculture in its waste of resources; the amount of wood left by workers is gigantic. According to experts it will take twenty to thirty years to collect this wood in the Ural regions alone (Ageev, 1984, p. 113). In terms of resource waste, hunting is not behind the logging industry. Of some 100,000 deer killed each year, only one-tenth are used in one way or another (*Komsomol'skaia Pravda*, August 29, 1987).

The construction industry is probably second only to agriculture and timber in waste of resources, building materials, and parts. The system of food distribution contributes to the spoilage of a significant amount of food. A recent study conducted by Anatolii Rubinov, famous for his muckraking reports on various aspects of Soviet life, showed that in at least half of all stores in the Russian republic where auditing was carried out spoilage was commonplace (*Literaturnaia Gazeta*, December 18, 1985; see also my article in the *Wall Street Journal*, March 20, 1986). The waste of raw materials is tremendous in other industries, especially in manufacturing of machinery, where up to 40 percent of all metal goes to waste (Bunich, 1986, p. 27).

## *The Mishandling of Capital Goods*

Capital goods, i.e., equipment, means of transport, and buildings, symbolize property much more than raw materials or agricultural products. Thus popular attitudes toward capital goods are even more indicative of the stance the Soviet people have regarding public property than are the data mentioned previously.

As in the case of raw materials, this waste cannot only be explained by people's lack of respect for socialist property. The nature of the Soviet economy per se accounts for a considerable part of it. As Marxist theory claims that labor is the single source of value, until the late 1960s the Soviet leadership regarded the growth of labor productivity and the saving of labor and wages as the main economic tasks. This disregard for the efficiency of capital goods contributed to people's carelessness about them.

Soviet sources describe in detail the deterioration through poor maintenance of trucks and agricultural machines. Without putting in the labor and parts necessary to keep them going, Soviet workers reduce the functional lifespan of heavy machinery and means of transport by a greater margin than technical standards would assume. Furthermore, over the last two decades the Soviet mass media has published numerous articles on the dismantling of machines in order to get parts (see, for instance, *Pravda*, January 20, March 22, 1986).

## *The Concern about Personal Property*

While displaying indifference toward socialist property, the Soviet people show themselves extremely zealous toward private property.

For example, the same farmers who cynically watch or participate in wasting the harvest or equipment of the collective or state farms are enormously careful and thrifty when it comes to their private plots. With only 2–3 percent of the arable land, they manage to product almost one-third of the agricultural products of the country.

Those who own private cars are much more prudent and fastidious in caring for them than their American counterparts. When the Soviet government started mass production of automobiles, it was assumed that the average lifespan of a car would be eight to ten years. However, twenty years later it was discovered that practically all cars bought in the early 1960s were still running, a circumstance which could only exacerbate the lack of parts in the country. The people mustered the same diligence with respect to all other durable goods, such as TV sets or washing machines, which served them much longer than in the West and than what was foreseen by Soviet planners. In no way can the longevity of privately owned durable goods be attributed to their high quality. The exact opposite is true. Only the great concern of the people to maintain their personal goods accounts for their superannuation.

Despite their low labor ethics in socialist production and indifference to socialist property, individuals demonstrate real concern for the maintenance and multiplication of goods when they are the actual owners.

# CHAPTER 3

# The Soviet Individual in Official Political Life

## The General Concept

The *homo politicus* Soviet individual differs radically from *homo economicus*. In economic activity the Soviet individual is much more in conflict with the leadership than in the political sphere. As we saw in Chapter 2, people in the post-Stalin period have been mostly ignoring the economic prescriptions of the leadership, going along with them only when their individual interests coincide with the official economic goals.

Ultimately, the Soviet people have won the battle with the government in the economic sphere, forcing the latter to adjust to the economic behavior of its citizens and to realize that this behavior cannot be controlled solely with ideological means. The famous Novosibirsk memorandum ascribed to Tatiana Zaslavskaia (1984), regarded as reflecting the views of party reformists, stated this explicitly.

But the people's political behavior, unlike economic, is much closer to official requirements. The Soviet individual obediently follows many political commandments of the system. A number of factors account for this dissimilarity.

First, in most cases, the political requirements do not impinge on the vital material interests of the people. These requirements do not usually present threats to the quality of life (i.e., income, housing conditions, access to food and consumer goods, education, medical and cultural facilities, job prestige, place of residence, and so on).

Sometimes, when a citizen responds to official appeals in the economic sphere, it may mean having to leave a big city moderately well supplied with consumer goods and facilities of various kinds for a village or a new settlement with more primitive conditions, or taking a less prestigious and harder position instead of an occupation that would bring more gratification. Nothing like this happens, however, when an individual demonstrates political loyalty. Moreover, this loyalty will help him or her enhance the quality of life.

Second, material success demands professional skills, experience, and hard work, often accompanied by stress and physical exhaustion. But observing political directives is relatively easy; it does not take such a heavy toll on the physical and psychological resources of the individual, especially if it is possible to ignore moral compunctions. After all, the bulk of political activity in the country is not substantial in essence and is reduced to various ritualistic performances that do not demand too much energy or perseverance from an individual. It requires only recognition of the legitimateness of the system (see Shlapentokh, 1986). In many cases, political obedience demands only public statements in the terms desired by the current leadership. With the steady decline of official interest in the genuine feelings and thoughts of the citizens, the ruling elite is more often satisfied with these rituals that show formal compliance with the system, and they do not expect real emotions or ideas to be injected into political activity.

Third, whatever the importance of the economy for the Soviet leadership, the role of politics is immeasurably higher. The Soviet system has basically acquiesced to low efficiency and poor workers, even if from time to time it undertakes drives against them as in the case with Andropov and Gorbachev.

Changes in the political life of the country in the post-Stalin period have led to the rejection of mass, blind terror as a means of indiscriminately frightening the public, to the softening of political repression against deviationists and nonconformists, as well as to more tolerant attitudes toward politically passive citizens.

At the same time, while significantly softening the official policy toward dissidents, the Soviet system has hardly made a step toward political pluralism, leaving intact, for instance, the election system with a one-candidate slate designed by Stalin in the mid-1930s. This preserves the one-party rule imposed on the country in 1918 and prohibits, according to the decision taken in 1921, any serious political debates inside the party. Thus the Soviet political system of the 1980s, as with any other period of its history, immediately reacts to any manifestation of disloyalty and punishes not only those considered a foe of the system or of the regime, but anyone who is even suspected of being such.

Today, as in the 1930s or 1940s, a citizen who simply does not show his allegiance to the system and the current leadership cannot hope to have a significant career, enter a good college or university, go abroad, or enjoy any other perquisites of good citizenship. The system continues, as it has in the past, to mete out punishment to anyone who directly challenges it.

The evolution of the Soviet system has been accompanied by an asymmetrical development in politics: the growing indifference to demonstrating political loyalty is combined with automatic punishment of those who deviate from the rules of political behavior.

## The Mythological and Pragmatic Levels of the Soviet Mentality in Politics

The Soviet individual is able to balance him or herself in the economic and political spheres by maintaining two different mental levels—pragmatic and ideological.

The relationship between behavior and mentality will be better understood if it is supposed that an individual, especially one in a field controlled by strong political power, can separate the pragmatic layer, responsible for decisions affecting material interests, from the layer responsible for creating the individual's self-image as a person devoted to the dominant ideology. The economic behavior of the Soviet individual is mostly under the control of the pragmatic level. Here economic behavior is considered broadly as any type of activity that brings rewards of any kind. From this point of view political behavior is also under the command of the pragmatic level insofar as it concerns achieving material goals—social status, high income, privileges, and so on.

But the substance of political behavior, its meaning and messages, is completely in the domain of the mythological level. When espousing socialist democracy, the superiority of socialist property over private, or supporting the Soviet invasion of Afghanistan, the Soviet individual does not take these statements seriously or as relevant to their behavior.

Separating the mythological and pragmatic levels eases the task of adapting to the Soviet political system, especially during the Brezhnev era when the leadership did not demand real unity between words and deeds and a person could take refuge in private life. In this period, with a sophisticated mind the individual could easily be a shirker at the workplace and active in politics. Brezhnev's two-decade period led to a multiplication of this type of personality that could combine extremely low professional skill and labor ethics with intensive political activity, a development which has been denounced often since his death.

## Participation in Government

The Soviet people are probably more unanimous in their attitudes toward their role in government than on any other political issue. Official studies, despite the highly loaded character of the questions asked, show that the majority of the people do not ascribe to the official dogma that they have any control over higher level policies or even local ones. Moreover, there is various indirect evidence suggesting that the majority do not seriously believe in such official slogans as "socialist democracy," which suggests that the people govern their own society. One conspicuous example is the well-known indifference of the voting public to one-candidate elections (see Zaslavsky, 1979). But there are other examples.

Rafael Safarov conducted a survey of 1,500 residents in the Kalinin region in 1972–73 to collect data on attitudes toward the role of public opinion in government. He found out that the majority of the respondents (despite the loaded character of the survey questions) did not believe public opinion had a significant influence on government policies. Thirty-one percent declared themselves incompetent to even evaluate local authorities (Safarov, 1975, p. 53). Only 6 percent thought they were competent to answer questions related to long-term planning (p. 56), the same number supposed that local authorities took public opinion into full account, 55 percent said that they did it partially, and 11 percent said they did not take it into account at all (p. 121).

The sociological study conducted by the Institute of State and Law in the Stavropol region found, in the view of two Soviet authors, a very low level of participation in local government. Less than one-sixth displayed some initiative in raising issues of social importance to local authorities. Only 12 percent took part in discussions of drafts of decisions advanced by these authorities, and only 4 percent spoke at meetings where the deputies reported about their activities (Lopata and Petukhov, 1986, p. 29). Their conclusions—and it is significant that they could be published in the Gorbachev era—are in stark contrast to the statistics concerning worker participation in government flaunted in the previous period.

Although people seem almost contemptuous of the official political games in democracy, the absolute majority of citizens vote regularly in various elections. Official Soviet data suggests that participation is always about 99 percent of those entitled to vote.

These figures are not reliable. As some studies show (see, for instance, Zaslavsky, 1979), many people try to escape the election, using excuses such as business trips, vacations, and other activities which presumably keep them away from voting centers. A number of people (especially among the intelligentsia in Moscow) regard the avoidance of elections as some sort of political sport. With the general loosening of the regime it has become easier and easier to skip participation in the election procedure, for instance by assigning one member of the family to vote for the rest. A few daredevils, by threatening to boycott the elections, blackmail the local authorities into giving them some concessions, such as getting the roof or bathroom repaired.

But only a minority can afford such behavior. The average citizen is afraid that refusing to vote will be considered a seriously disloyal political act. Therefore, on the Sunday when the election takes place, every citizen sets off for the election center where, usually without looking at the ballot, and of course without dropping into the booth where it is formally possible to rescind the name of the single candidate, performs his or her "civic duty," as this action is described in the propaganda. In the 1940s the good Soviet citizen was expected to vote at 6 A.M., as soon as the voting started, to show an impatience to vote; now the authorities are satisfied if the appearance is by noon or even later.

The majority of Soviet people do manage to ignore pre-election campaigns. Only a few (no more than 9 percent in cities; see Grushin and Onikov, 1980, p. 379) ever speak at pre-election meetings or visit the election centers, where voters can get advice on political and other issues.

But there is little doubt that a large majority of the 2.3 million people elected to government bodies (TsSU, 1985, p. 11) are genuinely glad they were chosen by the authorities for this position. Although they have no real influence on the government, these people enjoy some privileges—the number and kind in direct proportion to the level of the body—and are somewhat privy to the mechanism of power.

Another category of politically active citizen is those regarded as "active assistants" to government bodies. Official statistics count 40 million such people. Almost all of them work in various committees and fulfill various assignments as part of their sociopolitical obligations.

The average Soviet individual complies with the political elite and attends meetings when some official projects (i.e., drafts of the constitution, party programs, laws on higher education or labor collectives) are debated. If their superior asks them, they will take the floor and say a few words in support of the project, and as ritual demands, advance some comments and wishes which, of course, will be fully ignored by the government.

According to a nationwide survey conducted by the Institute of Sociology in 1981, up to 50 percent of the adult population participate in the debates on new laws (Levykin, 1984, p. 91). The draft of the new Soviet constitution in 1977 was almost universally known ten to twelve days after it was published. The text was known to 92 percent of the adult population, it was discussed at 450,000 open party meetings where 3 million people took the floor in debates and it was discussed at 1.5 million meetings at the workplace or residence (Kerimov and Toshchenko, 1978, p. 12; Tarasov and Kotunov, 1984, p. 94). The 1983 draft of the new law on labor collectives was debated at 1.2 million meetings where 5 million people spoke on the subject, advancing 130,000 ideas (Simonian, 1986, p. 38). The draft of the new law on schools in 1984 was debated in 1.3 million meetings where 7 million people took the floor. Including all forms of participation, it is estimated that 120 million people were involved with this school reform (Strizhov, 1984; Svininnikov, 1985, p. 104).

In all cases of so-called public debates on new laws, the political elite pretends that the drafts are supported unanimously by the people, who express concern only about some details and formulations. However, when sociologists were allowed for the first time to ask people how they felt about a new law, the results were quite different. A survey asking 1,000 people about their attitudes toward the new school law revealed, in sharp contrast to the image presented in the mass media, that only 43 percent completely endorsed the law (Voinova and Korabeinikov, 1984, p. 99).[1]

## *Subbotniks*

Along with elections and debates on new laws, the Soviet elite uses another way to muster support for official policy—"subbotniki"—

voluntary work on Saturday ("Subbota" in Russian). When a Subbotnik is declared, for instance, in connection with Lenin's birthday, all employees, students in high schools and colleges, and even pensioners are called on to take part in it. According to official data, no less than 80 percent of the adult population respond to the call (Levykin, 1984, p. 91). In most cases, the manual workers go to their usual workplace, while nonmanual employees are used for the cleaning of offices, streets, parks, and so on.

Usually the Subbotnik, which is supposed to help the economy by the use of nonpaid labor, is poorly organized by the administration and local party committees, and millions of people waste their time during this ritualistic action. However, the Soviet people have become accustomed to the irrational character of this enterprise and regard it as an unavoidable necessity. A few people even manage to find some pleasure in it because the Subbotnik, which lasts only a few hours (the administration is often forced to release people because it cannot find work for them), quite often ends up as a drinking party. Such was the case under Brezhnev, before Gorbachev's antialcohol campaign in May 1985. Quite often Subbotniks are used as a cheap means of catching up with an overbudget project, forcing employees to work without pay, which always causes resentment (see "Voluntarily but Compulsory" in *Literaturnaia Gazeta*, December 16, 1987; see also *Pravda*, July 13, 1986).

## *Participation in Surveys and Letters to the Mass Media*

The average individual generally does not avoid participating in surveys organized by official institutions. As a rule, these surveys, with the exception of a few heady years in the 1960s, contain politically insensitive questions and offer highly loaded choices to answer them. Soviet people view participation in a survey as a sort of social obligation. Hospitality also accounts to some degree for why they rarely reject the request for an interview. The rate of refusal in face-to-face interviews is no more than 3–5 percent, much less than in the West (Shlapentokh, 1973, 1976).

But the true attitudes of the people toward sociological surveys are revealed by data on mail surveys. No more than 5–10 percent of recipients send back questionnaires, much less than in the West, where about 30 percent respond to mail surveys without prompting (Shlapentokh, 1976).[2]

On the other hand, the amount of letters written to the editors of newspapers as well as to various government bodies is vastly superior to that in the West. In 1981–83 the Central Committees received 2 million letters and local party committees 10 million (Lopata and Petukhov, 1986, p. 39). Millions of letters come to newspapers; *Pravda* alone receives more than a half million each year (Novoselov, 1985, p. 13).

Each year one-sixth of all Taganrog residents, according to Grushin, send at least one letter to a newspaper or party committee. However, the majority of these letters are not responses to issues discussed in the mass media or to social or political events, but complaints about personal problems, a fact which the media, in boasting about the number of letters, tries to obfuscate, presenting them as if mostly dealing with public issues. Only 5 percent of the letters in *Izvestia* (Davydchenkov, 1970, p. 150) and 34 percent in *Komsomol'skaia Pravda* (Verkhovskaia, 1972, p. 144) are concerned with public events.

It is clear that the authors of the letters are the most active part of the Soviet population, geared to defend their interests even if it means getting into conflicts with the authorities. One-third (35 percent) of authors of the letters to the media are party members, and 25 percent are from those with a higher education (these categories overlap each other). This is twice as high as their proportion in the general population, another indication that these authors are the active part of the population.[3]

## Participation in Ideological Work

As was mentioned before, the good Soviet individual must take an active part in ideological work—being its object—by disseminating official views, and play a passive role as the consumer, as well as subject, of this propaganda.

### *Passive Participation in Ideological Work: Exposing Themselves to the Mass Media*

The majority of the Soviet people are exposed to ideological indoctrination from as young as five or six until old age, and to a great extent cooperate with it.

Much of this indoctrination is carried out through the mass media. Practically all families, in full accordance with the desires of the political elite, subscribe to Soviet newspapers and magazines, on the average of as many as two or three newspapers and four magazines. Television and radio, owned by 95 and 93 percent of all Soviet families, respectively, also play extremely important roles in the indoctrination of the population.

The demand for many Soviet periodicals often exceeds the available number of copies. In the 1970s, for instance, shortages occurred in such newspapers as *Trud* ("Labor"), *Komsomol'skaia Pravda* ("The Young Communist Truth"), *Nedelia* ("Week"), *Za Rubezhom* ("Abroad"), and *Literaturnaia Gazeta* ("Literary Gazette"). It was also difficult to get a subscription to many other periodicals that play a significant role in Soviet ideological dissemination.

Thus in some ways the Soviet people finance, even if partially (some periodicals are on subvention), the propaganda addressed to them. Yet people who read or watch TV look for information or entertainment, not political advertising. Soviet sociologists have found that the people pay minimal attention to purely propagandistic articles in magazines or in the audiovisual media. In a poll, respondents ranked these types of articles eighteenth out of nineteen different kinds of articles in *Izvestia* (Shlapentokh, 1969b, p. 21), and seventeenth among eighteen different kinds in the newspaper *Trud* (Shlapentokh, 1969a, p. 95). Many shun the solely propagandistic periodicals, party magazines in particular, and demonstrate a feverish interest in those journals with minimal ideological fillers, such as *Zdorovie* ("Health") or *Vokrug Sveta* ("Around the World"). According to Grushin's studies in Taganrog (1973), there were 9,000 subscribers to all party magazines, and 14,000 to *Zdorovie* (Grushin and Onikov, 1980, p. 132).

The same tendency was revealed with book choice. Avid book buyers, Soviets purchase far fewer than the authorities would like of books with political content, particularly ones written by Soviet leaders. Despite the extremely low price of this last type of book, many sources indicate that most end up being recycled.

However, in their quest for information Soviets expose themselves, as do many other people in different countries, to a systematic flood of government propaganda. They watch TV news regularly (in particular the program "Time"), as well as voluntarily attend public lectures. The society "Znaniie" ("Knowledge") alone offers more than 25 million lectures a year, with an average attendance of about 40 people (Panov, 1984, p. 21). In both cases, people expose themselves to well-orchestrated ideological processing. Soviet leaders in no way try to hide this, but instead underscore it as the major task of their mass media, quite often equating propaganda and information (see Iakovlev, 1984).

The number both of political books bought and ideological periodicals subscribed to would be significantly less if millions of people did not have to demonstrate their knowledge of Soviet politics in the system of political education and if—and this is particularly important—they did not themselves play the role of propagandist. Thus they need official materials to help them in this work. In a rare confession (which could only have been possible due to *glasnost*) Mikhail Nenashev, the head of the State Committee on Publishing Houses, speaking about political books published in recent decades, said, "Despite a strong desire to do so, I cannot name any book which has gained popularity among any group of readers—workers, engineers, the creative intelligentsia, war veterans" (*Pravda*, November 24, 1987).

With all this taken together, and despite some developments unpleasant to the authorities, the Soviet people, somewhat of their own will, are firmly rooted in the mass media and cannot escape from getting a solid portion of official propaganda each day. Well aware of the rejection of purely propagandistic materials by the majority of the people, the elite makes sure any ideological program or article is packed with useful information, making it nearly impossible to avoid propagandistic injections.

## *Attendance at Political Schools*

The majority of adults are supposed to attend political schools as part of the Soviet system of lifelong political education. As a matter of fact, attendance of these schools is practically obligatory for all people, and the administration and party committees see to the mass participation of workers, farmers, and the intelligentsia in political education. According to official Soviet data, 70 million people are "embraced by political and economic studies" with 2.5 million people as propagandists. An additional 4 million serve as agitators and 3.4 million as lecturers (Sbytov, 1983, p. 152; Shumakov, 1983, p. 53). Upon being asked why they decided to choose a certain form of political education, respondents in Moldavia in the mid-1970s almost openly pointed to pressure from superiors (72 percent). Only 20 percent referred to personal interest in the issues (Timush, 1978, p. 16).

Ideological indoctrination is a self-perpetuating and self-sustaining process. When people attending political schools were asked how they use the acquired knowledge, 39 percent pointed to their own ideological activity as the most important sphere of the application of this knowledge. Nineteen percent named their occupation as the sphere where they applied the knowledge, and the rest could not indicate how they used their political studies (Timush, 1978, p. 56).

The degree of pressure on one to undergo political education increases with the rise of social status and education. So the intelligentsia, party members, and of course the officials have to enroll, without exception, in one of the schools or seminars in this system, whereas people of lower status, such as farmers or blue-collar workers who are not party members, usually are not found on the list of students enrolled in political school.

Many people try to skip the classes and the seminar meetings in these schools. However, the majority of those who are supposed to attend are there to answer roll call in most cases. Attending a school of political education forces people to read and buy political literature in order to be "active" in class, prepare a presentation, or pass an exam. In this way, people have to imbibe the Soviet ideological texts, which (and this is the core of the issue) are used to exert influence on them, especially on the issues outside the realm of personal experience.

It is noteworthy how Soviet young people responded to the question in Brezhnev's time: Is "the deepening of political knowledge" important? Their responses varied according to the varying pressure on them exerted by the authorities at different levels of education. According to a 1978 survey of 11,000 students, 80 percent of all high school students gave an unreserved "yes." They were followed by students in higher educational institutions (73 percent) and the intelligentsia (also 73 percent). But only 51 percent of vocational school students and 65 percent of unskilled workers considered political education necessary (Alekseeva, 1983, p. 40).

However, during the developments in 1985–87, when people were allowed to express their thoughts and feelings much more freely than in the past, the political inculcation of the youth earned only very modest results. Only the whiff of freedom was enough to sweep away many, even if not most, Soviet dogmas. A study carried out by the Institute of Sociological Research in 1986 in nine cities (including

Moscow) found that "less than 26 percent of the students displayed a real interest in the social sciences as they are taught in higher schools." Some of the data produced by this study are even more dismal for Soviet ideologues—only 10 percent of the students are really interested in lectures on social issues, and 43 percent directly stated that they hold Soviet political literature in very low esteem (Vasilieva, Kinsburskii, Kokliagina et al., 1987, pp. 21–22).

While observing the relatively free debates on various social issues over a long period of time on the Arbat (a famous Moscow district which for a while during *glasnost* turned into a small version of Hyde Park), journalists from *Komsomol'skaia Pravda* realized that not one statement directed against Soviet ideology was rebutted by even one participant in the spontaneous discussions. They even gave their article the indicative title "The Defeat on the Arbat" (*Komsomol'skaia Pravda*, November 27, 1987).

## *The Individual as a Propagandist*

Being active in the ideological training of others is a significant part of the life of Soviet individuals. Their professional and social duties become instruments of Soviet propaganda. This is especially true of social scientists, teachers, cultural workers, managers, party apparatchiks, and military officers. According to my calculations, by a conservative estimate 12–14 million people, about 10 percent of all employees (there were 130 million employees in the Soviet Union in 1984, TsSU, 1985, p. 408), conduct ideological work on a daily basis in the framework of their profession (see also Klopov, 1985, p. 215; Morozov et al., 1984, p. 232).

No less than 8 million (this figure overlaps to some degree the previous one) are involved in ideological work "after 5 o'clock." It is important to note that both these categories of ideological workers compose the majority of the socially active part of the Soviet population. (In 1984 there were 18 million people with a higher education and 19 million party members, with significant overlap between the two groups.) Thus people who manage to achieve at least one of the means of making a career in Soviet society (see Shlapentokh, 1986b) are involved in ideological work in the Soviet Union.

By including the greater part of the Soviet population (and most of the socially and politically active people) in ideological activity, the

Soviet political elite has at its disposal a gigantic network for indoctrination, as well as a number of other networks covering the country. This network can also be used to intensify the indoctrination of the propagandists themselves. Being obliged to repeat official slogans, the propagandist, even with a highly critical attitude toward the system, begins to impute a bit of credibility to even the most absurd ideological dogmas, if only to maintain one's self-image and not appear as a coward or careerist parroting ostensible stupidities.

In this respect the recruitment of outstanding intellectuals as hack propagandists is especially noteworthy. The pressure on intellectuals and graduate students to take an active part in ideological work drastically increased in the 1970s. Many who are pushed to participate in such activities may ultimately accept the legitimacy of their actions in order to reconcile their internal conflicts about doing this.

Publicly alienating scholars from the intellectual community is an important part of this process. Rudolf Ianovskii, then a department head at the Department of Science of the Central Committee, wrote that such leading scholars as S. Vavilov, I. Kurchatov, S. Korolev, A. Alexandrov, M. Keldysh, M. Dubinin, and a number of others had become preoccupied with the ideological education of academics (1979a, p. 82; 1979b, pp. 107–16; see also Degtiarova, 1985, pp. 56–79; Stepanian, 1983, pp. 301–30). The party committee secretary of a chemistry institute of the Academy of Science, B. Sergenev, wrote in *Kommunist* that one leading researcher in his institute, a member of the Academy of Science, headed a seminar devoted to the study of the classics of Marxism-Leninism, and another led a seminar on the relationship between modern science and dialectical materialism (*Kommunist*, 1972, 6). Among the editors of the book, *Ideological and Political Education of the Technical Intelligentsia* (1982) are such prominent scholars as the chemist Nikolai Emmanuel, the biochemist Alexander Baiev, and the physicist Iurii Osip'ian, all full members of the Academy of Science (Ianovskii, 1982; about ideological indoctrination in medical institutions, see Golyakhovsky, 1984, p. 201).

## Soviet People in "Voluntary Organizations"

### *Membership in Organizations*

The political elite succeeds in including nearly every individual in the various organizations it created and controls. The most socially and politically active people, of working age in particular, are associated with two or even more organizations.

Almost all Soviet employees are members of trade unions. By the end of 1984 they had 136 million members, including not only working people (there were 117 million workers in state enterprises and institutions in 1984) but also retired persons (Panov, 1985, p. 17; TsSU, 1985, p. 408). Unless they are a member of a trade union, people are deprived of all benefits, such as sick leave, vacation, and so on. Thus everyone who joins the labor force automatically, without any special procedure, becomes a member of the trade union.

The formation of the second largest organization—the Young Communist League (Komsomol)—is not very different from the first. The majority of Soviet youth between the ages of fourteen and twenty-eight are members of this organization. At the end of 1984 there were 42 million Young Communists in the country. By comparison, in 1984 there were 8 million junior and senior high school students, and 6 million students in universities and colleges (Panov, 1985, p. 18; TsSU, 1985, pp. 512, 519). Official policy demands all young people of certain age be included in Komsomol, although for form's sake it is claimed that a teenager can be accepted into the organization only if he or she deserves it and is recommended by party members of Komsomol (Shishov, 1983, pp. 48–53). The Pioneer branch of Komsomol, which is composed of children under the age of fourteen, has 19 million members.

The third most important social organization—the Communist Party—comprised 19 million people at the end of 1984, about one-tenth of the adult population (Panov, 1985, p. 13). Unlike the two other organizations, access to the party is difficult and is strongly regulated by the political elite. There are many more people who want to join than the number the party leaders want to accept. Each office or enterprise gets its quota, and there is usually sort of a line of people burning with desire to become full-fledged party members. In fact, the party comprises the most active part of the Soviet population (i.e., people with high aspirations in terms of the quality of life and prestige), and, as Alexander Zinoviev once aptly observed, in practically any office or enterprise the party members, on the average, are superior in education, professional skills, and even in moral virtues as compared with nonparty members. This fundamental circumstance must be taken into account in any analysis of developments in Soviet society.

As the backbone of the political system, the party has to incorporate the majority of active people in the country, those who, for instance, were energetic enough to get a higher education and who are capable of taking part seriously in various forms of voluntary social work. Of course, all people holding more or less important positions, even at the district level (including history teachers in secondary schools), must belong to the party.

Despite all attempts to present the party as an organization of the working class, the proportion of party members is increasingly moving from farmers, unskilled, and skilled workers to the intelligentsia and intellectuals. Only 20 percent of skilled workers were party members, 10 percent of the semiskilled, and of the nonskilled 7 percent (Klopov, 1985, p. 202).

On the other hand, up to 60 percent of scholars and members of the Writers' Union are party members, and up to 90 percent of the delegates at the Writer Congresses (see *Sovietskaia Kul'tura*, June 8, 1985, p. 2; *Literaturnaia Gazeta*, December 18, 1985, p. 3; see also Shkaratan, 1982, p. 49).

Along with these three major organizations, there are a number of others that have a less prominent role in Soviet life, such as the Society of Inventors (13.5 million), the Scientific-Technological Society (12 million), sports organizations (53 million), the Voluntary Organization for Assistance to the Army, Aviation, and Navy (DOSAAF) (more than 100 million), the Soviet Red Cross, and the society Knowledge (for the dissemination of knowledge) (3 million).

## *Attitudes toward Organizations*

Various sources suggest that the Soviets use these organizations as a means to achieve their own purposes and are not concerned with the stated goals of these groups. The official organizations are regarded as arms of the state and the political elite and are incapable, in even the slightest way, of representing the interests of their members. The members of these organizations not only cannot seriously influence the formation of the leadership at the national level, but even in local branches and production units and are forced in a voting ritual to approve the candidates appointed from above.

Thus contrary to official expectation, only 14 percent of all respondents in the large study of young people in Byelorussia and Estonia (1981–84) ranked joining the Young Communist League as a great event in their life, which meant it gathered less votes than any other event included in the question as an alternative (22 percent pointed to marriage and 23 percent to the birth of the first child) (Babosov, 1985, p. 76). If a writer wants to portray life realistically, he either ignores Komsomol activities or presents it as having little to do with the real interests of youth. Even the contributors to the magazine *The Youth* avoid practically all subjects related to Komsomol activities. It is impossible, for instance, to find any novel that mentions Komsomol in *Younost*'s issues in 1986 (see *Younost* ("Youth") 1986, 1–6), and if an author even dares to touch the subject he describes Komsomol in a rather ironic style (see, for instance, Poliakov, 1985). The magazine tries to compensate for the absence of Komsomol in its fiction by publishing ideological articles devoted to it.

As for the trade union, it is presented in Soviet literature, plays and movies as a laughing stock (see, for instance, Shtemler's novel *Supermarket* or Riasonov's movie *Office Romance*).

In essence, the same rather detached attitude is in evidence toward the Communist Party, in deep contrast not only to the Revolution and civil war periods but even to the first three subsequent decades, when the majority of communists considered their membership in the party as one of the most important emotional facts of their life (see the memoirs of Grigorenko, 1982; Kol'man, 1982; Kopelev, 1975, 1978; Orlova, 1982). Although it has much in common with the trade union and Komsomol, the party does have some unique features in the role it plays in the lives of its members.

First, party members are much more concerned about their reputation than a member of the trade union or Komsomol. In fact, cases of exclusion from the last two organizations are very rare while the threat of exclusion from the party is real for any individual who has done something against the current party morals or political goals. Exclusion from the party, even if not accompanied, as in the past, with arrest, is in most cases the end of one's professional career and as such is a highly effective lever the authorities have at their disposal, allowing them to manipulate party members.

Second, the concept of democracy as applied to the masses was completely rejected by the Communist Party in November 1917, when Lenin dispersed the Constituent Assembly, which was freely elected by the Russian people after the February revolution. However, even though it has never been really implemented, the idea of democracy within the party still lingers among some party members who nurture neo-Leninist dreams about a democratically organized party ruling the country. This has echoes of the Athenian political concept—democracy for all free citizens and merciless control over slaves.

Under some special circumstances (if the party bosses have not made up their minds, or if a new regime starts a campaign against the previous leader and wants to mobilize party members against the old cadres, as was the case in the first years of Khrushchev's and Gorbachev's regimes), the party can offer members some freedom for expressing personal views on local matters as well as on the election of local party leaders. However, the cases when a party member feels himself or herself to be a real participant in the political process, even at the local level, are extremely rare, and the majority of party rank and file consider themselves ordinary soldiers obliged to obey their commanders.

Membership in the main three organizations calls for the performance of a number of ritualistic activities, such as attendance at meetings, participation in debates, and the fulfillment of various assignments.

The ritualistic nature of the activities of most party members does not mean that the party has no political or practical consequence on the rank and file. Observing the rituals, such as regularly approving the party leaders' speeches and the Central Committee's decisions, or supporting superiors, demonstrates political loyalty and readiness to obey any order. This could include taking part in a campaign to denigrate colleagues or friends.

Moreover, the regular observance of ritualistic games not only enhances one's political reputation with its personal safety (the low likelihood of becomig embroiled with the political police), but also opens doors professionally. Komsomol and the party, with the most active and educated part of the population, form a nationwide school for the selection and training of eventual apparatchiks. A considerable portion of party members take part in various assignments, in particular "election" to party bodies of various levels, because they have a passionate craving for some role in the party, whatever it may be. The same thing happens in the trade union and Komsomol, though prizes of lesser value are at stake. But there are some party members who as often as possible keep a great distance from any party activity. For the first group, membership is a springboard for promotion, for the second, a condition for survival, a safety device.

## *The Meeting*

The activity at meetings convened by an organization (the Communist Party, Komsomol, a trade union, or the manager) is of special significance. Since Soviet ideology proclaims the democratic nature of all public life, and in particular of social organizations, the meeting of their members is supposed to represent the highest example of this, and members' participation in discussions at these meetings is supposed to be the implementation of democratic principles. Organizational meetings take up 25 percent of all time spent on voluntary social work, with the rest spent on various special assignments (Artemov and Patrushev, 1979, pp. 69, 75; Plaksii, 1982, p. 89).

The majority of the Soviet people consider meetings that take a significant amount of their leisure time as useless formal ceremonials, in which the decisions are prearranged and can in no way be modified by the debates. Only 21 percent of the respondents of the survey sponsored by the Young Communist League said that meetings in this league are effective, and 16 percent said bluntly that they had no idea (Plaksii, 1982, p. 100).

Soviets regard the meetings primarily as a place where they have to be educated, taken to task, and berated, and not allowed to express their views or help in directing the organization. The superiors among the respondents were especially firm on this point (Voinova and Petrov, 1975, p. 163).

Attendance at these meetings depends on the status of the organization convening them and on the eventual punishment for missing such meetings. Party meetings have a higher attendance than any other. Officials claim that 96 percent of the party members answered roll call at the meetings devoted to the twenty-sixth party congress (Rodionov, 1984, pp. 143–44). The meetings in Komsomol and the trade union cells are usually attended much less regularly than party meetings, and it is always a problem to have the two-thirds quorum of members for the meeting which reelects the directive bodies. Considering all organizations, 67 percent of the population attend various meetings with varying regularity (Levykin, 1984, p. 91).

Many who are forced to attend meetings are not only annoyed by the waste of time, but by the hypocrisy and uselessness of them. These people have elaborated sophisticated techniques to while away the time at meetings. People read magazines and books, talk with each other (it is usually quite noisy at a Soviet meeting), exchange notes (if they sit far apart), play chess (in reality or else mentally), some women knit, they sleep, dream, and so on. Numerous Soviet jokes, anecdotes, and satirical songs and sketches, both legal and illegal, have featured the attitudes of the people toward these obligatory meetings.

The most reliable source of information on these meetings is probably the Taganrog study carried out by Boris Grushin in the late 1960s and early 1970s. He and his colleagues, however, could not avoid being influenced by Soviet mythology in the study; the questions as well as the answers were considerably influenced by the dominant ideological context. However, the Taganrog study still provides the best information on this subject ever produced in the Soviet Union (see Grushin and Onikov, 1980; see also the article of Grushin's graduate students Voinova and Chernakova, 1979). According to this study, only 11 percent of respondents said that their opinions changed because of debates at meetings. Only 35 percent assessed the decisions adopted at the meetings as "totally correct," a low figure in view of the character of the survey (Voinova and Chernakova, 1979, pp. 85, 90).

A unique study in Soviet sociology revealed that 87 percent of the decisions approved at meetings are abstract and do not specify the time when the recommendations are to be fulfilled. Without mentioning figures, the authors of the study noted that "discussions on amendments to the draft of a decision took place very rarely." Whereas 89 percent of all speeches contained some valuation of the office of enterprise, only 20 percent of all decisions took these evaluations into account, showing how little audience participation mattered. The study said that "as a rule the appraisal of the situation [in an office or enterprise] in the decisions is positive, with some modicum of criticism" ( Voinova and Chernakova, 1979, pp. 87–89).

The character of the speeches at the meetings is also noteworthy. Since speeches are expected to be critically oriented, 67 percent of all orators at the Taganrog meetings included some critical judgments in their talks. However, the criticism, as the sociologists confess, is usually abstract and addressed not to specific people but to "organs in general." What is more, one-third of all orators simply took the floor without raising any specific issue (Voinova nad Chernakova, 1979, p. 82).

But who are the orators at meetings in the Soviet Union? How many who attend them actually take the floor? In some ways the number of people who speak at meetings is an indicator of the political pressure on the population. All else being equal, the greater this number, the more insistent the political power has been that people publicly manifest their loyalty to the regime and its current policy. Since the post-Stalin period the authorities have significantly softened their pressure on the people. Now activity at meetings is necessary not so much for survival, as was the case in Stalin's time (see the description of meetings in 1937 in Chukovskaia's documentary novel *Deserted Home* [1981]), as for promotion or especially for preserving one's position or for gaining access to a desired job. Currently, no more than one-fifth of attendants at trade union and similar meetings are active, and up to 50–75 percent are active at party meetings.

In Taganrog only one-fifth of all citizens regularly asked permission to speak at meetings. Forty-five percent of all these "regular orators," as they are contemptuously called by the Soviet people, took the floor in nearly every meeting they attended, 31 percent in half the meetings, and 24 percent occasionally.

A comparison of the "regular orators" with the rest of the audience at the meetings (which is also weighted with respect to the general population) permits no doubt about the regulars' composition. Forty-two percent of them are supervisors (compared to 23 percent in the audience), 66 percent are party members (against 40 percent in the audience), and 66 percent officials of various social organizations (again with only 40 percent in the audience) (Grushin and Onikov, 1980, pp. 388–89; see also Voinova, 1976, p. 95).

Much less reliable studies conducted by Nikolai Bokarev, an active ideological sociologist, add some information about the behavior of party members at their meetings. Again, as in Tagangrog, party members—who are usually more active than nonparty members anyway—are also divided into two groups: those who spoke up regularly (62 percent) and those who did it rarely (32 percent). The first group clearly consists of highly ambitious people or those who already belong to the class of leaders. In the first group, 79 percent were managers or officials of an enterprise, in the second only 34 percent. Those who actively work in "the preparation of a party meeting," a ritualistic action, are mostly of the managerial class (44 percent of party members who participated in this activity were managers as compared to 28 percent who were ordinary engineers) or party members with some position in the local party hierarchy (60–84 percent) (Bokarev, 1979a, pp. 120–22).

## Voluntary Social Work

### *Official Data on the Motivation for Social Work*

Attendance and speeches at meetings are only one element of voluntary social activities expected of good Soviet citizens. Voluntary social work embraces numerous activities which the people are obliged to perform after 5 P.M., including disseminating propaganda, assisting the police in keeping order, taking care of children and the aged, organizing elections, and other similar tasks. Of less significance are diverse assignments which they must regularly fulfill. Avoiding social work is considered a serious political flaw that can damage one's reputation; it influences the content of references and with it the chance to go to a good college or get a prestigious job.

The study of Soviet attitudes toward social work is difficult. It is assumed that every good Soviet citizen has to like social work, and thus the sociologist who wants to know the genuine feelings about this work faces enormous problems. However, this subject is usually under the control of ideological sociologists who expect answers from their respondents to fit Soviet political doctrine. Despite this, the responses to ideological sociologists from people who know how to answer strongly loaded questions about social work are of some interest and can be used in our analysis.

Questions about the motives behind social work are of great importance in the questionnaires of ideological sociologists who, as if feeling their impunity (who will dare tell them it is impossible to get true answers to such questions?), expect their respondents to pick the politically correct choices. Indeed, the majority of respondents do not disappoint these sociologists.

Vladimir Sokolov, for instance, claims, with satisfaction, that 59 percent of young people in a large survey conducted in the late 1970s (11,000 people) claim they chose to do social work because "this [the participation in social work] is necessary for the collective and society." However, this means that 40 percent avoided giving such an ideologically obvious answer. Twenty-three percent preferred a neutral and rather individualistic alternative ("it is satisfying to communicate with people"). The same number of respondents also gave an ideologically unclear alternative ("it enriches me with knowledge and practical experience"). Ten percent brazenly declared that they "have to take part in social work because it could not be avoided," the same number said "social work will help me to solve some personal problems," and

13 percent gave an even worse motive ideologically—"social work is necessary for promotion" (Sokolov, 1981, pp. 94–95). Since each respondent could give multiple answers, it is impossible from Sokolov's data to learn the size of the "pure type," i.e., those who chose only ideological or only pragmatic alternatives. However, even these results clearly show the mental maneuverings of the Soviet people with respect to social work (Sokolov, 1981).[4]

In the Taganrog study, in which respondents were again allowed to use as many answers as they wanted (a fact very important in the evaluation of data), Edward Klopov shows that the number of votes cast for the most ideologically desirable reason for doing social work ("for the sake of society and the collective") and for individualistic reasons (it is useful "for communication," for the "enlargement of vision," and so on) were practically equal—47 and 41 percent, respectively. At the same time, 12 percent openly explained they spent time on social work for egotistical (Klopov calls it "instrumental") considerations (Klopov, 1985, p. 222; see also Baturin, 1984, p. 123).

The 1982 Taganrog survey gives some glimpses into the real attitudes of Soviet people toward social work. One question asked which type of social work deserved more attention. The type of work that got the most votes was that connected in some way with the genuine problems of Soviet life, far outranking the type of work regarded by the authorities as most important.[5] Thus 38 percent chose "work with children and youth," 34 percent "the protection of public order," and 24 percent "land development and conservation of nature," whereas "work in the party, trade union, and Young Communist League" got only 21 percent, "ideological work" 25 percent, and "self-management" 6 percent (Klopov, 1985, p. 220).

The first time-budget study in Pskov in the 1960s found that adults spend an average of ten minutes a day on social work, including 2.5 minutes on social assignments, 2.1 on political education, and 3.1 on meetings. Various regional studies conducted later confirmed this figure (Artemov and Patrushev, 1973, pp. 69, 75).

The gradual decrease of political pressure on the people and the transformation of political activity more and more into purely ritualistic exercises has quietly increased the possibility of avoiding social work.

Soviet sociological data demonstrate this process, such as that of Vasilii Patrushev, the main Soviet expert on time budgets. His unique longitudinal study of Omsk workers shows that between 1961 and 1976 the time spent on social work declined by 37 percent for men and by 80 percent for women. Among collective farmers (Rostov region), the decreases were even more dramatic (Patrushev, 1979, pp. 25–26; see also Mints and Nepomniashchii, 1979, p. 41).

The most recent data available demonstrate that the trend which began in the 1970s continued into the 1980s. A survey in Pskov in 1986, conducted under the guidance of Vasilii Patrushev (who supervised the city's first budget time study twenty years ago), found that the residents of this city now spend an average of only seven minutes on social activity (a 30 percent drop in two decades) compared to seventeen minutes on average among the residents of Jackson, Michigan (*New York Times*, October 26, 1987).

## *The Uneven Distribution of the Burden of Social Work*

While formally demanding active social work from each Soviet citizen, the political elite is in fact highly selective in this domain.

The pressure to perform social work is not the same on all people. As is the case with ideological work, a number of variables determine the importance of doing social work for each individual: education, age, the character of professional work, party membership, and class status. In general, the intelligentsia is under much more pressure than workers and farmers.

According to various sources in the 1960s and 1970s, 50–55 percent of all employees were involved in social work; broken down, it came to 30–40 percent of the farm workers, 40–50 percent of the blue-collar workers, and 60–80 percent of the intelligentsia (Klopov, 1985, pp. 212–13, 226; Shkaratan, 1978, pp. 82, 114; Sokolov, 1981, p. 89).

Another study conducted by the Academy of Social Science and the Institute of Sociology in seventy enterprises (1978) found that 13 percent of all respondents with an elementary education were involved in social work on a daily basis, 17 percent of those with a secondary education, and 25 percent with a higher education. Party members are at least 1.5 times more active in social work than nonparty members (Svininnikov, 1985, p. 127; see also Lopata and Petukhov, 1986, p. 48).

Active social work is much more important professionally for those who come into ideological contact with people than for those who deal with machines or nature. Teachers and professors, social scientists, and cultural workers are, for example, expected to be engaged in social work more than engineers, agronomists, or researchers in natural science. For the 14.5 million people who work in education, 9.6 million in culture, 1.4 million in science and higher education, and 4.5 million in social services, ideological activity is a more important duty than for the millions of people with the same education working in industry, building, or transportation, a fact clearly understood by students in college and the university. It is characteristic that first-year students differ strongly in their willingness to be involved in social work. Those who major in the humanities, education, or management regard this work as an important condition for successful careers and about 37 percent of them plan to spend a lot of time on this work. Among students who choose other occupations, the percentage who have similar plans is much lower. Among students whose major is mathematics or physics only 19 percent plan to spend much time in social work (Rubina, 1981, p. 91; Titma, 1981).

Just belonging to the Communist Party assumes an obligation to do active social work, and though there is great variance within the party the average member spends much more time on social work than the nonparty member. According to the principle that as many people as possible should be included in supervisory positions, the Soviet political elite enrolls into the ranks of so-called party activists up to 30 percent of all party members and in trade union activists about 5 percent of all trade union members (*Knizhka Partiinogo Aktivista*, 1979, pp. 31, 49; TsSU, 1982, p. 50).

The class divisions of Soviet society exert a direct influence on the distribution of social work in the country. There are about 2.5 million superiors (those who head some administrative unit, with a primary party cell), without taking into account their deputies and the party and Komsomol secretaries, which would probably make this figure four or five times higher (see Kerimov et al., 1985, p. 76; Rodionov, 1984, p. 105). Whatever their rank, they are expected to be much more active in social work than their subordinates. Certainly this division between supervisor and subordinate overlaps greatly the division of the population into party and nonparty members. However, it is important to remember that millions of party members are rank and file, whereas there are many managers, mostly at a low level in the hierarchy, who are not party members.

## *The Admirers and Haters of Social Work*

The stance of the Soviet people toward social work is not a simple matter even if we can discern major trends. It would be erroneous to take social work as it is described in Soviet publications at face value (see, for instance, Friedhut, 1977; Hough, 1977, 1979; and even much earlier, *Harper's* "Civic Training in Soviet Russia," 1929) or dismiss it as a heavy corvée imposed on all Soviet citizens under fear of punishment (see McClosky and Turner, 1960).

Even studies conducted by ideological sociologists show that the majority of people holds a highly negative, often contemptuous attitude toward social work and regard it—like organizational meetings—as meaningless, ritualistic, and a waste of their time. They consider social work as a toll on the political system and try as much as possible to reduce the size of this tax imposed upon them by their superiors. For these people social work is a constraint, a burden they have to evade or minimize as much as possible.

However, not everybody in the Soviet Union is hostile toward social work or tries to avoid it. According to some, the number of people eager to become activists in social work is probably about 10–20 percent (see Babosov et al., 1983, p. 71; Iakuba and Andrushchenko, 1976, p. 162).

There are four categories of people who hold a positive attitude toward this work and want the authorities to consider them as exemplary social activists: (1) those who connect their fate with the given political structure, such as party apparatchiks and ideological workers; (2) seekers of careers in the nomenclature; (3) poor workers; and (4) single people and pensioners. For these people, doing social work is not an exorbitant price to pay for its benefits and can even be a source of pleasure.

Apparatchiks and ideological zealots consider social work as part of their professional activity and as a means of preserving their jobs. For ambitious young people who have decided to penetrate into the party apparatus, the KGB, and other parts of the Soviet establishment, arduous social activity is a pass to this future.

Social work involvement also provides good protection for people with low or diminished professional skills, who hate their jobs, or are not conscientious workers. Soviet society has created a special type of social activist who, though despised by colleagues, can nevertheless weather criticism throughout his professional life. Many novels and movies have stigmatized this type (see, for instance, Riasanov's *Office Romance*). Even the Soviet political elite from time to time bristles against such people and against the performance of social work during working hours, but usually only for the sake of appearances. This type of social activist is a fixture in any Soviet enterprise or office and slices off a considerable amount of working time doing social work.

Thus the data of Tatiana Kozlova and Galina Subbotina are noteworthy. They asked scholars about the role of social work, along with other values (obedient behavior, creativity, and material well-being), in their life. It turns out that the role of social work rose in proportion with the increase in age. So, among scientific workers in the 21–25 age group, 25 percent consider social work an important sphere of their activity; among scholars in the 51–60 age group this figure is 34 percent (Kozlova and Subbotina, 1976, p. 192). This correlation between age and interest in social work seems to be in direct proportion to the decline of creative activity of many scholars after forty, a fact confirmed by American studies (see Lehman, 1953) as well as by Soviet ones (see the survey of studies on this subject in Kozlova, 1983, pp. 20–34). With age, many scholars try to compensate for their shrinking productivity with an administrative career or social activism.

Social work is often an outlet for the energy and emotions of many single people, mostly women, often pensioners, who see in the work an opportunity to make contact with other people. Pensioners stand out as a category of people among whom quite a number genuinely enjoy social work. For many the participation in social work means preserving the old style of life from which they often reluctantly parted. For this reason they prefer to continue their social work. In surveys about motivation, many pensioners did not hide this fact. From 36 to 40 percent of those asked why they were involved in social work gave as a reason "the pleasure of communication with people," while 29–34 percent chose "it is interesting," "preserves health," or "fills time" (Barandeev, 1984, p. 53; Shapiro, 1983, pp. 100–07).

In this respect it is noteworthy that pensioners are also among those who send letters to the mass media and authorities. According to data in the Taganrog study of the late 1960s and early 1970s, the number of retired people who send letters surpassed their proportion in the population by 1.4 times (Grushin and Onikov, 1980, p. 384; Tokarovskii, 1976, pp. 118–19). Among the authors of letters to the editor of *Izvestiia*, 76 percent were older than fifty-five, although this age group composed only 15 percent of the readers (Davydchenkov, 1970, p. 152).

Even people who usually despise social work and its activists will, under certain circumstances, develop some positive attitudes toward particular kinds of it if they see it as being genuinely useful to people and the country, and if it touches upon humanistic or patriotic feelings.

There are also situations when people use social work as an opportunity to socialize, givng them a pretext for drinking, flirting and having simple fun.

Social work is also attractive to many people because it can to some extent satisfy their need for power and to command others. In this respect I will discuss the relationship between social work and power in Soviet society.

## *Social Work and Power*

Social work must presumably be performed voluntarily and without material compensation. It consists of various activities roughly divided into two groups—directive and nondirective. In the first type, the individual performs some function in which other people are controlled, whereas in the second type, a person obeys the orders of a superior.

Superiors in social work include activists of the party, Komsomol and trade union committees at various levels, and numerous elected bodies in the government (soviets or councils). According to a recent study in Taganrog (1982) of all worker activists, who made up 48 percent of all workers, almost half (a quarter of all workers) were "secretaries of party committee members, and leaders of trade unions and the Young Communist League organization."[6] These soldiers of social activity work as agitators (there were 8 million of them in the beginning of the 1980s; see Brezhnev, 1981), as members of teams assisting police in keeping order on the streets (13 million), as members of various teams as well as committees created mostly for propaganda purposes at the place of residence (30 million), and as people fulfilling various casual assignments (Novoselov, 1985, p. 13).

There is a strong, directly proportional relationship between position in the hierarchy of social work and the orientation of the individual to do this work. The majority of those positively oriented toward it belong to the officer corps, whereas people with negative attitudes generally compose the rank and file. The number of officers in social work is enormous—millions of people. Five million communists (about one quarter of all members) serve on various party bodies (Rodionov, 1984, p. 146), 15 million serve on trade unions, and 10 million in the Young Communist League committees (Lopata and Petukhov, 1986, p. 31).

The huge army of people who have some position in the social worker hierarchy often have overlapping administrative positions (for example, the party secretary of a large production unit or of a research institute often shares power with the director). This involves a significant part of the Soviet population in the political system as bosses of various sorts, giving people in social work a chance to command. This reinforces the system, as does involving a considerable part of the Soviet population in ideological work, which, whatever its quality, forces people to identify themselves with the regime, whose policies they then praise.

## Contact with Illegal Critics of the Regime

In Stalin's time, not only "the enemies of the people," but also their wives and children as well as close friends were ostracized by their colleagues, acquaintances, and most of their friends. Those who maintained relations with people stigmatized by their connections with those arrested or exiled were considered heroes at that time (see Chukovskaia, 1981; Grossman, 1974, 1980; Kopelev, 1975, 1978; Panova, 1975).

In the post-Stalin period the situation changed significantly. Of course, the majority of the Soviet population, as in the past, avoid contact with those declared disloyal and even more with dissidents. The Soviet people rarely come publicly to the defense of those who are the target of official campaigns. This changed somewhat in the 1960s when a few people, mostly intellectuals, could publicly defend their friends and colleagues. There was a campaign to defend, for instance, the poet Joseph Brodsky, who was put on trial in 1964–65 for "social parasitism." This was followed a few years later by the decision of some authors to stand by persecuted writers—Andrei Siniavskii, Iurii Daniel, and then Alexander Solzhenitsyn. However, in the 1970s, with the political reaction in the country that came after Khrushchev's liberalization, public support of nonconformist people practically disappeared, and even the prominent intellectuals with liberal reputations, such as writers Grigorii Baklanov, Sergei Zalygin, Valentin Kataiev, Chingiz Aitmatov, Vasilii Bykov, or such scholars as Nikolai Semenov, Lulii Khariton, and Andrei Kolmogorov, took part in the orchestrated campaigns against Sakharov, Solzhenitsyn, and other dissidents.

The party apparatus in the 1970s could, with great effort, effectively organize meetings at which appointed people denounced their colleagues who decided to emigrate from the country. Only in very rare cases were there people courageous enough to publicly defend the right of people to leave the country (see Simis, 1982).

But if publicly a majority of Soviet people continued to behave toward heretics in almost the same way as they had under Stalin, their private behavior was considerably different.

Unlike in the past, a significant number of people defy the authorities and continue to entertain relations with people denounced as foes of the Soviet system. The attitudes toward would-be emigrants and dissidents is indicative.

I here refer to my own study, which I conducted for six months in the Soviet Union after my application for an exit visa in October 1978. During this period I kept a diary in which I collected information on the attitudes of people around me. In some respects, this study is an experiment in participant observation. My sample included about 300 people with whom I was in more or less regular contact before my declaration to go abroad (for more about the composition of the sample, see Shlapentokh, 1984, p. 232).

The would-be emigrant is considered in the Soviet Union a traitor, and contacts with him or her are interpreted as an unwillingness to comply with the stance of the political elite toward emigration. In my sample, 56 percent of all contacts increased or retained the same level of interaction with me. Only 24 percent stopped all contact with me, and 20 percent reduced them. Other emigrants also tell about the considerable number of people who stayed in touch with them during the painful period of waiting for the authorities to respond to their request for an exit visa (Simis, 1982; see also *Novoye Russkoye Slovo*, August 3, 1986, about the attitudes in Moscow to Gulko, a prominent chess player who was a "refusenik" for seven years). Even in a play *40, Sholom-Aleikhem Street*, which was staged in a Moscow theater, the hero, despite the objection of his father, escorted his girlfriend emigrating from the country to the rail station (Stavitskii, 1986, pp. 28–51). The memoirs of Soviet dissidents published abroad show that even committed dissidents such as A. Amalrik (1982) or Leonid Plushch (1979) were not eschewed by many people in private life.

The average Soviet individual, as in Stalin's time, avoids any gatherings not officially approved by the state, even the most politically innocent. The people know from birth that any attempt to create an unofficial organization is considered by the authorities as a direct threat to the regime, and those participating in meetings convened by such an organization run a serious risk. Individuals shun unofficial exhibitions, informal theatrical performances, and unofficial seminars devoted to cultural issues, not to mention any assembly with even the slightest oppositional flavor.

Of course, serious changes occurred in Soviet society after Stalin. It was especially evident in the 1960s, when a significant number of professionals, students, and intellectuals in particular took part in numerous unofficial gatherings. The bard movement—the many gatherings for hearing bards, or balladeers—the semiofficial festivals, and semiprivate and private parties for the same purpose, attracted thousands of people across the country. Then samizdat, the underground literature, became the cause of thousands of people in the nation's main cultural centers. Samizdat activity evolved for some people into campaigns to sign protest letters to the government, and to attend political trials and even opposition meetings and demonstrations (Alekseeva, 1984).

Since the mid-1960s, and especially after the Czechoslovakian invasion in 1968, the Soviet authorities, mostly through the KGB, began to crush the liberal movement. It took about ten years to suppress essentially all political deviance in the country, and to the end of Brezhnev's regime the average intellectual, as in Stalin's time, shied away from any form of unendorsed public activity. Certainly, as is always the case in history, the complete restoration of "the status quo ante bellum," of the political atmosphere of the 1940s or 1950s, was not possible. What the KGB could not destroy during the 1970s was illegal private political activity, mostly of a verbal character, which at short notice can evolve into public activity.

Particularly important in this regard is any public connection of the Soviet people with the church, or organized religion. Though evidence suggests (see, for instance, Iakunin, 1979; Solzhenitsyn, 1972; *Vol'noie Slovo*, 1976, vol. 24; 1977, vol. 28) that the Russian Orthodox church, as well as other religious congregations (Moslem, Judaic, Lutheran) recognized by the government are under strict control, apparently this is not enough for the leadership. The political elite, as it did after the Revolution, still regards attendance at a church or synagogue, the public observance of religious rituals (baptism, for instance), or public praise of religion as politically disloyal acts.

Recent official Soviet studies show that up to one-third of the population regards itself as religious. However, the number of those who attend religious services is much less (Iablokov, 1979, pp. 139–42; Podmazov, 1985, pp. 19–20). This difference derives not only from the universal gap between the belief and the practice of religion, but to a very considerable extent from fear. Even in the 1960s, the number of intellectuals who attended religious services did not grow significantly. But at the same time, the intelligentsia as well as young people from all walks of life revealed a growing interest in religion. This was done in many, and mostly private, ways, such as demonstrating a great interest in religious literature, especially the Bible (even with the extremely high price of Bibles on the black market—up to half or even more of the average Soviet monthly salary; see *Vol'noie Russkoie Slovo*, 1977, vol. 28, p. 16), in demonstrating an interest in religious objects, primarily icons, and in reading novels or seeing movies that treat religion with respect.

## Attitudes toward Acceptable Critics of the Regime

The Soviet elite expects that the average Soviet citizen will not express interest, let alone speak in support, of critics of the regime who are allowed to express their views.

When pursuing a policy of modernization from time to time, the political elite is forced to make some maneuvers and accommodate intellectuals, permitting them to criticize Soviet flaws. But at the same time the elite tries to separate the intellectuals making the critique from the mass intelligentsia and the rest of the population and strongly frowns upon the rank and file who join these intellectuals.

This intricacy of the Soviet system was clearly revealed in the period of liberalization in the 1960s. After having allowed Twardovskii's *Novyi Mir* ("New World") to publish highly critical novels and articles, the authorities then tried to curtail dissemination of the magazine, including eliminating it from army libraries. For the same reason, movies approved by the central authorities are often not allowed to be widely shown throughout the country, especially in the provinces. Such was the case in the 1980s with such movies as Bykov's *Scarecrow* (see Alexander Kazantsev's article in *Pravda*, May 23, 1986).

In most cases, the Soviet individual is capable of separating the signals addressed by the political elite to a small group of intellectuals or a foreign audience and signals directed to the masses. Understanding the deeply authoritarian nature of Soviet society and the natural orientation of its leaders toward repressive actions and their aversion toward any form of democracy or pluralism, the average Soviet citizen usually does not allow himself to be provoked into critical activity, even when such a critique is apparently invited by the leadership.

In fact, a majority of the population kept its distance from the legal critics even in the 1960s and shied away from public support of Solzhenitsyn's stories even when they were published in Soviet magazines. The critical campaign launched by Gorbachev in 1985–86, with its thrust against party officials, was also avoided by the majority of Soviet people.

Again, as in all previous cases, the majority of the people did not believe in the radical shift of the Soviet system toward openness and the ability to criticize superiors and various flaws in Soviet life. Even the mass media in 1985–86 published many letters in which people expressed their mistrust of the duration of such a policy and vowed not to take it at face value. The nationwide survey conducted by the Moscow Institute of Sociology at the end of 1985 found that only 38 percent of respondents, answering a loaded question, agreed that the atmosphere in the country (the degree of openness, freedom to criticize) had improved (*Literaturnaia Gazeta*, October 8, 1986). Thus the majority of Soviets did not trust Gorbachev's appeals for critical activism.

## Cooperation with the KGB

Soviet individuals reach their highest level of political loyalty when they agree to collaborate with the KGB.

The prestige of the KGB in Soviet society in the last two decades has significantly increased. Three circumstances account for this development. First, the period of terror when the political police was the main perpetrator of it is now in the remote past, and only a few people are left alive who witnessed its excesses. Second, since 1953 the KGB has only been used to persecute people who primarily seek confrontation with the Soviet political system, and people who are ready to comply with this system—the majority—have nothing to fear. Third,

Brezhnev's regime spent a lot of effort embellishing the image of the KGB, using novels and movies to describe it as a patriotic institution playing a positive role in Soviet society and KGB agents as heroic. A number of writers, such as Iulian Semenov, devoted their entire careers to praising the KGB (see, for instance, his collected works, 1983–84). This change in the status of the KGB, however, could not replace the revolutionary fervor that induced people to collaborate with it in the first decades after the Revolution.

But the general fear of the KGB, even if pushed into the subconscious of the majority of the Soviet people (meaning that fear of the KGB is not a frequent issue in communications between friends and family members), remains an important part of the Soviet mentality, and they automatically restrain from many actions that might get them into trouble with it, such as contacting foreigners, supporting dissidents, joking about politics, or disseminating information obtained from foreign radio.

The recruitment of informers was always a very important political goal of any Soviet regime, and was probably upgraded in importance by Brezhnev. Almost all memoirs of Soviets published in the West contain episodes of recruitment by the KGB (see Ashkenazy, 1985, pp. 77–84; Golyakhovsky, 1984, pp. 109–10; Polikanov, 1983, pp. 67–69; Terz, 1984; Vishnevskaia, 1984, pp. 133–39; Voinovich, 1985). Certainly, as is the case with social work, educated people have a much higher chance of being recruited than workers or farm laborers with only an elementary education and a low social status.

With the passing of time, a type of system such as the Soviet one gradually and inexorably enrolls a growing number of people in its network of collaborators. If in the beginning the number of informers in Soviet society could be estimated at a few percent, now, seven decades later, this figure is much greater. This principle (let us name it the "law of extensive reproduction of informers"), which postulates the involvement of a growing portion of the population in collaborating with the political police, is directly connected with another tendency (let us name it "the law of extensive reproduction of lawbreakers"). This postulates the gradual increase in the number of people in the country who have violated the law, even once, which gives the KGB a good means for recruiting people into service (lawbreakers are co-opted by threats of legal persecutions for crimes committed, and the KGB promises to ignore the crime if the individual will collaborate).

How do Soviet people react to recruitment by the KGB? Of course the response can only be approximate, because data on this issue is probably one of the best-guarded Soviet secrets. From various sources, mostly impressionistic in character, it is possible to deduce that a considerable part of the population does not withstand KGB pressure and joins the army of informers. Each recruiting operation is carefully prepared, with all details on the life of the candidate scrutinized beforehand. His or her weaknesses, including any violations of laws or morality (adultery, for instance) are checked in order to provide a means of eventually blackmailing that person into cooperation. Threats and promises to help the potential informant and his or her family cope with problems they may face are also used in recruiting candidates. But certainly, the whole recruitment process is presented by the state and party as an appeal to the patriotic feelings of a "true Soviet personality."

It seems that only a few people can resist this blend of threats, seduction, and demagoguery, while most convince themselves that the advantages (safety and protection) or service to this omnipotent organization outweigh the disadvantages (the contempt of friends and the fear of leaking information to acquaintances).

CHAPTER
4

# The Collective in Soviet Political and Economic Life

The concept of the collective—people with whom the individual works, lives, or participates in sports and hobbies—plays an extremely important role in Soviet ideology and politics as well as in the life of the Soviet people. According to *Pravda*, there are 2.5 million collectives in the country (September 24, 1984). Not only is each enterprise and office considered one, but the political elite regards each residential block a collective, i.e., a contingent of people who interact regularly with each other and as such, form a significant instrument of the government.

All the major official Soviet documents, such as the constitution (1977) or "The Program of the Communist Party" (1986), underscore the leading role of the collective and collectivism in Soviet society. The political elite deemed it necessary to adopt a special law about the labor collective (1983). The collective, as the main unit of Soviet society, is the leading arena for Communist Party activity, for the Young Communist League (Komsomol), and for many other official organizations. It is, especially in the workplace, the main area for indoctrinating the Soviet people.

## Official Functions of the Soviet Collective

The idea of collective fits in well with the general concept of power developed by the Bolsheviks. This concept postulates control of the country based on a network of various institutions which, with varying methods and duties, keep tabs on each individual from the day of birth. The party and the KGB is the hub of this multilayered network, which also includes the police, block administration, post offices, and any other institution that carries a roster of families and individuals. The production collective, where people spend at least nine hours a day working, is an important part of the network that makes up the basis of the Soviet political system. Collectives perform a number of functions. First of all, one must understand that collectivism (devotion to the collective) is one of the fundamentals of Soviet morality. This moral code presents the interests of society as superior to those of the individual.[1] However, Soviet ideologues realize that most people view the demand to make sacrifices for society as an abstraction (except in the case of war) and is not terribly effective. But the same demand in relation to the collective, a concrete entity where the individual knows many if not most members, is more humanized and therefore much more likely to be successful. Thus personal relationships which emerge on the job and, to a lesser extent, those which materialize at the place of residence, can be mobilized by the regime for its purposes.

In advancing collectivism as a leading moral value, Soviet ideology exploits various feelings such as altruism, comradeship, friendship, the human need for affiliation, respect for people in the same social surroundings, and even democratism (the obligation to obey the majority). At the same time, official ideology suggests the necessity of keeping friendship and other personal relationships in check, as they can be potentially hostile to the big collective and the state (I will discuss this later).

Collectivism has always been used in Soviet society as a means of extracting sacrifices from the individual, but practically never the reverse. The heroes of the collective, as depicted in the mass media, novels, or movies made in accordance with the principle of socialist realism, are people who neglect their personal life, their comfort, and material well-being for the sake of the success of the plant or collective farm. These so-called heroes are portrayed in the novels of many hack Soviet writers like Piotr Pavlenko, Semen Babaevskii, Vladimir Kochetov, and others.

However, the collective is almost never supposed to come to the defense of the individual against the state or party bosses. Cases when a collective, i.e., a majority of the colleagues, was involved in a struggle against the director of an enterprise, a local party committee, or a ministry have been extremely rare.

The second function of the collective demands that it serve as a watchdog over each of its members. The collective is regarded as responsible for the production, as well as the political and moral, activity of the people belonging to it. It is obliged to guarantee the political loyalty of its members and take an aggressive stance toward any activity the authorities regard as anti-Soviet. Colleagues in the production collective are supposed to prevent the violation of labor discipline and punish those who trespass against the rules. Soviet surveys are filled with questions about the participation of respondents in the control of their colleagues (Changli, 1979b; Plaksii, 1982; Smirnov, 1979).

The collective is replete with voluntary and involuntary informers and is a leading base for KGB operations against citizens. For the most part, the personal file on each Soviet individual is filled out with the help of reports submitted by his or her colleagues.

The collective is also the official moral educator of its members and watches whether moral requirements are observed in the workplace and in the family. It is entitled to reprimand an individual for all sorts of bad behavior. Spouses are encouraged to come to it for help in settling family conflicts, including adultery. Soviet schooling sees the collective as an organ that can force parents to pay more attention to the studies and behavior of their children.

Since the collective is endowed with the role of moral judge, it is supposed that in any conflict between the collective—representing the majority—and the individual, the collective is always right. To be "against the collective" has long been one of the harshest accusations leveled against Soviet citizens. Recently, a famous Soviet movie, *Scarecrow* (made by Rolan Bykov, a prominent film director and actor), in the first attempt to show a realistic picture of the "typical Soviet collective," portrayed a conflict between a collective and an individual with the former representing deception and cruelty and the latter, nobility and honesty. (For an official description of the collective, see Fedoseev, 1985, pp. 214–16; Il'ichev et al., 1983, pp. 264–65; Rumiantsev, 1983, pp. 97–101.)

## Popular Attitudes toward the Collective

The study of the attitudes of Soviet people toward the collective is a difficult task because almost all surveys on this subject have been conducted by ideologically oriented sociologists who offered highly loaded options to questions, prodding their respondents to extol the collectives in which they worked. However, even these data give the opportunity to get some idea of the real views of the Soviet people about the collective.

Analyzing these data, it is necessary to make a distinction between responses related to issues with differing political significance. It is one thing to answer questions about the role of the collective in self-management—a highly sensitive political issue—and quite another to respond to questions about the moral influence of collectives on the respondent, which is a relatively moderate political issue. Then it is important to discern questions eliciting abstract answers—for instance, about the role of the collective in general—from questions that require concrete ones.

It is possible to contend that at the abstract level the majority of Soviet people probably support the idea of the importance of the collective in social life and even the idea of the superiority of collective interests over individual ones. Soviet ideological training has been really successful in educating the people at the verbal, mythological level to negate individualism and revere collectivism and patriotism.

In the survey conducted by Vladimir Sokolov (1971–72), it was found that 97 percent agreed with the alternative "I cannot live without the collective." In another study (1978–79) by the same researcher, 74 percent of the 11,000 young people polled evaluated "the opinion of the collective about his or her work" as very important (Sokolov, 1981, pp. 123–24).

However, a growing number of people do not want to join the cult of the collective. This development is especially noticeable at the pragmatic level in which people define their personal attitudes toward the role of the collective but still in rather abstract terms.

According to Sokolov's data, when asked on whom they rely in achieving a difficult goal, only 20 percent of young people chose the best alternative ideologically, "to the same extent on myself as on the collective," whereas one-third plainly declared that they "rely only on themselves." Fifty percent chose an alternative which leaned more to the belief in individualism than in collectivism—"I rely on myself in the first place but to some degree on the collective also" (Sokolov, 1981, p. 125).

The general indifference of the majority of Soviet people to the collective with which they work revealed that poor relations between people rarely is a major cause of labor turnover or low satisfaction with work. According to various sources, less than 1 percent of the workers name a bad collective as a reason for leaving their workplace or explaining why they were dissatisfied with their job (see Antosenkov and Kupriianova, 1985, p. 118; Ratnikov, 1978, p. 180).

All popular Soviet novels and movies either derogate the collective (see, for instance, such movies as Roman Balaian's *Day and Night Dreams* [1983], Sergei Mikailian's *Fell in Love at One Request* [1982], Leonid Zorin's *Kind People* [1980], and many others) or ignore them. No respected Soviet author has ever tried in the last three decades to describe positively the role of the collective in the life of Soviet people.

Pointing to the radical difference between the official image of the Soviet collective and the reality does not mean that in many cases people do not become quite attached to an enterprise or a research institute in which they work and enjoy its highest prestige. All other things considered, the average Soviet individual, as well as the American, likes to work in a well-known enterprise that attracts the attention of the public with its achievements.

What makes the collective such an important place for the Soviet individual is the chance to communicate with other people, a circumstance recognized by many Soviet researchers (see Kovalev, 1975). The job is the main place where the individual strikes up acquaintances that often lead to close friendships and camaraderie with others. The job is also an important place for people of the opposite sex to meet (about 40 percent of married people met their partners on the job or at school, Kharchev, 1979, pp. 215–16). For the Soviet individual the workplace as an arena for personal contact is especially significant because close personal encounters in other places—clubs, cafeterias, etc.—are either totally impossible or else very restrained because of the difficulty in developing a mutual trust. Sociological surveys show, for example, that when asked about their motivation for working, two-thirds of all female respondents indicated social communication (Boiko, 1980, p. 178). A recent Soviet movie, *The Most Attractive* (1985), vividly describes the life of a Soviet collective—a department of a design institute—whose members are preoccupied by their personal relationships.

The majority of the Soviet people make up their own informal groups within collectives, which play significant roles in their lives and which have nothing to do with the collective as it is presented ideologically. This can create an impression of how vital the collective is to the Soviet people, an illusion many of them share, not making the distinction between their informal groups and the organization inside which these groups function. This circumstance significantly blurred the answers of respondents concerning their attitudes toward collectives.

These informal groups, as well as the network of friends and acquaintances, are the arenas for the outlet of collectivistic feelings—of the desire to make some contribution to a common cause—of many Soviet people, in opposition to the great number of individualists who reject any form of cooperation with people unless it brings them immediate benefit.

Moreover, these informal groups (Soviet authors write about two levels in the collective—macro and micro) are often regarded by their members as refuges from the big, official collective, a fact well recognized by social scientists, who see in informal groups, not without reason, danger to the official political system (Bueiva and Alekseeva, 1982; see also Rusetskaia, 1984, pp. 75–76).

## Attitudes toward the Collective as the Moral Authority

If, as was mentioned, many Soviet people, in praising collectivism, express doubt about the support which they can find in the collective, even fewer of them are ready to accept their collective as a judge of their behavior, a view based on widespread skepticism regarding others' morals.

A study of young people in Byelorussia and Estonia (1984) provides us with some data on the perceptions of Soviet youth on the moral values of others. Only 9 percent found among their peers the qualities of honesty, 8 percent unity between words and deeds, 6 percent selflessness, 15 percent diligence, 7 percent devotion to the dominant ideology, and 15 percent collectivism. Seventeen percent of the respondents agreed to describe the relations in their collective as really good, with "exactness," friendliness, and mutual help as the dominant features (Babosov et al., 1985, p. 137).

In another survey, only 20 percent of the respondents could bring examples attesting to the virtues of members of their collective (Sokolov, 1981, p. 267).

Blinov, Titma, and their colleagues tried to establish the influence of various institutions on the moral perceptions of young people in Russia, the Ukraine, Byelorussia, and Estonia (1981–83). The data collected clearly showed that the role of the collective is not great. Despite the loaded character of the questions, only 10 percent of all respondents attributed to the collective decisive importance in the formation of moral views. Private institutions, such as family and friends, exert, according to the answers, a much more significant impact—17 and 18 percent, respectively. The collective was assessed especially low by young people when they were asked about the "sensitivity" and "tactfulness" of various institutions. Only 7 percent highly praised the collective for those qualities, with 33 percent attributing this to friends, and 63 percent to family (Babosov et al., 1985, pp. 52–54; Blinov and Titma, 1985, p. 12).

With a poor view of their own collective and the growing ideology of individualism, Soviet people quite often, even in surveys conducted by ideologically minded sociologists, demonstrate their hostility toward the collective's interference in their private lives. This phenomenon became clear in a study of Soviet attitudes toward dating services (Shlapentokh, 1984a). Sokolov has also acknowledged that the majority of young people feel the collective has no such prerogatives (Sokolov, 1981, p. 125).

But even though they may not feel the collective has any right to judge them, people in no way disregard the opinion of them held by their colleagues and in many cases are eager to be highly esteemed by them. Of course, of special importance in this are the views of their informal groups within the collective.

Contrary to official expectations, people do not regard the collective as having a good psychological climate when its members are demanding and exacting (which is the official ideal of the collective), but when people are mutually tolerant of bad labor discipline, embezzlement, and other labor violations. As various studies show, no more than one-third of respondents verbally condemned the misbehavior of their comrades and even less undertook any action to punish them (see Chapter 3).

The nature of satisfaction with the psychological climate in the collective is similar to that of work—in many cases high satisfaction is combined with low productivity and labor discipline. Soviet sociologists and psychologists usually, as with job satisfaction, assumed that the better the psychological climate, the higher the compatibility of the collective's members, which would lead to better productivity. Apparently they digested the sociometric concepts developed in the United States which are used for the study of interpersonal relations and praised those collectives where everybody liked each other according to their sociometric matrix (see, for instance, Shorokhova and Zotova, 1980).

Only since the mid-1970s has the idea emerged in the Soviet Union that the collectivist is the ideal figure for Soviet society and the conformist is a negative personality in all modern societies, and that the two can be confused with each other. This idea was really developed with the plays of two authors—Il'ia Dvoretskii and Alexander Gel'man (particularly in Dvoretskii's *Man from Outside* and Gel'man's *We Who Signed*). It later spread to popular publications (Ivanov's *Collectivism or Conformism*, 1980), and also showed up in some scientific works (Dontsov, 1984, pp. 146–48; Parygin, 1981, p. 63; Rumiantsev, 1983, p. 98).

## The Collective and Self-Management

As skeptical as they are of the moral authority of the collective, people take even less seriously the official image of the collective as a self-governing organization, a part of real civil society. The respondents in surveys sponsored by such institutions as the Academy of Social Science at the Central Committee of the Communist Party or the High School of the Young Communist Leagues are well aware of the significance of this myth in official ideology and respond to the questions very cautiously.

However, even the data collected by ideologically oriented sociologists reveal that a majority of the Soviet people reject the official idea about the role of the collective in management as well as official statistics about participation of workers in various forms of self-management. Many of them were bold enough to do this even under Brezhnev.

In 1976, two ideologically loyal sociologists, Yuri Volkov and Vladimir Mukhachev, referring to the study conducted under the auspices of the Young Communist League school, contended that 48 percent of all workers in the country "actively participated in the management of their enterprises" (Volkov and Mukhachev, 1976, p. 174). When they asked workers directly, "Do you feel like the master of your enterprise?" only 34 percent responded that they definitely felt so and behaved accordingly, and 12 percent confessed that while they did feel this was so, they did not always act as it demanded (Volkov and Mukhachev, 1976, p. 80).

In another survey in the same period (1978) ideological sociologists elicited a positive answer about participation in management from only 25 percent of the respondents; the investigators suggested that 45 percent of these people already took part in government but half of them were not aware of this (Svininnikov, 1985, pp. 109, 123).

The survey conducted by Plaksii found that 60 percent of young workers rejected the answer to the question which said workers had a high role in management. These respondents picked other, less ideologically ridden, alternatives (Plaksii, 1982, p. 97).

The genuine interest of Soviet workers in self-management was revealed in the Taganrog survey in 1983. When asked about the sphere of social activity that deserved their special attention, only 6 percent chose the alternative related to self-management (Klopov, 1985, p. 220).

The ludicrous character of the myth of the role of the collective in government becomes more clear when the answers of workers to questions about concrete forms of their participation in management are considered. In general, meetings of the collective, including "Permanently Active Production Meetings," highly praised in official propaganda, play mostly ritualistic roles, which has even been recognized from time to time in Soviet publications, and what is more, in official documents.

Edward Klopov, in his book that served as an apologia about the Soviet working class, using very euphemistic terminology, confesses that "workers' meetings still do not fully play the role which is ascribed to them in the development of socialist democracy and in the strengthening of the social and political activity of the working class" (Klopov, 1985, p. 209). He cites data showing that only 51 percent of the workers in the huge Cheliabinsk Tractor Association were inclined to respond affirmatively about workers' meetings as "a form of social management," disregarding other forms even more resolutely (Klopov, 1985, p. 209).

According to Blinov's data based on a sampling of workers in several cities in 1976–77, only 20 percent took part in the debates on production plans and only 23 percent on the organization of labor (Blinov, 1979, p. 65).

## New Trends in Attitudes toward the Collective in the Post-Brezhnev Period

The widespread corruption in the country forced the new Soviet leadership to change reluctantly the tenor of propaganda on the role of the collective, primarily the idea that "the collective is always right in the conflict with the individual."

During the 1970s many collectives, from being an agent of the state and the watchdog of state interests, even against managers, turned into servants of the directors and local party bosses. By involving many of their subordinates in collusion for embezzlement, falsification of statistical reports, and the recruitment of cadres loyal only to them, while allowing sloppy work and idleness, managers and regional party officials turned collectives into a base for blatant violations of Soviet laws and deception of the leadership.

Since Andropov and later Gorbachev saw the purge of corrupt bureaucrats necessary in order to overhaul the economy and accelerate technological progress, they could not avoid some modifications in the stance toward collectives even while praising collectivism as the basic tenet of Soviet society. These modifications, not easily perceptible, were intended to demolish the arguments of corrupt officials that their actions were supported by "the collective." This change in the analysis of the collective began to be reflected in ideological literature and the publications of social scientists who, following journalists, started to speak about "quasicollective," "false collective," and so on (see Simonian, 1986, pp. 72–74; see also *Pravda*'s editorial which, in the new spirit, retreats from the postulate that "the collective is always right," November 2, 1986).

In 1983 and especially in 1985 and 1986, the Soviet mass media, assigned with cleansing the party apparatus, inundated the public with articles denouncing the collectives. They covered the mishandling of production affairs, protectionism, embezzlement, and many other misdeeds of managers and party officials. The press even dared call these collectives the "Cosa Nostra," acting as mafialike organizations in almost open defiance of the state (see, for instance, *Pravda*, July 20, 1985; March 11, 1986; May 10, 1986; July 25, 1986; *Nedelia*, #21, 1986, pp. 15–16; *Sovietskaia Kul'tura*, June 28, 1986).

Liliia Beliaeva, a *Pravda* journalist, can be singled out as the author who realized the full-scale deleterious consequences of the cult of the collective for Soviet society. In various articles she attacked the corrupted collective—"communities of liars" as she named them in one of her articles—and sided with individuals who dared challenge their collective and the majority (see *Pravda*, April 11, 1986).

Some Soviet authors started to analyze relatively objectively the evolution of Soviet collectives into organizations whose leaders deftly exploited the official cult of collectivism in order to protect themselves against public interference. Chingiz Huseinov's *Family Secrets* (1986), Anatolii Tkachenko's *You Know Him* (1986), and Mikhail Kholmogorov's *Wait for a Guest* (1986) are among the new novels beginning to describe the true role of many collectives in Soviet life.

# CHAPTER 5

# Soviet People and the West

Among the requirements demanded by the political elite of the people, hostility to the West is one of the most important. Hatred of the West as a political, social, and national enemy is inculcated by all the ideological apparatus in each individual from childhood. The amount of energy and resources spent directly on anti-Western propaganda is enormous. Each mass periodical devotes a significant part of its space (the major newspapers up to one-fourth) to it. The same is done by all textbooks on social issues, official literature, and plays.

The attitude toward the West is probably the most important indicator of political loyalty in the country, and any investigation of political reputation by the party or the KGB starts with its study.

I will now discuss what the real attitudes of the Soviet individual are toward the West and analyze to what degree the Soviet state is successful in controlling its people in this respect.

## Soviet Behavior and the West

Even with gigantic pressure to comply with the official stance toward capitalist society, popular attitudes toward the West are extremely contradictory.

In some ways, it can be said that the official policy is rather successful. As in the past, Soviet people consider the Western countries, above all the United States, as committed adversaries of Russia and the Soviet Union. According to computations based on various surveys conducted by the author as well as on other sources of information, 50–70 percent of the Soviet Slavic population (about 71 percent of the entire Soviet population in 1979) support the foreign policy of their government. The number of strong critics, in my opinion, does not exceed 3–8 percent (see Shlapentokh, 1984b).

The perceptions of the Soviet people about the West, as far as they are revealed in official surveys (even if the responses do not correctly reflect the genuine views the Soviet people discuss among themselves), fit the official doctrine very well. Even in the late 1960s, when the Soviet people still lived in an atmosphere of relative political relaxation, they shared very loaded ideological images of the West. According to Grushin's survey of Taganrog residents, only 2 percent of the respondents considered the level of democracy in the United States to be "very high" (the figure for Britain was 3 percent); in contrast, 60 percent viewed Bulgaria and 34 percent viewed East Germany as models of democracy. Only 2 percent thought living standards were "very high" in the United States, France, and Great Britain; the figures for Czechoslovakia and Bulgaria were 63 and 49 percent, respectively (Grushin and Onikov, 1980, p. 306). Another nationwide survey conducted in 1977 showed respondents ranking the Soviet Union four on a five-point scale rating quality of life compared to an average ranking of only two for countries in the West.[1]

Of course, the Soviet population is not uniform on this, as well as on other, aspects. People with a higher education, especially intellectuals, and those engaged in creative activity, are much less conformist in support of foreign policy than the bulk of the Soviet population. This was already revealed in the 1960s when people were asked to evaluate articles on foreign affairs in Soviet newspapers, a good substitute for direct questions on attitudes toward official foreign policy. The highest educated people in all surveys evaluated these articles much lower than those with less education. In *Izvestia*'s survey in 1966, 33 percent of those with a higher education, compared with 22 percent of those with only a secondary education, demanded an improvement in information on capitalist countries (Shlapentokh, 1970).

A majority of the Soviet people under normal circumstances (i.e., not at times of crisis) do not disseminate in public information they got from foreign radio or from other foreign sources of information (newspapers, magazines, contacts with foreigners inside the country, and so on). Even the materials of the magazine *America*, which is distributed legally in the Soviet Union under the provisions of an international agreement, are not usually discussed in offices and workplaces.

The average Soviet individual, as is expected, shuns contact with foreigners unless it is an assignment from superiors. As all visitors of the Soviet Union have contended, it is very difficult to get an invitation from ordinary Soviet people to visit their homes, which is in stark contrast to typical Russian hospitality (Shipler, 1983; Smith, 1976).

At the same time, generally if a Soviet individual does meet a foreigner, even without special instructions he or she will defend official policy and try their best to embellish the image of the country. The average Soviet apparently sticks to the idea that almost all foreigners are looking for various secrets and is indeed cautious in discussing even the most innocent subjects with foreigners.

When visiting exhibitions from abroad in the Soviet Union or visiting foreign countries, the average Soviet rarely praises Western achievements and tries to find the seamy side of any apparently positive developments. Soviet novelists who describe heroes traveling to the West probably plausibly depict the reaction of Soviet people to Western life. Yuri Bondarev is a prime example of this. In all of his last novels—*The Coast* (1975), *The Choice* (1980), *The Play* (1984)—he forced his heroes to reason on the Western mode of life in a rather negative way. Sergei Kondrashov provides another example of this attitude; in his documentary novel the main hero, a Moscow correspondent in the United States, as well as all other Soviet personages, behave hostilely toward America and its people (1985).

Although they comply with many official demands about public attitudes and behavior toward the West, average Soviet individuals at the same time in many ways not only privately but also publicly express highly positive views and feelings related to capitalist society.

## Preoccupation with the West

In spite of their outward, and in some cases, inward, compliance with the official stance, average Soviet citizens are extremely absorbed with the West and its mode of life, which they try to imitate in many respects. Of course, people everywhere are interested in other countries, and the desire to imitate foreign lifestyles is universal. Western Europe and recently Japan attract the attention of many Americans as do the cultural and consumer goods created in these countries. However, the role of foreign countries in the life of the American citizen is minimal in comparison with the Soviet counterpart.[2]

There are three groups in the Soviet population especially strongly influenced by the West—the apparatchiks, the intelligentsia, and the youth. Prestige likely plays a great role in the life of these groups. The infatuation of Soviet youth with the West, its style of life, its culture—often not their best features—is one of the most sensitive political and social issues in the country. Admiration of the West among young people is so high that in a survey conducted by *Literaturnaia Gazeta* and *Sotsiologicheskie Issledovaniia* in four large cities in 1987 one-third of all teenagers openly declared (despite the utterly negative stance of ideology toward the Western lifestyle) that "imitation of the West" was one of their main values. Fifty-eight percent of the same teenagers were not ashamed to say that obtaining Western goods was among their life goals. Rock music was admired by 67 percent of the young people (Shchekochihkin, 1987, p. 13). In various ways Soviet writers, movie directors, and jouranlists have alarmed the public with the danger emanating from this blind imitation of Western lifestyle. Mikhalkov's movie *Kinship* grotesquely depicts a young, educated lady who stupidly tries to follow a Western lifestyle. Evtushenko makes the same lament in his poems and prose (see, for instance, his poem "Canned Culture" in *Pravda*, June 8, 1986, p. 3, and his novel, *Berry Field*, 1982).

The same issue, with a different degree of aggressiveness and condemnation, is regularly raised by Soviet politicians. At a meeting celebrating the sixtieth anniversary of the Komsomol, first secretary Victor Mishin depicted the influence of the Western mode of life as a dangerous plague and went so far as to equate the adoration of Western goods and lifestyles with political treason. "The distance from sloppy dressing, imitation of Western lifestyle, and the absorption of Western mass culture to antisocial behavior is sometimes not very far. Moral collapse, as Lenin warned, always leads to political collapse" (*Komsomol'skaia Pravda*, July 20, 1984).

## *Interest in Information on the West*

While repeating the official statements on the West, the average Soviet individual avidly hunts for information on life in capitalist society.

Various surveys I conducted in the 1960s and 1970s as well as those of former colleagues have unanimously established that interest in foreign affairs in most cases is stronger, or at least as strong as, interest in domestic news, with the exception, of course, of extraordinary events. This is in high contrast to the United States. As *Pravda* surveys carried out in 1968 and 1977 showed, about 90 percent of all readers more or less regularly read the articles on international issues, whereas only 70 percent on economic issues, 68 percent on moral and educational ones, and 60 percent on Marxist theory (Chernakova, 1979; Evladov et al., 1969).

The behavior of other newspaper readers is practically the same. Those who read central newspapers start with materials on international issues, as did two-thirds of *Izvestia*'s readership and almost the same amount of *Trud* and *Literaturnaia Gazeta* readers, based on surveys in the 1960s and 1970s (Shlapentokh, 1978a, p. 262; 1969a, p. 100).

Even readers of local newspapers, who supposedly have to be interested in local news in the first place and who in most cases already subscribe to national newspapers, also prefer international materials to all others; only 25 percent of Taganrog newspaper subscribers ignore foreign affairs articles, while articles on industry are ignored by 62 percent of all readers and on municipal bodies by 46 percent (Grushin and Onikov, 1980, pp. 228–39; see also Sbytov, 1983, p. 175).

A study in 1979 found that, as its author put it, "82 percent of Leningrad residents display stable personal interest in the information about events abroad. The similar figure for domestic information is 75 percent" (Losenkov, 1983, p. 48). International issues attract the first attention of TV and radio audiences.

Any legal source of international information attracts a gigantic following. The Soviet magazine, *Za Rubezhom* ("Abroad"), which has published articles translated from the foreign press since its inception in 1960, immediately became one of the most popular despite its tendentious selection of material. In the early 1980s its circulation was one million, which could not satisfy even a part of the demand for it. Among *Literaturnaia Gazeta* readers, in 1973 the number of subscribers to *Za Rubezhom* (it was very difficult to subscribe) was 15 percent, whereas the number of those who were subscribers to all regional party newspapers (there was no limit for subscriptions to them) was 23 percent (the number of subscribers to *Pravda* was 45 percent, Fomicheva, 1978, p. 39). The results of Grushin's Taganrog study (1973) also showed the extremely high popularity of *Za Rubezhom* among city residents (Grushin and Onikov, 1980, p. 127).

The yearning of Soviet people for information of foreign origin was also revealed in the study by Irina Fomicheva and her colleagues.

Upon being asked what sources of foreign information they prefer, 66 percent of *Literaturnaia Gazeta*'s readership voted for original foreign materials (28 percent even asked for no Soviet commentary) and only 14 percent chose Soviet authors (Fomicheva, 1978, p. 57).

Soviet surveys also found that one of the chief claims Soviet people level against their mass media is the insufficiency of international information. Grushin asked various groups of Taganrog residents about their satisfaction with the information on national, city, and foreign events. The largest group favored additional international information. More than half (52 percent) of the people who attended political schools, for instance, expressed their grievances on this subject as compared to 33 percent who wanted more information on national life and 25 percent who wanted more on their city (Grushin and Onikov, 1980, p. 330). Even more significant is the conclusion made by Nina Chernakova on the basis of a nationwide survey of the adult population (1977). The survey suggested, according to her, that "the population experiences a deficit of information on several problems of life in our country and especially on the problems of international life" (Chernakova, 1979, p. 23).[3]

International topics also dominate the interests of those who attend public lectures organized by the society Znaniie ("Knowledge"). Citizens in Moldavia in the mid-1970s put international issues in first place (70 percent) as a desirable subject of public lectures, whereas such issues as "problems of communist construction" were felt by only 29 percent to need more lectures (Timush, 1978, pp. 89, 145).

International affairs also seem to be the first topic of conversation among Soviet citizens, as opposed to the idea that they should be more concerned with domestic affairs. According to a Leningrad study (1979), 67 percent of people speak with their friends and family members about foreign events, whereas 61 percent exchange information and views on internal political developments, and 43 percent on economic problems (Losenkov, 1983, p. 61).

Interest in Western developments does not seem to vary according to demographic and social variables (sex, education, social status, place of residence, etc.). Women and men, rural and city residents, people with higher and elementary education—all avidly devour international information. However, the impact of all these variables on interest in domestic information is much more pronounced (see Firsov, 1981, pp. 107–09; Losenkov, 1983, pp. 49–54; Shlapentokh, 1969a, p. 26).[4]

It is unlikely that the high interest of Soviet people in international information stems from the desire to get data confirming the official Soviet images of Western society or is dictated by the fear of war. The last supposition (see Alekseev, 1970, p. 183; Losenkov, 1983, p. 48) does not hold because this interest in foreign affairs was very intense during one of the calmest periods in international relations, the détente era. Indirect data suggest instead that people find foreign news attractive, despite its censored character, because it depicts the diversity of life abroad. This contrasts with the monotonous tenor of domestic news and even with the dreary character of Soviet life itself,[5] which was recognized by Gorbachev in his first speeches upon assuming the leadership (Gorbachev, 1985, 1986).

## *English in Soviet Life*

In great contrast to Americans, the Soviet people greatly appreciate the knowledge of foreign languages, a tradition with roots deep in the nineteenth century, when Tolstoy could write pages and pages of *War and Peace* in French and when the study of foreign and classical languages took the lion's share of students' time in secondary school.

Under Stalin, especially in the late 1940s and early 1950s, the knowledge of foreign languages aroused suspicion and could be used as an additional sign of political disloyalty. After 1953 the authorities radically softened their attitudes in this area, allowing the Soviet people to give vent to their desire to learn foreign languages, among which English became dominant. Reading in English is quite widespread, especially among educated people.

In the present-day Soviet Union, as in pre-Revolutionary Russia, knowing other languages, especially English, is an indicator of social prestige and status. So far, this knowledge is essentially monopolized by two groups in the population—intellectuals and apparatchiks—especially those who deal with foreign countries. However, it is the dream of most parents to send their children to schools where languages are the major subject of study.

The knowledge of English and to a lesser degree French, German, and other Western European languages, opens the possibility of skirting the obstacles created by the authorities for gaining any familiarity with Western culture. This knowledge helps overcome some of the jamming of foreign radio broadcasts in Russian by allowing people access to radio broadcasts that have not been translated, and also aids in communicating with foreigners.

## *Interest in Western Culture*

The average Soviet individual not only gulps down all the international information he or she can find, but also displays a keen interest in Western movies, music, and even literature. Unlike general news of the West, which is devoured by people of all educational levels, interest in Western culture is rather strongly correlated with educational level, even if people with an elementary schooling are attracted by various elements of the Western mode of life. But in view of the steady growth of education and the number of those in the intelligentsia with a connection to the masses (a result of high social mobility), educated people exert a tremendous influence on all strata of the population.

Interest in Western culture is so enormous that it is revealed even in studies where the authors had absolutely no intention of drawing notice to this phenomenon. Moscow University sociologists asked *Literaturnaia Gazeta* readers in 1973 (when the crackdown on liberals was in full swing) "what publications in the newspaper" they preferred. The number of those who expressed their preference for "foreign authors" turned out to be almost 50 percent higher than those who pointed to "native authors," while the majority demanded publications of both types of authors (Fomicheva, 1978, p. 52).[6]

*Literaturnaia Gazeta* readers clearly display a keen interest in Western cultural life. They read articles on "foreign culture" (86 percent) nearly as often as the most popular materials of the newspaper (domestic life—96 percent, art—91 percent, "international developments"—88 percent) and more than materials on Soviet literature (71 percent). What is more, 22 percent of all readers demanded an increase in material on Western culture (only moral issues generated a greater number of readers demanding more space devoted to it—37 percent) (Fomicheva, 1978, pp. 22, 47, 63).

But even more remarkable is data found by Grushin in his Taganrog study based on a representative sample of the population. The majority of citizens turned out to be extremely well versed in foreign culture, in any case much better than their counterparts in the United States. Seventy-five percent knew "the prominent foreign works in literature and arts that had appeared in the last two to three years," 78 percent knew "the important discoveries in foreign science and technology," and 86 percent knew "outstanding foreign political figures." Only 6 percent of Taganrog residents did not know the major American political figures of the twentieth century, and 5 percent did not answer correctly the questions about French political leaders.

Taganrog residents were quite well acquainted with Western history, and only 9 percent could not answer the question about main events in U.S. postwar history, 10 percent about French postwar history, and 17 percent about British postwar history (Grushin and Onikov, 1980, p. 323).

Two groups of the Soviet population especially open to the influence of Western culture, even to its different elements, are the intelligentsia, especially its cream—the intellectuals, and youth. The impact of Western culture and lifestyle on Soviet young people is one of the most sensitive political issues in the country. It is regularly raised by Soviet officials, sometimes quietly, sometimes aggressively.

### MOVIES

Few Western movies are available to the average Soviet citizen. Of 250–300 films shown each year in the country, the number of foreign origin does not exceed 25–30, a ratio of 10 to 1. Although there is no direct data on the attendance at foreign movies, there is much indirect evidence that shows they are quite popular, often more so than Soviet ones. According to official data, among the ten most attended movies, two were foreign (*Iskusstvo Kino*, 1984, 12, p. 18), which means that the average popularity of a Western movie is at least two times higher than a Soviet film. Soviet newspapers regularly lament the popularity of Western movies, blaming various people and institutions for this (see, for instance, *Literaturnaia Gazeta*, November 12, 1986, p. 8).

The possibility of seeing a Western movie not run in general movie theaters is one of the greatest privileges enjoyed by members of the party apparatus and the cultural elite. Since Stalin's time the Soviet political elite can regularly see private showings of foreign movies. This privilege is also extended from time to time to those apparatchiks and party intellectuals who are assigned to prepare drafts of party documents or leaders' speeches at the special country houses close to Moscow. Access to such places in Moscow as the Filmmakers' Club, the Writers' Club, and especially the Archive of Movies or other institutions that more or less regularly show foreign films privately is a dream of any Moscow resident as well as of visitors to the capital.

The international film festivals always create an atmosphere of high excitement in Moscow, as well as in other cities where some movies from the festival are shown. The famous movie, Men'shov's *Moscow Does Not Believe in Tears*, recreates quite well the feelings such a festival creates among Muscovites, especially younger ones.

The introduction of video recorders in the Soviet Union has to some degree broken the monopoly of the Soviet dominant class on foreign movies, because they are used almost exclusively to see foreign films. This has become of major concern to Soviet authorities, who, since the early 1980s, have repeatedly brought this issue in the most important political speeches and declarations (see, for instance, KGB chairman Chebrikov's article in *Kommunist*, 1985; see also the interview with Alexander Vlasov, Minister of Internal Affairs, *Komsomol'skaia Pravda*, January 12, 1987).

### MODERN WESTERN MUSIC

Modern Western music is the target of Soviet youths' admiration. Soviet authorities have tried over many years to suppress interest in it and destroy its appeal to its numerous fans (see Alekseeva and Chalidze, 1985, pp. 58–60; Starr, 1983; Volkov, 1982, pp. 44–50).

Valentina Alekseeva cites data about the musical preferences of Soviet youth which show that, almost regardless of education and status, they rate variety music and jazz not only higher in popularity than opera and symphonies, but also higher than folk music, which, in contrast to jazz, is a genre strongly supported by official ideology. Even young workers who with their more traditional tastes have to be less captivated by Western music ascribed a score of 4.5 (on a 5-point scale) to jazz, whereas folk music got 4.0 and opera 3.4 (Alekseeva, 1983, p. 67). According to data on Sverdlovsk workers in the late 1960s, 70 percent in the 18–19 age group prefer jazz to all other types of music. The respective figures for the 19–20 age group is 60 percent, and for both 21–25 and 26–30, 41 percent (Kogan, 1970, p. 260). In a recent study of students in Zaporozhie, Stanislav Kataiev found that 53 percent preferred foreign variety music, 39 percent Soviet rock and variety, 28 percent foreign rock. At the same time only 21 percent named symphonic music and 2 percent folk music (Kataiev, 1986, p. 107; see also *Komsomol'skaia Pravda*, September 5, 1987; *Sovietskaia Kul'tura*, October 20, 1987).

Finally, the authorities have had to virtually capitulate to the youth, legalizing numerous discotheques, bands, and ensembles that disseminate Western music across the country (see *Sovietskaia Kul'tura*, May 23, 1985, and January 10, 1987). What is more, by the end of 1986 Gorbachev's regime recognized rock, the "rockers" movement, and even allowed the creation of a special institution to encourage, and of course supervise, the legalized "rockers" (*Komsomol'skaia Pravda*, January 18, 1987).

Soviet novels and stories that wish to objectively describe the life of Soviet girls and boys can hardly omit this important detail of youthful lifestyle, so the infatuation of Soviet youngsters with fashionable American and other Western performers and musical ensembles, such as Michael Jackson (see, for instance, Evtushenko, 1986, as well as Poliakov's 1985 novel *The Extraordinary Event*, where he describes how the first Komsomol secretary visits the discotheque in his district and is forced to listen to Western rock).

WESTERN LITERATURE

Interest in literature is especially affected by educational level. Soviet data show that even those with only a secondary education eagerly read foreign novels, especially from the West.

The Soviet magazine *Inostrannaia Literatura* ("International Literature"), which publishes foreign literary works in translation, is extremely popular in the Soviet Union. According to a survey in the sixties, readers of *Literaturnaia Gazeta* rated only two other periodicals more important than *Inostrannaia Literatura*—*Novyi Mir* ("New World") and *Iunost'* ("Youth"), both known at that time for their liberalism. Forty-one percent of all respondents read *Inostrannaia Literatura* against 51 and 53 percent, respectively, for the other two magazines (Shlapentokh, 1969b, p. 154).

In the next decade, when the political reaction forced the latter two magazines to lose their liberal reputation, the popularity of *Inostrannaia Literatura* among *Literaturnaia Gazeta* readers increased dramatically. The number of subscribers to *Inostrannaia Literatura*—28 percent—was five to nine times higher than the number of subscribers to the next most popular magazine—*Iunost'* with 5 percent, *Oktibar'* ("October") at 4 percent, and *Novyi Mir* with 3 percent (Fomicheva, 1978, p. 40).

*Inostrannaia Literatura* not only figures prominently among readers of *Literaturnaia Gazeta*, who are mainly highly educated people, but Grushin's 1973 Taganrog study found that the number of subscribers to this magazine was 5.5 times higher than that of *Novyi Mir* and even more compared to other Soviet literary magazines (Grushin and Onikov, 1980, p. 132). Even among young workers (in the city of Cheliabinsk, 1970) this magazine ranked third in popularity, behind two magazines addressed specifically to youth—*Iunost'* and *Molodaia Gvardiia* ("Youth Guard") (Kogan, 1975, p. 114).

The Western classics as well as Western modern literature in general successfully compete with Russian classics and even with modern Soviet literature. This occurs despite the natural difference between the number of books published by Russian and Soviet authors and by foreign authors (the ratio of the number of books published in 1983 was 7.7:1 and in the number of copies, 4:1; Knizhnaia Palata, 1984, pp. 62–63). It is important to note that the lion's share of Western literature published in the Soviet Union consists of the classics, and only a modest part of it is modern literature (see Dobrynina, 1978, p. 39).

The demand for popular literary books, novels, and poems has always been unsatisfied in the Soviet Union, but this is especially true with respect to foreign authors. The sociologists of the Lenin Library singled out four categories of literature—pre-Revolutionary Russian, Soviet Russian, Soviet non-Russian, and foreign. After analyzing the popularity of various books in Soviet libraries in the 1970s, they found that 78 percent of all library users took out works of Soviet Russian writers, 47 percent of foreign authors, 32 percent of Soviet non-Russian writers, and 25 percent of pre-Revolutionary Russian authors. Taken in total, the number of people interested in foreign authors is extremely great. What is more, as the educational level of the library users increased, the difference between Soviet Russian and foreign literature as the object of interest decreased. For professionals, the difference in percentage points was only 25, and in Moscow libraries it was even less—11 points (Frolova, 1976, pp. 25, 26).[7]

Other studies by the same sociologists reveal the keen interest of all Soviet people, even of those who live in small cities and villages, in Western literature. Eleven percent of the residents of Ostrogozhsk, a small city in the Voronezh region, were found to read foreign classics while only 10 percent read Russian classics. Five percent also read modern Western literature and 65 percent Soviet Russian literature. Again, people with higher education read foreign authors more than others.

A survey of rural residents (1973–75) based on a nationwide sample (I designed this sample and helped design the program of the study) found that the number of people with even elementary education who read foreign literature was 36 percent in Lithuania and 21 percent in the Ukraine (the figure was lower for Central Asia—4.9 percent) compared to 46 and 53 percent who read the native literature (Ukrainian and Lithuanian), and 53 and 28 percent for Russian literature. For rural people with a secondary or higher education, the reading of foreign literature is much greater—

33 percent for the Ukraine and 57 percent for Lithuania (Solovieva, 1978, pp. 34, 35).[8]

Other sources corroborate the data of the Lenin Library sociologists. According to Nikolai Mansurov, his survey in Moscow found that the number of people interested in Russian and Western classical literature was the same—18 percent (Ermolaiev, 1979, p. 69; Mansurov, 1979, p. 129). The study of literary interests of young workers in Cheliabinsk found that among the five most read writers, three were Western (Émile Zola, Theodore Dreiser, and Alexander Dumas) (Kogan, 1975, p. 113).[9]

### WESTERN CLOTHES

For many in the Soviet Union, clothes seem to be superior to any other item of Western lifestyle. Since the mid-1960s Soviet society has been in the grip of Western fashion—jeans, sheepskin coats, T-shirts, and other garments.

But not only these three types of clothes are in fashion in the Soviet Union. In fact, every element of dress, from top to bottom, including the most intimate articles of the toilette, are in high demand if they are of Western origin.

A survey carried out by *Literaturnaia Gazeta* and *Sotsiologicheskie Issledovaniia* in 1987 found that Soviet teenagers yearn to possess Western (*firmennye*, i.e., produced by Western firms) goods—80 percent clothing items and the rest hi-fi equipment. The average price of such items ranges from 119 rubles in Leningrad to 448 rubles in Erevan (the average Soviet salary was 190 rubles in 1985) (Shchekochikhin, 1987, p. 13). It is a special pleasure of the Soviet individual, particularly for women, to claim there are no Soviet-produced articles on the body. In fact, female teenagers in Moscow were asked whether they would date young men who did not wear jeans. To the great surprise of the Soviet sociologist who cites the data, the majority said "nyet" (Alekseeva, 1983, p. 62).[10] The heroes of Soviet novels and movies are almost all dressed in jeans and a sheepskin coat and they possess many other things of nonlocal origin.[11]

The devotion to Western attire is so great that Soviet factories have begun to produce shirts, blouses, and sweaters bearing various Western commercial logos printed in England, such as Marlboro, Mercedes-Benz, or Levi-Strauss.[12] The manufacturers attempt to pass them off as Western products. Given the ideological climate in the country in the 1980s this action by factory directors is truly remarkable (see *Komsomol'skaia Pravda*, July 20, 1984).[13]

### WESTERN DURABLE GOODS

Western or Japanese electronic gadgets, such as stereo systems, portable radios, tape recorders, and more recently, video recorders, are much coveted items in the Soviet Union, as are appliances of foreign origin for the kitchen and bathroom. The latter are among the most desirable objects for those who have a chance to acquire them. Even sophisticated and brave intellectuals like Galina Vishnevskaia and her husband spared no effort to bring from the West equipment for the kitchen and bathroom, which after this became the place of excursion for all guests who visited their Moscow home (Vishnevskaia, 1984).

CHAPTER
6

# Privatization of Soviet Society

## The Withdrawal of Energy and Emotions from the State

A major development in Soviet society since the mid-1950s has been the state's gradual loss of authority over all strata of the population—from the top apparatchiks to ordinary laborers and farm workers.

An increasing number of Soviet people have become indifferent to any work in social production as well as to official political activity. They have lost confidence in their managers as decision makers or as capable of objectively evaluating the performance of subordinates and rewarding them while keeping in mind the interests of the country and the state. By the 1970s, with overwhelming apathy and cynicism people had practically abandoned any critique of shortcomings in their enterprises or of their superiors.

This strong alienation from the state and its apparatchiks, as well as a deeply rooted disbelief in any positive results from personal intervention for the public good, was fully manifest in the post-Brezhnev period. At this time the mass media began to reflect the mood of the Soviet population to some extent.

In this respect the discussion of social critique in *Literaturnaia Gazeta* was noteworthy. Many participants (and the newspaper clearly was not objective in its presentation of various views, preferring optimistic letters) plainly expressed their reluctance to come to the defense of the interests of society. Readers angrily rejected the appeals of some authors to persist in the fight for the common cause. One reader, after telling a number of sad stories about his attempts to fight for the interests of the state, said, "I became a realist and I promised myself to follow the proverb that silence never makes mistakes." Another reader suggested that "the number of people who avoid any conflict in their professional life is growing" (see *Literaturnaia Gazeta*, September 26, 1986; see also the same newspaper, February 8, March 21, May 9, June 6, August 15, December 19, 1986). Even *Pravda* journalist Liliia Beliaeva describes the growing passivity of the Soviet people when confronted with actions directed against the interests of the state (see her articles in *Pravda*, June 4, 1985, and *Pravda*, March 23, 1986).[1]

## Types of Privatization

There are various types of privatization which differ from each other in the degree of state interference and their deviation from existing laws and norms.

The growing role of totally private institutions, such as family and friends, in the lives of the Soviet people, as well as those of less accepted institutions such as "friends of friends" and lovers is probably the most accepted type of privatization.

The "second," civil society, with its stormy and expanding unofficial public life is another form of privatization that is much more significant to the future of the Soviet Union than the first type. It combines the illegal or semilegal means with legal ones.

The third type of privatization is the most significant as it conflicts the most with official society and undermines the Soviet system from within. It assumes that everyone—from minister and first regional secretary to the orderly in a hospital or a sales clerk in a rural shop—will exploit their position for their own personal interests against the interests of the state and official policy.

## Soviet People—Heroes of Privatization

The Soviet people in general, preoccupied with their own interests, are no different than people in other societies, even if we take into account the most fervent party activists in the first decades after the Revolution. Putting aside a few exceptions, the average Bolshevik, even in the heyday of the Revolution and the civil war, was an ambitious individual who liked prestige, power, and material privileges (if these did not jeopardize the prestige of being an ascetic revolutionary). The October revolution knew very few self-effacing commissars who served the cause in obscurity.

The heroes of novels written in the 1920s and 1930s about this period—Iurii Olesha's *Envy* or Il'ia Ehrenburg's *The Second Day*—were portrayed as energetic masters of life, in no way humbly looking for an opportunity to drop from the limelight. The few available memoirs about this period (Berberova, 1983; Grigorenko, 1982; Mikoian, 1975; and Ulanovskaia, 1982) describe the average party activist the same way—full of aspirations, eager to be promoted in the party apparatus, and enjoying popularity and especially the control they had over others. Material well-being definitely did not play a leading role in the life of apparatchiks in the first decade after the Revolution. However, though some of them liked to demonstrate, often for purposes of vanity, their ostensible puritanism in everyday life, the majority relished those modest, by current standards, privileges which the poor young revolutionary state bestowed on them (Ginzburg, 1985).

Even the official Soviet legends about the leaders of the Revolution and the civil war cannot present them as Spartan heroes for whom anonymous service to the Revolution and the party was enough. Of course, the lifestyle of these early heroes differed greatly from Soviet rulers in the 1930s and especially in the 1960s and 1970s. Brezhnev, with his notorious passion for cars and luxury goods, was far from Stalin's ascetic life. But even Stalin had many country homes, where he enjoyed revels with his colleagues, as was so vividly described by Milovan Djilas (1970; see also Alliluieva, 1967, 1969).

Lenin, "the most modest man," as his official icon suggests, really was by all accounts indifferent and perhaps even hostile to a sumptuous lifestyle. But during the harsh years of the civil war even he rested in a large country house in the outskirts of Moscow and hunted.

The fundamental difference between the Soviet apparatchiks of the 1920s and the 1970s and 1980s lies not in the intensity of their personal interests but in the degree of their identification with the interests of the state. The Bolshevik in the 1920s and even early 1930s was convinced that his ego would prosper only with the progress of the state, which he regarded as his own "company" with himself as stockholder. This is how Alexei German's movie, *My Friend Ivan Lapshin* (1984), much acclaimed by Soviet intellectuals (it was censored for a time), presents people in the year 1935. They were consumed by diligent public activity and reduced their private life almost to nothing.

Today, the apparatchik looks at the state only as a means of satisfying his own needs and is ready to sacrifice the interests of the state at the first occasion that arises if it would benefit him. He is absorbed with his private life and evaluates everything in public life from a narrow, egotistical point of view. Mikhail Voslenskii depicts this image of a typical apparatchik in his book *Nomenclature* (Voslenski, 1980).

If the radical shift from public to private life is typical for the Soviet apparatchik, the dominant class, it is even stronger for ordinary people, who even at the height of the civil war cared for their own individual interests before anything else. However, even those who hated the new order could not help both respecting and fearing the state born of the Revolution. Most of them looked for survival and a career under the new regime by conscientiously cooperating with the state, fulfilling its commands in professional and social life. This was especially true for young people, who were driven to consider public life as the primary goal of their existence (Shlapentokh, 1986).

The main result of the Soviet evolution in the post-Stalin period was the gradual decrease of the role of public life for Soviet citizens. The individual of the 1970s and 1980s identifies little with public goals and is far from the official normative image of the Soviet citizen. This individual tries to minimize efforts in his work life. If he cannot withdraw from official political and social life, he feigns participation in them, performing various ritualistic obligations. At the same time he does his best to exploit the state for his own personal interests, even violating elementary morals and laws if he thinks he can escape punishment.

If Western society is protected against wild egotism by the network of institutions that not only curb it but channel it more or less successfully for the common good, Soviet society so far has been practically helpless against privatization and can confront it only with mass repressions.

With the decline of official public life, the role of private institutions and with it new forms of unofficial public life—illegal and semilegal civil society—have been growing in Soviet society almost uninterruptedly in the last three decades.

While advancing the concept of the privatization of Soviet life, I do not want in the least to contend that on the surface official public life became less visible and did not take as much time from the people as did their occupation and social work. The point is that the majority of the Soviet people do not see their efforts for the public good and for the interests of the state as rewarding and consider their activity in the private zone as much more remunerative.

Formally, Soviets working in industry spent about forty-three hours a week on their job in 1977, an increase compared to 1963, when they worked forty-one hours, with about one hour spent on social activity (which has declined, as was mentioned, during the last fifteen years). However, during the last two decades the emotional involvement of the Soviet individual with the public sphere declined significantly, leading to a decrease in productivity, a regression in labor ethics, and the growing ritualization of political participation and social work.

This emotional withdrawal does not imply that there are not any who are passionately involved in their work. However, for the majority of Soviet workaholics, the driving force is not the interests of the state but their desire for self-fulfillment or professional prestige, and the social importance of their work is accepted with pleasure as an additional bonus, but not as a major goal in life.

The real correlation between public and private life in the Soviet Union can be found in those literary works and movies considered by the public to be a realistic portrait of Soviet life. It is interesting to contrast these works with the novels written in the 1920s and 1930s. Such writers as Yuri Trifonov (1982, 1983a, 1983b), Yuri Bondarev (1980, 1985), Georgii Semenov (1985a, 1985b, 1986), Iosif Gerasimov (1985), and Timur Pulatov (1984) are among those who created novels about urban life. Valentin Rasputin (1980, 1985a, 1985b), Vasilii Shukshin (1970, 1982, 1984), and Victor Astafiev (1984a, 1984b, 1986) are regarded as the representative writers of "rural prose." These authors became prominent mostly in the 1970s. Authors of the 1980s who have gained public attention include Vladimir Krupin (1985) and Vladimir Makanin (1984). These authors are acknowledged by the authorities, who have awarded them numerous prizes and medals, as well as by public opinion as the best Soviet writers of the last two decades. None wrote a novel or story where the heroes were agitated by public events. They are all consumed by their private lives and reflections, which have nothing to do with official ideology. The Communist Party, Marxism, socialism, and similar concepts are simply ignored.

Yuri Bondarev's novels are especially noteworthy in this regard. The author, a party member, holder of many official positions in the Soviet hierarchy, and the winner of state prizes, in his last novels—*The Choice* (1980) and *Game* (1985)—completely ignores public life. His heroes are absorbed by relations with their spouses, children, friends, and lovers. They reflect on the meaning of life, religion, and many other things but almost never even mention official slogans, public institutions like the party, or if they do it is in a rather contemptuous way.

Georgii Semenov (see his *Urban Landscape* [1985a], *The Smell of Burned Powder* [1985b], and *The Fox Intellect* [1986] as well as his numerous stories published in the 1980s) presented his heroes as even more isolated from official public life than Bondarev. Semenov's characters are fully engulfed into the mosaic of extremely complex human relations and come in touch with the official world only rarely.

Unlike authors in the 1920s, contemporary Soviet writers are incapable, without destroying elementary facts well known to their readers, of describing heroes devoted to state interests who would sacrifice everything for the motherland. Only those authors who wrote about scientists could present heroes who were as moved by the process of creative activity as they were by personal ambition, but again they were far from being patriots in everyday life (see Gerasimov's "The Gap in the Calendar," 1983; Grekova, 1983). Ruslan Kireev, another writer, blatantly discussed "the phenomenon of retreat," clearly meaning the retreat from public life (*Literaturnaia Gazeta*, June 4, 1986, p. 12).

The lack of positive heroes in Soviet literature for whom the common cause is the major object in life has been the subject of interminable debates in the Soviet press and in numerous conferences and meetings, but to no avail. The preoccupation with personal interests and private life is so overwhelming in real life that only hack writers can risk (and even then less and less often) including such heroes in their works.

In 1984 and 1985 *Literaturnaia Gazeta* published a special discussion initiated by a reader, Irina Karpova, who criticized Soviet literature for its complete absorption with private life, its special emphasis on the intimate relations between heroes, and its neglect of public activity. Only a few participants in the discussion dared deny these facts and most of the prominent writers accused of such things were called on to vindicate their novels as reflecting real life (see *Literaturnaia Gazeta*, January 23, July 4, 1984; August 28, 1985, p. 3; August 21, 1985).

The Il'ia Shtemler case provides an excellent example. This writer, evidently imitating Alex Haley's production novels, wrote a number of works of the same type—*Supermarket* (1984) and *Train* (1986). However, his heroes, described against the backdrop of their professional work, are evidently moved by prosaic, individual interests, and even the positive characters can easily exploit their official position for individual, even semilegal, goals.

Only one author—Chingiz Aitmatov—dared in his novel, *The Executioner's Block* (1986), to create a hero completely absorbed with a public good—the struggle against drugs. However, he assigned this role to a former Orthodox priest who was determined to resurrect Christianity in a new form.

Soviet filmmakers have also failed to create heroes for whom official goals are their own. The best Soviet movies, those which attract large audiences, are lauded in the press, and win prizes at various competitions, depict only their heroes' private life. Balaian's *Autumn Marathon*, Riasanov's *The Rail Station for Two*, Todorovskii's *War Romance*, Balaian's *Night and Day Dreams*, Mikailian's *Fell in Love at Own Request*, Gubenko's *From the Life of Vacationers*, and others either completely ignore official public life or mention it in a derogatory way.

## The Lie as an Institution of Privatization

Private life in Soviet society could not have existed in most cases if it had not protected itself against the state and official public life with deception.

Lying is not necessary in those cases when personal decisions are recognized and allowed by the state, such as choices in occupation, place of employment, forms of entertainment, partners for marriage, and friends. However, most of the private life of the Soviet people, especially in the "second society" and in pursuit of illegal goods within official society, would be impossible if they did not hide it from the state and deceive the authorities. People have to pretend in private with their families and friends that they are as loyal politically as in public. They have to conceal their black market deals, apartment exchanges, tricks to help them get into a hospital or a higher school, moonlighting, private lessons, extramarital relations, and numerous other activities.

People easily protect their private life because they are forced to lie regularly in their professional work, faking reports on their production activity, pretending to fulfill orders, and participating each day in the various rituals described in preceding chapters.

All of Soviet ideology and education have been geared over the decades to bring up obedient and conformist people, which forced the citizenry to resort to lying as a means of survival in a world where free and critical thought was persecuted. When, in 1985–86 the Soviet people and their mouthpiece, the intellectuals, got the opportunity to discuss some sore issues of Soviet society for the first time in decades, they named the dominance of lies as a leading problem (see, for instance, Alexander Gel'man's article "What Is at the Beginning, What Is Later," *Literaturnaia Gazeta*, September 10, 1986; Natalia Morozova's article, "And a Daredevil Became a Good Boy," *Sovietskaia Kul'tura*, August 2, 1986; Maia Ganina's article, "The Game in the Naked King," *Literaturnaia Gazeta*, January 15, 1986; see also the articles of Alexei German and Vasilii Bykov in *Literaturnaia Gazeta* [May 14 and June 18, 1986]; Alexander Buravskii and Mikhail Shatrov in *Sovietskaia Kul'tura* (July 3 and September 18, 1986); Grigorii Baklanov in *Nedelia*, 1986, #15).

## The Growth of Private Property

The dialectic of Soviet development in the post-Stalin period is that the political elite is to a great degree responsible for the privatization of Soviet society, a process undermining the fundamentals of the political and economic system. This is because, for various reasons, the elite has fostered the growth of private (or personal, in official Soviet terminology) property.

The major contribution of the ruling elite to this process was the policy which gradually turned millions of people into owners of significant amounts, by Soviet standards, of property, radically changing their psychology and behavior. The decisive step was taken by the Soviet rulers when they changed their attitudes toward private plots of land.

In the decades since the Revolution, the political elite was a consistent enemy of private property. Private plots were reluctantly tolerated by the leaders as a temporary and unavoidable evil, which was seen as the sole way to prevent starvation in the countryside. Khrushchev, a great Soviet reformer, shared the same official traditions, fulminating many times during his rule against private plots, private cars, and private country houses.

However, private property as such survived even under Stalin, and not only in the form of private plots but also as private houses in which, for lack of state apartments, lived three-quarters of the Soviet population, two-thirds of which were in cities (TsSU, 1985, p. 441). As standards of living rose after 1953, private property became more widespread, despite Khrushchev's views.

During the Brezhnev regime, in total unison with the whole process of privatization rampant under his rule, two events occurred that prompted an increase in private property. With growing food shortages and the need to increase food production, Brezhnev's regime turned sharply in the mid-1970s from reluctant acceptance of private plots to their enthusiastic support. A special decision of the Central Committee was adopted (though not published, for ideological reasons) which not only removed many legal obstacles to farmers working on their plots, but also ordered the official ideologies to shift from condemnation to praise of the plots and to materially aid the farmers with their family agricultural businesses.

This radical shift in official policy toward private plots was reflected in the new Soviet constitution adopted in 1977. An article in this constitution confirmed the right of the people to have their private plots and declared that "the state and collective farms have to assist citizens in keeping their private plots" (*Konstitutsiia* (*Osnovnoi Zakon*) *Souza Sovietskikh Sotsialisticheskikh Respublik*, Moscow 1977, p. 10). In his report to the twenty-sixth party congress (February 1981), Brezhnev spoke of support for private family plots as a fundamental element of Soviet agrarian policy and as if this policy had always been supported by the state (Brezhnev, 1981, p. 64).

It is also worthy of note that at this time the farm family had begun to be regarded as having an important place in economic activity. In numerous articles the Soviet press appealed to farmers, particularly the young, to understand how good it was to have a cow, some pigs, or chickens in their household, and not depend on the vicissitudes of the state food supply. The "family farm," a production unit where only members of the same family work, became a leading idea in Gorbachev's 1985–86 economic plans to revamp agriculture (Gorbachev, 1986).

In the late 1970s the government not only encouraged farmers but also city dwellers to have private plots. The consequence was to endorse an increase in the number of country houses, although this was not its primary intention. As indicated previously, Gorbachev's regime has only accelerated the movement in this direction. Now more than half of Soviet families are owners of their own parcel of land. The craving to own their own plot in the countryside represents a flight from urban civilization to nature, a development which has allowed city dwellers to retreat even further from all forms of public life in their place of residence (see *Literaturnaia Gazeta*, February 27, 1985, p. 13; a Soviet television program aired in February 1987 also showed how much urban dwellers are absorbed with their private gardens and country houses).

Of no less significance to privatization was a second development. As a remedy against the apartment shortage, the government introduced a new institution—the condominium. Members of the condominium (about 5–10 percent of big city residents now live in condominiums) became owners of their apartments, in contrast to other city dwellers who live in apartments belonging to the state or in old private houses deprived of facilities and usually in nonprestigious districts of a city.

But an even more important factor in the privatization of Soviet society was "automobilization." In the 1960s Soviet leaders decided to start mass production of cars for personal use, and by the mid-1980s no less than 10 percent of Soviet families had become car owners (in Moscow alone there are 500 thousand privately owned cars) (Babosov et al., 1983, p. 262; Bigulov et al., 1984, p. 91; Eko, 1985, #5, p. 103; Raig, 1986, p. 36; *Komsomol'skaia Pravda*, July 31, 1987; Pozdniakova, 1987, p. 60).

As various sources attest, having a car has significantly changed the lives of their owners. With a poorly developed service system (only 25 percent of private car owners are satisfied with service, Eko, 1985, #5, p. 105), car maintenance demands tremendous energy on the part of owners and regular contacts with people in the second economy (*Literaturnaia Gazeta*, May 9, 1984, p. 13; June 29, 1983; *Nedelia* 1984, #20, p. 7; see also the movie *The Extraordinary Event*, which shows how a good car mechanic can live the life of a nabob in the Soviet Union).

Owning a car makes it necessary to have a garage, as under Soviet conditions it is highly probable that a car parked on the street will be stripped of almost everything. The problem of obtaining garage space pushes the Soviet individual even further down the road of suspicious, mostly illegal, activity. The passion around garages was brilliantly described by El'dar Riasanov in his famous movie, *Garage* (1980).

The government abets the privatizing instincts of its citizens in another way, one also connected with technological progress. Soviet industry, although slow, is obliged to produce various electrical products and consumer goods that now make up a significant part of the personal property of Soviet citizens. Almost all have refrigerators, TV sets, and radios, and many have tape recorders (34 percent of all families), cameras (33 percent), washing machines (70), vacuum cleaners (37), and other goods (TsSU, 1985, p. 460).

The government also tries to provide the population with such consumer items as furniture and rugs as well as allowing, with great reluctance, the purchase of some luxury goods as china, glassware, and jewelry. In 1984 the Soviet people spent 3 billion rubles on jewelry (4.7 billion in 1981) and 4.8 billion on rugs (5.4 billion in 1982). The magnitude of these figures can be better evaluated if we compare them with the expenditures on furniture and electrical appliances—7.1 billion and 3.8 billion, respectively (TsSu, 1985, p. 485). In general private (or personal) property of the Soviet citizen has increased from 1970–84 by 2.5 times (Ulybin, 1986, p. 108; see also *Moskovskiie Novosti*, June 21, 1987).

Passing on material goods from generation to generation has allowed the majority of Soviet people to possess a considerable amount of personal property, a factor which now affects many of their decisions, actions, and thoughts. According to a nationwide study in the early 1980s, about a quarter of the industrial workers and farmers own quality furniture as do 36 percent of the intelligentsia. Fourteen percent of the workers, 7 percent of the farmers, and 25 percent of the intelligentsia have "expensive jewels" (Bigulov et al., 1984, p. 91). According to a Leningrad study, more than 50 percent of all residents own jewelry, about 60 percent expensive glassware, and 40 percent high quality furniture (Protasenko, 1985, p. 197).

The increase in the number of durable goods, including luxury ones, allowed people who already had them to accumulate more and influenced others to do the same. According to one study, 13 percent of workers and farmers and 15 percent of the intelligentsia want to buy jewelry, even more want to possess cut glassware (26 and 22 percent, respectively) and fashionable clothes (23 and 52 percent respectively) (Bigulov et al., 1984, p. 91).

The policies of the Soviet government, whatever its intentions, have led to the emergence of a society in which, despite its socialist principles, private property has become a leading factor in the life of a majority of the population.

# CHAPTER 7

# Legal and Illegal Private Life: Primary Groups

For Western readers the most conspicuous and understandable type of public life in the Soviet Union is the sphere of society where people deal with each other in small groups in which everybody knows each other well and where the relationships have strong emotional overtones—family, friends, and lovers.

## The Family: An Agent of the State or a Personal Refuge from the State?

Actively supported by the state and ideology, the Soviet family, since the mid-1950s, no longer plays such a strong role as an institution effectively used by the state as a means of social control. Since 1953 the Soviet family has gradually emerged as a cohesive unit that confronts the state, rather than serves it, and has become the leading institution in privatization.

The family is now the locale where one can completely relax ideologically and express genuine views on current events. Here individuals, from members of the Politburo to ordinary workers, receive what they are deprived of in official life.[1]

Soviet studies, even those conducted by ideologically oriented sociologists like Nikolai Mansurov, indicate that the majority of Soviet people regard the family (along with friends) as the place where they can really elaborate their views on developments in the world.

Family and friends are much more important in this role than school, the workplace, or any other area. When asked who influences them the most in the formation of their opinions on vital matters, in a 1976–78 study, residents of the Vladimir region put family decisively in first place, ahead of school, mass media, and social organizations such as trade unions (Mansurov, 1978). A survey conducted by *Literaturnaia Gazeta* and *Sotsiologicheskie Issledovaniia* in 1987 found that all groups of Soviet youth value friendship most (96 percent named friendship against 94 percent naming love and 90 percent naming an interesting profession) (*Literaturnaia Gazeta*, September 2, 1987, p. 13).

The survey of 3,500 young people in Byelorussia and Estonia clearly shows the prevalence of private institutions—family and friends—over public ones in forming the value system of the respondents. As was mentioned, 23 percent of them ascribed a role of authority to their work collective, 33 percent did the same with friends, and 41 percent with family (Babosov et al., 1985, p. 52; see also Goriachev et al., 1978).

The family also plays a central role in relations surrounding the "second economy," the enormous unofficial system of distributing goods and services parallel to the official economy. Members of families trust each other completely about their activities in this realm (e.g., illegal production, bribery, etc.) and serve as important connections in assisting each other in obtaining what they need. Had intrafamily relations remained unchanged from the Stalin era, the "second economy" would never have approached the scale it has during the last two decades.

The growing antagonism between the state and the family is revealed in another phenomenon, one no less important than the "second economy." This is the problem of protection and nepotism among members of the elite, both national and regional.

The relative disentanglement of the family from the state, and their confrontation as conflicting social values, has become very much a part of the public mind. The family has become a symbol of the institutions opposing the state, a development commonly found in nondemocratic societies. The ideological atmosphere in the Soviet Union has been shaped by the struggles of the state and the populace to mold the family to suit their conflicting needs.

Paradoxically, the official recognition and support of the family as a positive social value has made it possible for individuals to turn this support to their own advantage. For example, university students are expected to repay the state for their education by accepting work assignments, often in far-flung regions of the country. Yet, by appealing to the official support of the family as an institution, some graduates can avoid such assignments, arguing that severe familial disruptions would result.

## The Family as a Dominant Personal Value

Soviet sociologists have accumulated a certain amount of data on the place of marriage and the family in the value system of the people, and it is noteworthy that there is some consensus among the results obtained by different Soviet sociologists on the subject. Moreover, data from other socialist countries (Poland, Bulgaria) are perfectly consonant with Soviet data.

The major finding of studies on the personal values of people in socialist countries is that the family, directly or indirectly, is given a leading, often the leading, position on any list of values ranked by respondents. It can be said that a "drift to domesticity," if we measure it by the change in the role of the family in the system of personal values, has always been one of the most important social and political trends in socialist society (see Inkeles, 1980, p. 49).

In the surveys conducted by Zakhar Fainburg among workers and engineers in the Ural city of Perm in the 1960s, the family ranked first in importance (1969, p. 93; 1982, p. 73). The same was found by Iuri Arutiunian among the Moldavians in the early 1970s and 1980s (1972, p. 18; 1980b, p. 151) and by Gevoris Pogosian in Armenia in the late 1970s (1983, p. 164), as well as by many other authors (see, for instance, Sychev, 1974, p. 151).

The data of Vladimir Iadov in his long-term investigations in Leningrad led to the same conclusion. In Iadov's first study, done with Andrei Zdravomyslov in the mid-1960s, he discovered that there were more young workers oriented toward their families than those with any other orientation: 42 percent of the young workers were family-oriented, 23 percent were education-oriented, 8 percent job-oriented, and 12 percent civic work-oriented (Iadov et al., 1967, p. 248).

Iadov's next study was devoted to Leningrad engineers. This time the dominant role of the family as a "terminal" value (or goal) emerged even more clearly. In the list of eighteen terminal values, the family was outranked only by peace and health. In this survey, as in the surveys of Fainburg and Arutiunian, the family outstrips such values as work, social recognition, and an active life (Iadov, 1979, p. 56).

The dominance of the family as a value was revealed even more strongly in a study that categorized respondents according to their values orientation in more or less homogeneous groups. Of eight groups, only the four smallest included those who did not consider family a dominant value, and combined they formed only 16 percent of all respondents. Thus, 84 percent of all respondents found themselves in groups characterized by a strong family orientation. What is more, only one group was felt by the researchers to have a "balanced" orientation toward family and job. Other groups, composing 55 percent of all respondents, are described as predominantly oriented toward the family. In evaluating these data, it should be taken into account that a considerable proportion of respondents—one-fifth—were not married, and one-fourth had no children (Iadov, 1977, p. 229).

It is curious that such a bureaucrat in Soviet sociology as Anatolii Kharchev, the editor-in-chief of the only Soviet sociological journal and a man who very cautiously (and in many cases very deftly) wandered through Soviet ideology and politics, did not understand (or refrained from doing so) that the data he collected in his 1976–78 study revealed a denigration of official Soviet values by respondents. About 1,000 people in the Vladimir region, asked about the influence of various social factors on them, gave conspicuous priority to the family. School, the mass media, social organizations, the party, the Young Communist League, trade unions, and labor collectives were ranked lower. The same rankings were revealed, Kharchev said with satisfaction, in the 1969 survey of students in high schools and college (Kharchev, 1982, p. 17).

Data collected by sociologists in Sverdlovsk show that the general mood of the people depends much more on the quality of their family lives than on other factors, including work. The sociologists categorized groups of people by whether they were satisfied or not satisfied with three elements of their lives: work, family, and leisure. Then it was determined what proportion of the people in each group considered themselves as happy or unhappy. A comparison of the groups indicated that people satisfied with their family lives are more likely to be happy with their lives as a whole. Among those who were satisfied with all three elements of their lives, 46.7 percent considered themselves to be "completely happy." Among those who were satisfied only with work and leisure, the proportion indicating complete happiness was only 20.7 percent, a difference which should be imputed only to family. The respective difference for work was 22.8 percent, and for leisure, 22.9 percent (Kogan, 1981, pp. 172–73).

As Abel Aganbegian, a prominent economist, described the process of privatization in 1987, the low role professional work plays in the life of Soviet workers causes them to cease thinking about work even in the workplace and to cherish the idea of coming home to watch TV. The interest of the workers withdraws into their apartments, cars, country homes, and vacations. Work is now associated only with unpleasant feelings (Aganbegian, 1987, p. 14).

## Privatization within Private Life: The Disappearance of Large Families

The process of privatization has not only diminished the area of public activity but has also brought significant changes within private life itself, replacing forms which require interaction among many people by forms which reduce regular communication to only a few.

The gradual decrease in the number of extended families, that included three or even four generations, is an example of this process. It is especially noticeable in the Slavic regions as well as in the Baltic republics. The nuclear family consisting only of parents and their nonadult children is now the most typical family form in the Soviet Union. In 1970, couples with their parents or other relatives made up only about 20 percent of all families; in 1979, 18 percent (Kharchev, 1979, p. 236; Sonin and Dyskin, 1984, p. 146). According to other calculations, the ratio of the number of nuclear to large (multigenerational) families rose from 3.4 in 1970 to 4.2 in 1979 in cities, and from 3.1 to 3.7 in the countryside (Volkov, 1986, p. 218).

The number of large families is directly influenced by the process of modernization and the social changes it brings—rise in educational level, employment of women, etc. In Estonia, a republic usually in the vanguard of such changes, in 1970 only 16 percent of all urban families were large, but in Armenia 32 percent and in Turkmenistan, 29 (Riabushkin, 1978b, p. 47). The number of extended families in the countryside is greater than in the cities—24 percent compared to 22.

Living with one's parents is now looked upon more and more often as terrible not only for young couples but even for adult single children. About 80 percent of all newlyweds do not want to live with their parents at all (Kharchev, 1982, p. 46; Volkov, 1986, p. 220).

Soviet demographers consider living with parents as a serious threat to the survival of marriage for young couples. But with the apartment shortage especially hard on young families, many of them must live with their parents. Those who do, in contrast to tradition, more and more often conduct their household separately from the older couple. In Leningrad, for instance, 28 percent of all families that combine old and young couples had no common budget (Ruzhzhe et al., 1983, p. 17).

Privatization is manifest in the growing reluctance of young people to be materially dependent on their parents or be directed by them in any way. More than half of all married children, contrary to old traditions, do not ask their parents for advice (Kharchev, 1982, p. 44). Parents and children do not even try to live close to each other. In Leningrad only 13 percent mentioned desire for family proximity as a motive for exchanging apartments (in Baku, 25 percent). For families with four or more members, this motive was even weaker—only 2 percent. In general, families of such size are especially reluctant to live with parents, and the number of such families who live with parents declined in Leningrad during 1972–79 by almost eight times (Ruzhzhe et al., 1983, p. 41). The desire of young couples to separate themselves as much as possible from their parents arouses the lamentation of parents, who, in line with tradition, regard such behavior in their children as indecent and cruel (*Sovietskaia Kul'tura*, August 8, 1985).

The yearning for privacy is also expressed by older people, who more and more often, following the American style, prefer to live separately and not be burdened by the concerns about their adult married children or be a burden to them. The historic decision of Khrushchev to radically raise the old-age pension was greeted heartily not only by the young, who before bore the burden of sustaining their parents, but primarily by the old.

The desire to help raise grandchildren is today a rather weak motive for retirement. Only 16 percent of Moscow old people mentioned it as the stimulus for retirement (Shapiro, 1980, p. 48). In general, as Soviet experts contend, old people are not oriented to doing domestic chores and are not anxious to devote, as in the past, the time left to them to helping their children in the household (see Kharchev, 1982, p. 50; Sonin and Dyskin, 1984, p. 156). Only 17 percent of all pensioners considered helping their extended family as their main goal after retirement (Shapiro, 1980, p. 87). Only 49 percent of retired parents think that "it is necessary to help children as much as possible," whereas the rest feel this assistance should depend on certain conditions (31 percent "if they show respect," 10 percent "if it does not hurt parents' interests," and 19 percent "if they help you too") (Shapiro, 1980, p. 125).

Material conditions, especially housing, force almost two-thirds of young couples to start married life in their parents' apartments (Kharchev, 1982, p. 46). Young couples cannot do without the financial and physical help of their parents for a long time even with the desire for independence and separation. Forty-one percent of urban children are cared for by their grandmothers (*babushka*), generally until three years old. When a grandmother retires, her activity increases. Sixty-one percent of *babushkas* in Leningrad actively helped their children with domestic chores (Ruzhzhe et al., 1983, pp. 53, 57). Sixty-four percent of all working parents and 26 percent of all retired parents still financially help their adult children (Shapiro, 1980, p. 129; Volkov, 1986, p. 222). But recently public opinion has turned against those young who, preferring an easy life to independence and privacy, exploit their parents, forcing them to take care of young couples (*Sovietskaia Kul'tura*, December 5, 1985).

## Friendship as a Private Value

Friendship, now one of the most important pillars of morality, is another private institution in which Soviet people oppose the state.

The notion of friend in the Soviet Union is different than in the United States. Americans use the term "friends" even for persons with whom they entertain only the most superficial relations (see, for instance, Pogrebin, 1986, who treats neighbors or confederates as friends). But a friend, to Soviet people, is an individual with whom you have deep emotional, intimate relations. Friends in Soviet society characteristically maintain very intense contact. As Semen Lipkin, a Soviet author, became friends with Vasilii Grossman, the famous writer, they began to "meet each day" (Lipkin, 1983), and no Soviet reader would be amazed by this statement. The same frequency of contact was maintained between Anna Akhmatova, a prominent poet, and Lidiia Chukovskaia, a writer (Chukovskaia, 1976, 1980).

According to a Soviet study, 16 percent of all respondents met their friends each day, 10 percent two to three times a week, 22 percent weekly, and 31 percent several times a month. The rest (21 percent) met with friends more rarely (Kogan, 1981, p. 177). A survey in the 1970s by Michael Farrell and Stanley Rosenberg established that the average rate of contact with friends for young single people in the United States was 4.5 times per month and between 3.1 and 3.5 for married men with children (Farrell and Rosenberg, 1981, p. 196).

While Soviet ideologues have never engaged in vituperations against friendship, they have never bestowed upon it the title of a significant social value either. This may seem strange, given the role of collectivism as a fundamental of Soviet ideology. Indeed, friendship, as well as less intensive relations such as comradeship, can be treated as manifestations of collectivism (or at least as its initial forms). Some authors, such as Vladimir Sokolov (1981) and Veniamin Zatsepin (1981), are actually inclined to approach them in this way.[2] However, official ideology and the most sophisticated writers, such as Galina Andreleva (1980), repudiate (usually implicitly) any identification of friendship with collectivism because the latter involves the interactions of many people. Friendship, in contrast, is normally dyadic and a personal, even private, type of relationship, closer to the individual than to the collective. Moreover, in the Soviet context, the collective presupposes the existence of external control, which endears it so to the mentality of a Soviet apparatchik. However, the essence of friendship is the rejection of the idea of intervention or control by any third party.

Thus, it is not possible to find in official documents any hint of the importance of close relationships between individuals. The mass media does use the term "friendship" profusely; however, this is almost always at a "macro" level, as in "friendship among the people" or "friendship between the working class and peasants." In the entire period of Soviet history one can scarcely find a single editorial in *Pravda* devoted to personal friendships between Soviet individuals, although editorials are frequently addressed to issues of much less social significance. The few articles in which personal friendship is touched upon generally praise it in the context of the military or workplace, where it will benefit society or the state, but almost never as a relationship that may be valuable for individuals per se.

If *Pravda*'s lack of interest in friendship can at least be partly explained by Soviet ideology, the absence of even a word on friendship in such a lengthy party document as "Main Directions in Reforming General and Professional Education" (which took up almost the first two pages of *Pravda*, January 4, 1984) can only be accounted for by an ideological opposition to friendship. Devoting a special paragraph to the "moral and legal education" of students, the Central Committee, official author of the document, insisted that "collectivism and mutual exaction" be inculcated since early childhood. No mention is made of friendship, mutual support, or understanding between two or more people, though party officials could not ignore that friendship played one of the most important roles for children and youth.

The Soviet system has serious grounds for being, if not hostile to, at least suspicious of, close relationships between people, and especially of close, intimate friendships. In this respect, it does not differ from any other society with a nearly omnipotent government. The leadership in such societies prefers to have an individual completely isolated from other people and thus more at the mercy of the authorities. Evgenii Zamiatin and George Orwell skillfully grasped this important feature of the totalitarian society: friendship is an obstacle to the absolute dominance of the state over the individual. Moreover, friendship frequently constitutes the basis for the creation of underground organizations and antigovernmental activities of any sort.

Of course, the state and the political leaders do not regard all friendships like this. They are virtually indifferent to close relationships among persons who do not hold significant positions in society, in particular among blue-collar workers or farm laborers. However, as a person's social status increases, personal relationships become a focus of greater and greater attention on the part of authorities, especially of the political police.

With the softening of the Soviet system and the "humanization" of official ideology, friendship is mentioned more and more in the mass media as a positive value, without any reservation. In the post-Brezhnev era, a number of periodicals have published articles recognizing the major role of friends in the life of the Soviet people (see *Rabotnitsa*, 1985, 11, pp. 24–25; Voina, 1984).

## *Friendship against the State*

Friendship as an institution serves the Soviet people against the state in a variety of ways. In many cases friends are sources of information that cannot be obtained from the official mass media. According to our studies, as well as those of other sociologists in the Soviet Union, no less than one-third of the population regards word-of-mouth information as a vital source of knowledge about the outside world and especially about the internal life of the nation (Shlapentokh, 1969a, 1969b, 1970; see also Losenkov, 1983, pp. 60–79; Mickiewicz, 1981).

This exchange of information takes place only when people trust each other. For this reason, information flows most readily between friends. Only friends, for example, will swap news they have learned from listening to foreign radio. And only with friends is it possible to discuss freely and without reservation impressions of trips abroad or even of travels within the country.

Even more important is the role of friendship in an emergency. Since early in its history, political persecution has been regarded in Russia as the strongest test of friendship. Those who did not desert their friends when they were faced with government harassment have been regarded as among the most noble of people. However strong and intimate a friendship is, the cost can be high. This was especially true in the Stalin era, when persecution could rapidly extend to those who stayed friends with people treated as enemies of the state. As the Stalin era memories have receded, however, more and more people are standing by their close comrades who find themselves in conflict with the government.

The role of friends in the life of a dissident has been skillfully described by A. Amalrik (1982). Although in virtually permanent confrontation with the Soviet authorities for nearly two decades, Amalrik generally assesses quite positively the behavior of his friends toward him. Similar impressions can be drawn from the memoirs of P. Grigorenko (1982) and Terz (1984).

In the 1970s, Vladimir Sokolov conducted several surveys regarding moral issues. He discovered that 15 percent more people, at least verbally, are much more willing to make sacrifices for a friend or a loved one than for society (Sokolov, 1981, p. 79).

## *Friends in Everyday Life*

It would be erroneous to reduce the role of friendship in Soviet society to purely political factors and underestimate the other stimuli that drive individuals into close relationships with each other. But to be sure, friendship plays a central role in the lives of people in nondemocratic countries. For many in the Soviet Union a friend means, above all, an individual to whom you can pour out your soul, who recognizes your virtues and is tolerant of your weaknesses, who is your advisor in intimate spheres of life, and with whom it is pleasant to spend your leisure time.

Soviet people provide each other with considerable assistance in "beating the system." Friends play an extremely vital role in procuring necessary goods, for they constantly buy each other food, clothing, shoes, or other items should the chance arise, i.e., should these items appear in stores. Even more important is the assistance of a friend who has access to closed stores or cafeterias. It is considered perfectly ethical for people to ask their more privileged friends to bring food or clothes from places that are generally inaccessible to them.

Friends are extraordinarily active in providing other assistance in everyday life. They help their friends find a job, place children in a good high school or college, or get into a hospital or health resort. The importance of friends is directly proportional to the unavailability of goods or services, and is inversely proportional to the importance of money in obtaining hard-to-find items.

The mutual financial support between friends and to some degree colleagues and neighbors is also one of the most significant aspects of Soviet private life. According to some data, up to three-quarters of Soviet people regularly borrow money from each other (Pavlov, 1975, p. 115).

Thus it is natural that the prominent role of friendship in the everyday lives of Soviet people is closely intertwined with the "second economy" and the relations based upon it. There are, however, two types of radically different relations involved here. On the one hand, people involved in the "second economy" maintain relations based largely on bribes, extra payments, and covert exchanges of goods and services. Friends, on the other hand, render services to each other without material reward or compensation aside from emotional gratification. Yet, rendering services for friends sometimes forces people to infringe upon rules or even break laws. Thus friendship and family obligations—in the Soviet context—contribute significantly to the maintenance of the "second economy," and to the corruption and general moral decay of the society.

The obligations of friendship, as well as those of the family, also tend to undermine objectivity in public life. For example, professional performance, which should ideally be the only guide for the distribution of rewards in a society striving for efficiency and justice, may become subordinate to access based on whom one knows.

It is characteristic that L. Buieva, a Soviet social psychologist, and her coauthor V. Alekseeva, underscore that "true collectivism" and "the defense of [one's] own people" (the authors preferred not to use the term "friendship") are incompatible with each other. They write, "the struggle against the relapses of Philistinism is above all the active denial of communication and the knocking together of informal communities (and sometimes even of whole offices) based on the principle of 'you-me, I-you,' and also denying the submission of social activity to narrow egotistical interests" (Buieva and Alekseeva, 1982, pp. 39–40). Having essentially denounced friendship as it really exists in Soviet society as Philistinism, the authors reflect on a major problem in this society—people in close relationships aligned against the state and official ideology.

## *The Cult of Friends*

The available data suggest that the Soviet people place a greater value on friendship than Americans do. In a survey by M. Rokeach, conducted in the early 1970s, Americans ranked friendship tenth on a list of terminal values (There was variation according to educational level. Those with some college education ranked friendship twelfth, while those who completed college rated friendship a bit higher, in seventh place.) A study of Leningrad engineers by V. Iadov, conducted at about the same time, found that friendship was ranked sixth on a list with the same number of values (Iadov, 1979, p. 90; Rokeach, 1973, p. 64).

Similarly, a study of married people in Leningrad revealed that when they were asked what was most important for a happy family life, 15 percent named friends, while only 12 percent cited "interesting leisure time in the family," "good job standing," or "desirable education" (Boiko, 1980, p. 105).

As in other societies, the value placed on friendship is particularly strong among young people. A survey of Estonian students conducted in the late 1970s also revealed that "communication with friends" ranked first on a list of nine life values, with a score of 3.29 on a 5-point scale. "Communication with a loved person" received only 3.01, while "studies in school" scored 3.10 (Titma, 1981, p. 77). An earlier study, conducted on young Leningrad residents in the late 1960s, showed that 88 percent of all respondents pointed to "finding reliable friends" as their most important goal in life. Only the goal of "finding interesting work" surpassed the importance of friends among the respondents (Ikonnikova and Lisovskii, 1969, p. 91).[3]

The survey of students (in the late 1970s and early 1980s) conducted by Oleg Karpukhin and Vladimir Kutsenko showed that, when asked about their goals in life, they placed having friends (23 percent) in second position ahead of interesting work (15 percent), family life (11 percent), and self-fulfillment (5 percent) (Karpukhin and Kutsenko, 1983, p. 124). In another study conducted by Babosov and Titma in the late 1970s and early 1980s, the young people, responding to questions about their goals in life, put friends in first place (79 percent), before interesting work (78 percent), being useful to society (44 percent), and others (Babosov et al., 1985, p. 145).

## *Friends of Friends*

The Soviet individual carefully classifies people with whom he or she regularly maintains contact and separates friends from acquaintances. These acquaintances make up the core of the network of connections that allow a person to find solutions to various problems encountered in Soviet society. With only a few really close friends, it would be impossible to find access to dozens of various offices and enterprises, often in different parts of the country, and to overcome the difficulties with semilegal or illegal means.

Friends, however, still make a great contribution to this network, not so much with their own efforts in providing for their friends but by placing their own network at the disposal of one who asks for help. The friends of friends, as well as the acquaintances of friends, turn the whole of Soviet society into closely interwoven networks where there are only one or at most two individuals between you and an official or salesperson whose favor you need.

Friends of friends, unlike acquaintances, are not always people the individual meets regularly. Contact with them is usually only through communication with the common friend or at certain occasions, for instance, at birthday parties. However, people recognize that the bonds of friendship are such that friends of friends can be immediately mobilized to assist a person who is their common friend.

The contingent of acquaintances is recruited differently from that of friends. Since trust is a main criterion in selecting friends, Soviet people prefer to have as friends those they know from childhood or at least from their university or college. Forty percent of the friendships of the respondents of one survey began in high schools or other schools (Gordon and Klopov, 1972, p. 152; see also Goriachev et al., 1978, p. 46). Acquaintances, however, are found mostly at the workplace, or in resort places, on tourist trips, and at meetings and conferences.

## Love, Sex, and Lovers as Private Institutions

Along with friends, friends of friends, and acquaintances, lovers make up an important social element in the private life of the Soviet people.

The great role of lovers in Soviet life is directly connected with the importance Soviet people attribute to romantic love and to having sexual encounters with diverse people. Under Stalin, love was a refuge for Soviet people from the harshness of life. Yet, the state and mass terror were stronger in many cases than passionate love, and Soviet history knows many sad stories of people betraying each other despite the strong emotions that connected them. Recently, the Soviet movie, *Scarecrow*, raised this subject, placing its heroes in a secondary school and showing how, under the influence of demagoguery, clearly of official origin, people can betray their beloved.

With the decline of political repression and state interference in private life, the role of love and especially sex as a realm where Soviet people could let themselves go emotionally grew immensely in the post-Stalin period.

As many as 80 to 90 percent of Soviet people ranked love as one of the highest values (Fainburg, 1977; Kharchev, 1979; Kharchev and Matskovskii, 1978). Using M. Rokeach's scale of eighteen "terminal values," Iadov's sampling of engineers showed that love was ranked fifth in importance, ahead of other values such as material well-being, social recognition, independence, and freedom (Iadov, 1979, p. 90). A survey of young Leningraders found love ranked fourth among a list of thirteen values (Aseiev et al., 1981).

Of course, in real life the role of love is much less prominent than can be inferred from the verbal statements of the Soviet people. As soon as they have to analyze their own feelings in concrete situations, people render much less homage to love than in cases when they express their views in the abstract. Newlyweds rank love only as fifth among eighteen motives for marriage, and no more than one-quarter of married people regard mutual love as an important condition for family happiness (Golod, 1977, p. 50; Kharchev, 1979, p. 200; Tiit, 1978, p. 143).

What is more, with the growth of privatization and strong individualism, and the accompanying unwillingness to make sacrifices, even for a lover, love begins to recede before pure sexual pleasure (see Zhukhovitskii, 1986).

Soviet sociologists so far cannot ask people about the role of sexual pleasure in their life since bigotry and hypocrisy have been important parts of official ideology. However, Soviet literature and movies which, as was already mentioned, generally document Soviet life better than social scientists, provide ample information on this subject, leaving no doubt how important sex is in people's lives. Novels, stories, movies, and plays are replete with heroes absorbed with sexual issues. Leading Soviet authors, without speaking about the legion of mediocre writers, fill their novels and stories with numerous sexual scenes, a development which has even aroused the concern of ideologists (see *Literaturnaia Gazeta*, November 2, 1983; February 29, 1984; March 21, 1984; *Pravda*, March 17, 1986).

As people are so strongly involved in love and sexual activity, both premarital and extramarital, a lover becomes a fixture in the life of many Soviet people and therefore a participant in the concerns of everyday life. In the role of most intimate friend, as a lover is in some cases, a lover will engage in various activities to help the partner, such as finding a job, getting the partner a promotion, writing a dissertation or defending it, getting scarce goods, and obtaining access to the best hospital. The heroes of Trifonov's (1983b) or Gerasimov's (1983) novels, for instance, are extremely energetic in this sphere as are the characters of many Soviet movies, such as Roman Balaian's *Day and Night Dreams* (1983) or Leonid Zorin's *Kind People* (1980) or Georgii Danelia's *Autumn Marathon* (1979).

## A Dying Private Institution: Neighbors—Victims of Privatization

In the past, neighbors were also an important part of the private life of Soviet people, especially in the countryside where the traditions of old Russian communal life were quite strong for a long time despite the destructive effect of collectivization on human relations.

However, with the movement of the majority of city dwellers into single-family apartments, the concept of neighbor has lost its former role in urban life. Sixty percent of the residents in the new Moscow districts do not have any contact with neighbors and many do not even know them. On the whole, in Moscow and Leningrad no more than 10–12 percent of the people see their neighbors regularly (Iankova, 1979, p. 138; Kozlov and Lisovskii, 1986, p. 155).

It is important to note that the decrease in the role of the neighborhood in the life of Soviet people is also mostly the result of the process of privatization. Certainly, relations with neighbors are still a part of private life, since these relations are not under regular state control. However, the neighborhood involves personal relations of a lower order than friendship, because neighbors are people who are imposed on each other by external circumstance and happen to live in the same building or district. They are not associates completely freely chosen by the individual.

The importance of this factor can be seen from the data collected by Zoia Iankova, who established that Moscow residents are in closer relations, not with neighbors who live on the same floor or landing, but with those who live in other sections of the building; in the latter case, people visited an ailing neighbor 1.5 times more often than in the former (50 percent compared to 36). As Iankova noted, people select as associates those who match them best from the pool of neighbors. It is not surprising considering all this that the majority of Moscow respondents, when asked about their relations with neighbors, declared that they preferred to meet them outside their apartments. Since psychological and cultural compatibility in the selection of friends is more important than the mere fact of their proximity, it is not strange that with a rise in educational level the intensity of relations with neighbors decreases. Iankova compared people with a higher and a low education and found the intensity of relations decreased by three to four times (Iankova, 1979, p. 137).

As various sources show, people now rarely recruit their friends from among neighbors and quite often have no contact at all with those who live next door (Kharchev and Golod, 1971, pp. 101–03; Kozlov and Lisovskii, 1986, p. 155). Some scholars hope that some sort of collective relations will emerge between owners of adjoining gardens and country houses, with the backdrop of nature encouraging those city dwellers who own them to establish contacts with neighbors (*Nedelia*, 1986, #41, p. 3).

The developments in the countryside have almost completely destroyed relations between neighbors. The high mobility of villagers and their growing individualism have removed the neighbor as an important figure in the life of villagers, who in the past often resorted to a neighbor for assistance. Valentin Rasputin, in his novel *Fire* (1985b), vividly depicted the evolution of a Siberian village, from the prewar era when cooperation between people had been very strong to the 1970s when people were almost completely isolated from each other (see Ivan Vasiliev, 1986; see also *Pravda*'s article about the disappearance of relations with neighbors even in the Caucasus where they had been especially strong, July 27, 1984).

Though relations with neighbors are now relatively weak in comparison with the past, they still play a visible role in the life of the Soviet people. Twenty percent of city residents regularly borrow money from their neighbors, 17 percent seek some information from them, 16 percent exchange recipes with each other, and so on. The most active in these relations are retired people, especially women, and single women with children (Iankova, 1979, pp. 137–40; Kharchev, 1982, p. 52).

## Privacy in the Soviet Mentality

The gradual decline in the importance of public life for the Soviet people has led to a growing respect for privacy.

The high focus of Soviet ideology on the primacy of social over individual goals and on the right of the state, the collective, the party, Komsomol, and the trade unions to interfere in people's personal life made a claim for privacy (or in Soviet terms, "nonintervention in personal life") tantamount to a political challenge to the state.

The discussion in party or Komsomol meetings of so-called "personal issues"—adultery, divorce, the refusal to marry a pregnant woman or pay alimony, drinking habits, bickering with neighbors, illegal or semilegal moonlighting, etc.—were normal features of Soviet life under Stalin. The party was especially demanding and assumed that its members were ready to discuss any detail of their life with superiors. Not to be "sincere" with the party was regarded as a capital crime for a party member.

The majority of party members, as well as others who actively support the Soviet system, seemed to willingly comply with these demands and considered, especially in the 1920s and 1930s, the party or Komsomol cell as the fulcrum of their life. They practically refused to separate their public and private (or personal) lives from each other. In a movie about life in the 1930s, *My Friend Ivan Lapshin*, the heroes lacked any privacy whatsoever.

Another circumstance also accounted for the lack of a clear concept of privacy in the Soviet mentality of the past. The majority of city residents lived in communal apartments, i.e., in apartments where several families had to share the same kitchen, bathroom, and telephone. A single family occupied one room for itself (rarely two rooms) and quite often several generations—grandparents, parents, and children—shared this one-room apartment. In such a case there was absolutely no isolation for an individual. People could not even have sexual relations there without other members of their family present, who pretended to sleep while sexual intercourse was going on (see Berg's article on her neighbors in communal apartments in Leningrad, "Barbarians in the Debris of Utilization," 1984; see also Lidia Chukovskaia's documentary novel *Deserted Home*, 1981).

Relations between neighbors in such apartments were highly intensive, and among other things, provided a great deal of communication, mutual support (for single people this support was of vital importance), and concern for others' internal warfare. But this made the isolation of a family in such an apartment minimal, and as a rule it was not necessary to knock in order to enter the room of a neighboring family. Obviously there could be no private life in such an apartment. Viacheslav Nikiforov's movie *Fruzia* (1982) describes the life of a young woman living in a communal apartment and completely deprived of privacy by her neighbors increasing prying into her affairs, particularly those of an intimate nature.

The lack of privacy in communal apartments, in particular the necessity to use the same telephone in the lobby, was a situation actively exploited by the political police, who demanded neighbors spy on each other and report any suspicious event that happened in the apartment. Informers pressed into service were joined by millions of voluntary ones who often settled personal scores with neighbors. Motives for informing might be envy, sadism, the hope of taking over an additional room (in case the individual would be jailed), and so on.

The behavior and values spawned by communal apartments fit very well into collectivistic ideology and strongly affected the mentality of the Soviet people. They greatly contributed to the feeling that life without privacy was normal.

The general process of privatization as well as the move of millions of the people into individual apartments has led to the emergence and spread of the concept of privacy in Soviet life. It has begun to become one of the major personal values of the Soviet people.

In the begining, privacy as a concept was directed mostly against outside interference—from the state, colleagues, and neighbors—in family life, but gradually this concept started to pertain to those within the family. Individuals had the right to keep his or her personal life closed to other family members, even a spouse.

One rare indicator of this tendency can be seen from some of our data from the 1977 survey of readers of *Literaturnaia Gazeta*. Our questionnaire contained a question designed to elicit if unmarried respondents were inclined to recommend the use of a dating service to their relatives and close friends. In considering this data, we should take into account that only 1 percent of all respondents were opposed to the existence of such services. While one-fourth of the respondents said they would not recommend a dating service to friends or relatives, and about one-half answered that they would do so, the remaining one-fourth rather unexpectedly responded that the matter was a person's private business and that they would not impose their advice on others.

Although this alternative was available to respondents, given the public support for dating services, we assumed that few respondents would select this option of response. Thus, I must confess, we overlooked the possibility that some respondents would focus on an aspect of the question other than utility of dating services and view it in connection with the right of individuals to make their own decisions in such personal matters. It is noteworthy that this position was most commonly taken by the youngest and most educated readers of *Literaturnaia Gazeta.*[4]

## The Privatization of Entertainment

The private sphere of the Soviet individual—family, friends, friends of friends, lovers, and even neighbors—successfully withstood in the mid-1980s the blandishments of the gigantic network of cultural, social, and entertainment activities the state offers the individual for leisure time.

The state operates 138,000 clubs, 151,000 movie theaters, 134,000 libraries, and 720,000 amateur talent societies, as well as about 2,000 museums and more than 600 theaters (TsSu, 1985, pp. 532–43).

Strongly preferring to see people pass their leisure in public places of entertainment as much as possible, the authorities expend tremendous effort to lure them to public cultural institutions. But the authorities failed to turn the clubs into places where people were eager to spend their free time. Only a small fraction of the population (no more than 10–20 percent) can be considered by Soviet officials as regular club visitors (Kapelush et al., 1985, p. 67). Even in the countryside no more than 30 percent attend regularly (Khabibullin, 1980, pp. 128–29). Complaints about the unwillingness of the people to go to the clubs, in the village as well as in the city, have been common since the 1930s. Only the lack of movie theaters forced most people to step over the threshold of a club (Kapelush et al., 1985, p. 69; Khabibullin, 1980, p. 129; Striganov, 1981, pp. 46–48; *Sovietskaia Kul'tura*, November 13, 1986, p. 3). Now that there are movie theaters in almost all villages, not to mention the cities, the official club has lost whatever attraction it once held for the Soviet people. The dances that officials can hold in the club (which also served in the past as an inducement for young people to attend) became too obsolete even for young people in the most remote settlements (about this "boycott," see *Sovietskaia Kul'tura*, October 12, 1986; *Literaturnaia Gazeta*, December 9, 1987). Only a few prestigious clubs, such as for writers or filmmakers, in the big cultural centers (primarily Moscow) are popular.

Even official data on the number of participants in amateur art circles (the number of people taking part in these circles is clearly overestimated) shows a decrease of 6 percent in 1981–84 for this strongly supported state activity (TsSU, 1985, p. 540).

On an average evening in 1982, Soviet theaters were 72 percent filled (59 percent in Georgia), but this percentage has been declining (Zinin and Diskin, 1985, p. 109). Even famous Moscow theaters, the best in the country, attract fewer and fewer people. From 1970 to the mid-1980s the number of visitors declined by 20 percent (Gimpelson and Shpilko, 1987, p. 51).[5]

The 300,000 libraries in the Soviet Union have lost the importance which they once held in the lives of the people. Now they contain eight times fewer books than the citizens themselves, 5 billion against 40 billion (*Nedelia*, 1987, #33, p. 3).

The process of privatization has also affected museums, even in Moscow, where sixty-seven museums attract guests to the capital. Despite the increasing number of visitors to the city, the number of museum visitors has declined by 13 percent in the last fifteen years (Gimpelson and Shpilko, 1987, p. 51).

The spread of TV in the country has contributed enormously to the privatization of entertainment. Attendance at movie theaters declined 26 percent (by one-third in the cities), and attendance at drama theaters showed almost no increase in the 1980s and then began to drop in the middle of the decade (TsSU, 1985, pp. 544–45; Zinin and Diskin, 1985, pp. 186–87).

The introduction of video recorders in the 1980s was another serious blow to official public entertainment. With the gradual distribution of video recorders and especially the flow of videocassettes from abroad, the inducement to visit movie theaters shrank even more. The Soviet press reveals the mushrooming of private movie theaters that show films inaccessible to the public at large and which previously could be seen only by the elite. This development notes Valerii Kichin, a prominent journalist, outrages not only the authorities but also people with low incomes who look at the owners of video recorders (a very expensive convenience—4–5,000 rubles) with hatred (*Nedelia*, 1986, #15, p. 3; see also *Sovietskaia Kul'tura*, February 20, 1986).

In general, since the appearance of transistors in the 1950s, each step of technological progress only accelerates the privatization of cultural and entertainment activity. Although copying machines are inaccessible to the Soviet people, they still make their contribution in the dissemination of underground literature. And the extremely gradual penetration of personal computers into Soviet life will make its own, perhaps significant, contribution to this process.

Alcohol is also a serious factor that influences the character of leisure time. Steady imbibing in its own way keeps people from public places (except for restaurants and similar establishments) and in the home. The antialcoholism campaign conducted by Gorbachev in 1985–86 greatly contributed to the privatization of this sphere of life.

The growing role of hobbies is another manifestation of the private character of the interests of Soviet people in their leisure time, even if the state tries, unsuccessfully, to control this sort of activity through various clubs. According to the data cited by Edvard Klopov, time spent on hobbies rose from 1963 to 1977 by almost five times. This tendency continued in succeeding years, but somewhat slower (Klopov, 1985, p. 265). Now about 70 percent of the Soviet people have some hobby (*Nedelia*, 1986, #31, p. 2).

The dynamics of the amount people spend on state entertainment is an eloquent indicator of privatization in this domain of Soviet life. Between 1970 and 1984 expenditures on entertainment remained practically the same despite an increase in real income (per person) by

59 percent. As a result, the proportion of these expenditures in a working family's budget declined from 1.0 to 0.7 percent (Churbanov, 1986, p. 43; TsSu, 1985, p. 426).

Privatization of leisure time and entertainment ("domestication" or "individualization" in Soviet terminology) is seen by Soviet officials as a negative process that must be reversed. Vadim Churbanov, director of the Research Institute at the Ministry of Culture, considers "the growing role of state institutions in the cultural life of the population" as the most important task of his ministry for the immediate future (Churbanov, 1986, p. 57). However, he could not produce evidence that implementing this would be realistically feasible.

## Companionship, Gangs, and Associations

Private companionship plays a great role in the leisure time of Soviet people, significantly higher than in the United States. According to various sources, at least one-third of the Soviet people spend most of their free time in such groups, composed mostly of colleagues. Among people below thirty, the number who regard spending time with friends and acquaintances as very important increases to 60–70 percent (Alekseeva, 1983, p. 200; Erme, 1977, p. 117; Golod and Sokolov, 1977, p. 35; Plaksii, 1982, p. 117).

When asked how they would use additional free time if they got it, young people in the longitudinal surveys in Taganrog (1967–68 and 1978) in both cases ranked spending time with friends and acquaintances first (Klopov, 1985, p. 279).[6] This correlates well with information about where young people spend their leisure. Approximately 50 percent of the respondents indicated the "home of a member of the clique," whereas less than 20 percent mentioned clubs, houses of culture, and other places controlled by the state. With age, home entertainment rises in importance; older people spend 60 percent of their free time at home compared to 6 percent in clubs, etc. (Odintsov, 1976, pp. 124–25). In another study, young childless couples were asked about their attitudes toward collective and private forms of entertainment. Only 24 percent preferred the former, 46 percent preferred to spend time with their groups, and 29 percent with family (Plaksii, 1982, p. 172).

These groups, especially among young people, have become hotbeds for Western lifestyle dissemination as well as of various forms of social deviation, a development the authorities find frightening. By various means the state tries to discredit these groups and prevent them from influencing the youth (as an example of a very hostile description of these cliques, see Kozlov and Lisovskii, 1986). It is not amazing that Edvard Klopov, reflecting official views, expressed his concern about the amount of time spent by people in "cliques" (Klopov, 1985, p. 279).

Some cliques of teenagers who left home in the early 1970s and 1980s came to the streets of the big cities, where they formed gangs headed by a strong leader (at least in 30 percent of all cases). These gangs started fighting with each other as well as attacking those young people outside their gangs. In Moscow groups of fans for some soccer clubs formed gangs; later young people resorted to various other pretexts to form their groups, such as participation in ice skating. A new term emerged to designate the participants in this movement—*fanats*—probably stemming from the English term *fan* and its original form, *fanatic.*

The most characteristic feature of the fanats is their aggressiveness toward society. Fanats consciously dress in a way designed to arouse the anger and outrage of ordinary citizens. In some ways their appearance and behavior resemble that of Western "punks," although the Soviet version is seemingly more militant and self-assertive—more like urban territorial youth gangs in U.S. cities. Intergroup rivalry is expressed by gang fights. Fanats have reportedly attacked innocent citizens on the streets, and there are accounts of sadistic actions against boys and girls who are not members of these groups. Fanats have not only broken the state monopoly on authorized organizations, but they have also indulged in their own "publicity" through displays of graffiti on walls, fences, and other public areas. Such actions are virtually without precedent in recent Soviet history (about fanats see *Literaturnaia Gazeta*, June 6, 1984; July 4, 1984; Alekseeva and Chalidze, 1985, pp. 57–58; Kozlov and Lisovskii, 1986, pp. 124–26; *Strana i Mir* 1984, No. 1–2; *Rabotnitsa*, 1986, 6, pp. 26–27).

Some of these youth groups, as well known as the fanats, have their own insignias. One of them, centered in Kazan, was described by Kozlov and Lisovskii. Eschewing the attire worn by other gangs, this one preferred quilted jackets, a material heretofore generally regarded as very plain, and little hats with pom-poms, which gave them their name—"pompomists." However, the style of behavior of this group was the same as others—a clear orientation toward aggression and the cult of physical strength (Kozlov and Lisovskii, 1986, pp. 123–24).

In the 1980s new forms of cliques emerged: "the systems," associations of young people who try to satisfy their various needs and make themselves independent of society; "metallists," who proclaimed themselves to be admirers of "heavy metal" rock music; *rokery*, admirers of rock music; *breikery*, adorers of break dancing; *poppery*, young people whose goal is to get as much pleasure as possible from this life; *liubery*, young people with strong anti-Western feelings; groups dealing with the conservation of historical monuments (many members of these groups share Russian chauvinistic views); and many others (see *Pravda*, December 14, 1984; *Komsomol'skaia Pravda*, August 16, 1986, December 11 and 19, 1986, and January 12, 1987; *Literaturnaia Gazeta*, June 4, 1986 and August 5, 1987; Sundiev, 1987).

The growing role of large street gangs is an extremely significant development in Soviet life, another hallmark in the process of the withdrawal of the Soviet people from official public life.

## Private Political Activity

During the Stalin era the level of repression was such that not only was unofficial public political activity impossible, but even private communications on important social and political issues were rare. In the 1930s and 1940s, in exchanges between close friends people often avoided discussing issues in ways divergent from official policy.

After 1953, private communications gradually became more open. As it became clear that the mass repression of the 1930s was over, intellectuals and other segments of the population began to talk more freely. Following the twentieth party congress of 1956, conversations between individuals opened up even further. Of course, even at this point, few people would openly discuss whether the atrocities of the Stalin era were a natural outgrowth of the Soviet system, and conversations generally followed the interpretation that had been officially advanced for the period. Even in 1962, Anna Akhmatova did not mention in conversation the names of people who provided her with some information, and angrily rebuked those who violated this rule (Chukovskaia, 1980, pp. 412–13).

As each year passed without any mounting repression, people became increasingly less restrained in their interpersonal contacts. By the early 1960s, after a decade without Stalinist repression, the situation changed markedly and discussions of political matters occupied a central place in the conversations between intellectuals. Developments in this period, such as the bard movement, samizdat, the end of jamming of foreign radio, tourism abroad, the "Gulag's theme" in literature, as well as articles in *Novyi Mir*, *Iunost'*, *Internazional'naia Literatura*, and *Literaturnaia Gazeta*, all provided countless topics of discussion for gatherings at work and at home. To some degree, the level of activity suggested that people were trying to make up for the decades lost in hypocrisy and timidity under Stalin.

Salons emerged in a number of locations, providing places for intellectuals to meet and discuss political and cultural issues. Besides Academic Town in Novosibirsk, the first Soviet campus, salons operated in other academic centers, such as Pushchino and Chernogolovka, as well as in Moscow and Leningrad (for the figures on these gatherings, see Zinoviev, 1978).

This private political and cultural activity reached its peak in the 1960s, although in Leningrad, private cultural gatherings again became popular at the end of the 1970s (Kolker, 1985, p. 110). With the political reaction in full swing in the 1970s the intensity of private life significantly diminished.

## Intellectual Interest in Private Life

The Soviet people display a tremendous interest in the private lives of their fellow countrymen. Of all domestic issues, private human relations are most appealing to the Soviet people when reading newspapers and magazines.

This was established by us as early as the late 1960s when I conducted the first nationwide surveys of readers of the major national newspapers. No less than two-thirds of the readers of *Izvestia*, *Trud*, *Pravda*, and *Literaturnaia Gazeta* regularly read articles about moral problems, mostly related to family, youth, and other issues clearly far from the public issues (which attracted two or three times fewer people). In most cases, only international issues could compete with private ones for the attention of the Soviet people (Evladov et al., 1969, p. 36; Shlapentokh, 1969a, pp. 92–93; 1969b, pp. 172–73; Skvortsov, 1968).

The same tendency persisted in the 1970s, according to a study that found that issues on private life (family, children, household) were the predominant subjects for newspaper readers, TV viewers, and radio listeners (Fomicheva, 1976, pp. 86–87; 1978, p. 59; Prokhorov, 1981, pp. 95–96).

Magazines which specialize in materials relevant to private life are the most popular. Among them are *Rabotnitsa* ("Female Worker") and *Zdorovie* ("Health"), which, despite limits on subscriptions in Taganrog where Boris Grushin conducted his study in the 1970s, had more subscribers than all party, literary, and professional magazines combined (Grushin and Onikov, 1980, p. 132).

The interest of Soviet people in private life explains to a great degree why Soviet authors, as soon as they got a modicum of freedom, moved from writing "production novels" to works that fully concentrated on the private life of their heroes, with an almost conspicuous disregard for public life.

# CHAPTER 8

# Civil Society: Semilegal and Illegal Private Activity

Along with the legal forms of privatization, other forms of private life, mostly illegal, have been growing rapidly in Soviet society in the post-Stalin period. I refer here to Soviet civil, or second, society, which is mostly illegal or semilegal. As was mentioned in the introduction, civil society is a sphere of social life where people as private citizens interact with each other, creating their own various organizations not controlled by the state. The second society includes practically the same sectors of activity as the first, official one.

The degree of state hostility toward the second society varies according to its different aspects. Also, each political regime shapes its own policy toward the second society and its individual elements. The policy can vary from radical rejection of any private activity to the support and legalization of some of this activity.

Some aspects of the second society are almost completely legal, such as the private farm plot, while other aspects of it are strongly proscribed by the state, such as dissemination of foreign literature or foreign currency transactions. Aron Katseneliboigen developed this idea in his article on black, gray, and other "color" markets in the Soviet Union (1978).

## Economy

The famous second, or shadow, economy certainly plays the leading role in the second society, attracting much energy from wheeler-dealers as well as Soviet officials. Millions of Soviet people take part in the second economy as producers; consumers include practically the entire Soviet population (about the second economy, see Grossman, 1977, 1982).

The most important role in production in the second economy is that of privately owned plots of land in agriculture belonging to some 47 million families (Shmelev, 1985, pp. 3, 5). The form of agricultural production really falls into both societies—official (because it is legal) and unofficial (because so many violate state rules and regulations). How large an economic role those plots fill is shown by the fact that 2–3 percent of the arable land in the country produces almost one-third of all its agricultural products—22 percent of the meat, 32 percent of the milk, and 60 percent of the vegetables and potatoes (Levin and Petrovich, 1984, p. 133; Rimashevskaia and Karapetian, 1985, p. 84; Ryvkina, 1979). According to the calculations of Soviet economists, the labor expenditures on private plots are almost the same as on collectives and state farms—about 20 million full-time workers are involved, and the plots account for about 30 percent of farm-worker income (Dumnov, Ruthaiser, and Shmarov, 1984, pp. 107–08; Rimashevskaia and Karapetian, 1985, p. 86). In recent years Soviet authors have been able to discuss one of the prohibited issues of the past—the comparative efficacy of social production and private business. Various data published by them show, for instance, that the productivity of private plots usually exceeds that of collective and state farms by three to five or even more times (*Pravda*, June 23 and September 20, 1987, *Moskovskiie Novosti*, August 30, 1987, *Literaturnaia Gazeta*, June 24, 1987).

As was previously mentioned, various developments in recent decades (food shortages, the yearning for property, and the flight from overcrowded and polluted cities, among others) have induced 20 million city families (when all members are counted it amounts to 60 million people, about one-third of the urban population of the country) to become owners of private plots. On these small holdings outside cities (these plots are officially named "garden plots"), usually with a country house, the owners grow vegetables, berries, fruits, and in many cases potatoes.

Private plots in the countryside as well as the "collective gardens" in many ways channel resources from the state to the private sector. Marina Mozhina and her coauthors of *The Family and the Standard of Living in a Developed Socialist Society* found a strikingly high correlation between the amount of income from social production, or production for the common good, and the income derived from private plots. The more people earn in a collective (or state) farm, the greater the productivity of their private plots. The correlation between the amount of income from the private plot and the amount of products in kind received from a collective (or state) farm was also found to be very high. Soviet economists reasonably explain this fact by contending that the active role of an agricultural worker in the collective farm allows him or her to more actively exploit the resources of this farm for the benefit of his private economic activity (see Rimashevskaia and Karapetian, 1985, p. 91; see also Shokhin, 1986, pp. 40–41).

Moonlighting (or work outside of one's main job) is the next most important sector of the second economy, which, according to data published in the Soviet press, involves well over 20 million people who hold positions in the official economy. According to the calculations of two leading Soviet experts—Vladimir Kostakov and Valerii Ruthaiser—only 17–18 million moonlighters (about 15 percent of all employees take part in this activity) are involved in serving the population (*Sovietskaia Kul'tura*, January 8, 1987; see also Shokhin, 1986, p. 36). Moonlighting is especially widespread in the repair of apartments and electrical appliances, transportation, and the role of middlemen in trade (mostly selling agricultural produce). This private sector makes up as much as half of the service which is rendered by the huge state sector. According to special studies, about 60 percent of privately owned car repairs are done by moonlighters, and the private sector—those working for themselves—in this service is growing (Eko, 1985, 5, p. 112). The private sector repairs half of all shoes, 40 percent of all apartments, and 30 percent of all electrical appliances (Shokhin, 1986, p. 43).

Moonlighting, considered a private activity, has been treated differently under various regimes. The best period for it was the two decades under Brezhnev's rule, when the authorities completely acquiesced to it, with the full support of public opinion. This ended all hope of the state agencies to develop the capacity to satisfy the needs of the population. Since moonlighting, as any private economic activity, is closely intertwined with corruption, Gorbachev, as part of his anti-corruption crusade, has tried to put moonlighting under state control, for example, by insisting people declare sources of income (*Pravda*, May 28, 1986). This effort led to some curtailment of moonlighting as well as other activities in the second economy, and according to Leonid Zhukhovitskii, a prominent journalist, almost created chaos in Soviet life, especially a few months later when the government started to beat a retreat from this stance (*Literaturnaia Gazeta*, October 15, 1986, p. 11). This was when Gorbachev drastically changed course and started to encourage private activity in service and commerce (see "The Decree about Individual Labor Activity," *Pravda*, November 21, 1986).

The third sector of production in the second economy is composed of free-lance builders who after forming teams of laborers, roam the country looking for lucrative orders. These famous *shabashniki* have for over three decades been a fixture in Soviet economic debates—should they be regarded as helping the official Soviet economy or as its committed enemies? (see, for instance, *Literaturnaia Gazeta*, January 14, 1987, p. 13; Krutova, 1985, p. 21).

Working on individual contracts with their clients, mostly collective and state farms who pay them unofficial rates, *shabashniki* became a symbol for the hard work that could be stimulated by private initiative. In the Rostov region, for instance, their productivity was at least three times higher than that of builders in public enterprises. Many teams of these free-lance builders work sixteen to eighteen hours a day and guarantee the high quality of their products (see *Izvestia*, April 4, 1986).

Along with these free-lance builders, mostly Armenians, who are engaged in building activity practically the whole year (55 percent of them are not formally on the payroll in the public sector), are hundreds of thousands of other Soviet people, including engineers, teachers, and scholars, who use their vacation time for the same purpose and unite in teams of the same character as that of the *shabashniki*. They go to the north or the countryside, offering their building services to various organizations. The scope of this activity is such that in spring official construction organizations are almost completely deserted as workers set out for other regions of the country as private builders (see *Literaturnaia Gazeta*, July 15, 1987; *Pravda*, April 9, 1983).

The fourth sector in the second economy is the underground production of consumer goods. This activity flourished especially in the Caucasian republics in the 1970s and was the target of harsh prosecution after these republics had a change of leadership in the second half of the 1980s. However, underground business was not extinguished in these or other regions of the country. In the late 1970s and 1980s it was attested to by the appearance of T-shirts with labels indicating their foreign ("firm") origin, as well as by the sales of other fashionable goods or those in short supply.

This underground industry is more closely intertwined with the official economy and the party and state apparatus than the other sectors in the second economy, because it requires stolen raw materials and equipment and the use of the network of state stores for selling its products (about the connection between the "shadow economy" and the state apparatus, see Zaslavskaia, 1986b, p. 67).

### *Informal Economy*

A special sphere of the civil society—the informal economy—is closely intertwined with the formal, legal economy. If the second, illegal economy uses illegal means to achieve illegal goals (personal enrichment at the expense of the Soviet state), the informal economy embraces illegal activity which pursues legal objectives—the fulfillment of plans set by the state. The peculiar character of the informal economy explains why Soviet courts as well as public opinion has always been very ambivalent about those managers who violate laws in the interests of their enterprises (see Agranovskii's famous article about the trial of good managers, Agranovskii, 1982, pp. 293–308; Simis, 1982; see also various articles in *Literaturnaia Gazeta* about managers who were forced to resort to private, usually illegal, means in order to fulfill their duty, August 20, 1986, and January 14, 1987).

The informal economy prospers in all areas of Soviet society, but especially the supply of raw materials and parts and in the building industry. A considerable part of people's work outside their official job goes back into the official economy but for a higher reward. Millions of people take part as private individuals in construction work for state enterprises in cities and especially in the countryside, in servicing computers belonging to the state, and in repairing machines used by state plants and offices. In order to get raw materials, parts, and equipment, Soviet managers regularly bribe each other, using millions of schemes to get what is necessary for the fulfillment of plans (see Grossman, 1982, pp. 105–07).

The informal economy forms the basis for economic autonomy, i.e., the setting up of in-house production of parts and instruments which the enterprise would normally acquire from plants specialized in their production. The connection between autarky and the informal economy is especially strong in the construction industry. According to incomplete official data, in 1982 in-house construction, i.e., construction done by the customer himself and not special building firms, made up 10 percent of total production, and in the countryside up to 84 percent (*Pravda*, February 4, 1983). (For more about the informal economy see Kontorovich and Shlapentokh, 1986.)

## Education

Although not nearly as important as the economy in the second society, education became in the 1960s a serious branch of it, especially in big cities. Consumers of services were youngsters whose parents wanted them to pass entrance exams for university or college. With increasing competition for entrance to prestigious higher schools and with the general decline, because of the demographic situation, of the chances of getting into a university, a ready market opened up for this type of activity.

The number of tutors in mathematics, physics, Russian, literature, and history, among other subjects mushroomed in the 1970s, eliciting significant sums of money from ambitious parents and diverting the energy of many thousands of teachers and scholars from their official pedagogical and research work. The scale of entrepreneurial activity in this sphere is reflected in the fact that the monthly rate for training has been between 70–120 rubles, almost one-third or one-half of the average salary and even more (see *Nedelia*, 1984, #15, p. 6; *Literaturnaia Gazeta*, March 20, 1985, p. 11; see also Poliakov's novel *The Work with Mistakes*, 1986).

There are not only tutors for exams, but hosts of people teach foreign languages, music, and to a lesser degree painting. The high prestige of these cultural attainments places a significant value on this sphere of activity (about private music lessons see, for instance, Vishnevskaia's *Galina*, 1984).

In 1986–87 the idea of the privatization of education made significant steps forward. Various people began discussing the creation of private schools, the legal right of parents to teach their children at home, as well as the creation of classes in state schools for the teaching of some subjects as a special reward (*Komsomol'skaia Pravda*, December 5, 1987; *Literaturnaia Gazeta*, July 15 and August 26, 1987).

## Health Service

With the state monopoly on health service, the impossibility of getting modern medical equipment for private use and what is especially important in this respect, the fact that all medical services are free, private medicine could not develop as a serious branch of the second society, even in comparison with education. Although private practice is growing, especially in dentistry, opportunities are very limited and with little prospect for progress. Probably only illegal abortion (in spite of the fact that abortions are officially permitted) flourishes in the country outside of hospitals. In some areas 80 percent of all abortions are done illegally and one-fourth of them by medical workers or those who assumed their role (*Nedelia*, 1987, #38, p. 12).

Real private medicine, however, flourishes inside state medicine. Current practice assumes that relations between medical workers and patients are regulated by two codes—official and unofficial—and the quality of services rendered to a patient obviously depends on which code is prevailing in the given case. As an author wrote in *Kommunist*, Soviet medicine with its free services is increasingly influenced "by commodity-money relations and the horrors of the shadow economy" (*Kommunist*, 1986, #17, p. 67).

Unless placed in a hospital for the political or cultural elite, a patient cannot expect the services of first-rate doctors or the attention of nurses and orderlies. Of course, there are exceptions. Soviet doctors are highly devoted to their profession and their patients. But the quality of service can rise dramatically, however, if the second, unofficial code is in effect.

Money is not the only remuneration used in private medicine, but gifts (cognac, a box of candy, cosmetics, and of course, all sorts of foreign goods) and especially services (including access to special stores, travel agencies, barbershops, and so on) can be offered by a patient on the basis of reciprocity (see Vladimir Golyakhovsky's *Russian Doctor*, 1984, p. 104; see also *Literaturnaia Gazeta*, December 9, 1987).

## Culture

Privatization in culture has had since the very begining clear political overtones, thus encountering the particular hostility of the state.

Two developments in the 1960s initiated the "second culture" in the Soviet Union: the bard movement and samizdat.

## *The Bard Movement*

In the early 1960s, a completely new cultural phenomenon emerged in the country: the appearance of the bards, who performed their own musical compositions. This was perhaps the first spontaneous movement in Soviet history to encompass hundreds of thousands of people, initially the intelligentsia and students and then the whole population. As tape recorders became widely available at that time, the songs of the bards became accessible throughout the country, out of the control of the authorities. Moreover, the bards performed publicly in various institutions in Moscow, Leningrad, Novosibirsk, and elsewhere. The most famous bard was Bulat Okudzhava, followed by such singer-composers as Alexander Galich, Vladimir Vysotskii, Viktor Kim, Iuri Visborn, and a number of others of varying quality.

Listening to songs of the bards became an important incentive for social gatherings, and the songs' themes often turned such gatherings into political discussions. Interest in bardic compositions was a reliable indicator of a person's liberalism, and as a result the songs served to bring together people of common political views (see Sundiev, 1987, p. 57).

## *Samizdat*

The dissemination of government-suppressed literature had begun before 1964, the year of Khrushchev's dismissal, and started probably in the late 1950s or even a bit earlier.

However, the real upsurge of samizdat began in the mid-1960s and was directly stimulated by Solzhenitsyn's works, both published and unpublished. *Cancer Ward* and *The First Circle* were two of the first major pieces of samizdat to circulate. Other important works, such as Eugeniia Ginzburg's *Into the Whirlwind*, Boris Pasternak's *Doctor Zhivago*, some stories by Shalamov, and the testimony of Anatoly Marchenko, also became highly popular works of samizdat. In the 1970s, the most popular works were Solzhenitsyn's *Gulag Archipelago* and Nadezhda Mandelshtam's *Memoire*, along with the novels of Vladimir Voinovich, Georgii Vladimov, Vladimir Kornilov, and others.

A number of enthusiasts took great risks by typing and disseminating the literature themselves, and they were joined by others who contributed to the cause.

In fact, the volume of samizdat was so great in the first half of the 1960s (according to some sources, more than 300 authors gave their works to samizdat; see Alekseeva, 1984, p. 243) that many among the intelligentsia would read almost nothing but unofficial literature. The more courageous would even accumulate these works and build their own libraries of samizdat, although many of them were later arrested and sentenced to significant jail terms (such as a Riga mathematician, Lev Ladyzhenskii). During a search of the Soviet dissident Pimenov's apartment, KGB agents found 250 samizdat publications in his library (*Vol'noie Slovo*, 1973, vol. 8, p. 7).

Over time, the proportion of nonfiction works distributed by samizdat began to grow and included a variety of historical investigations of secret official documents, transcripts of political trials, memoirs, and collections of political materials. Samizdat also included translations of the works of foreign authors prohibited by the authorities, such as George Orwell's *1984*, Milovan Djilas's *The New Class*, Arthur Koestler's *Darkness at Noon*, and Hemingway's *For Whom the Bell Tolls*. By the 1970s, nonfiction materials were definitely dominant among samizdat works.

Some of the most important samizdat contributions were the underground periodicals. The authorities were particularly hostile toward these forms of samizdat, because they were well aware that part of Lenin's success in his struggle against tsarism had been due to the organizational role of such Bolshevik newspapers as *Iskra* and *Pravda* (about this, see Litvinov, 1976). Along with samizdat, illegal or semilegal exhibitions of painters have also become an important element of Soviet civil society since the mid-1960s (see *Literaturnaia Gazeta*, August 19, 1987).

## *The Dissemination of Foreign Literature*

Another important element of private cultural life is books published abroad and disseminated in the country through private channels. This literature includes all sorts of works—from detective stories in foreign languages, mostly English, to serious fiction, books on various scientific subjects, materials related to social issues, and emigrant publications in Russian. Foreign magazines circulating in the Soviet Union range from *Penthouse* and *Playboy* to the *New Yorker* and emigrant periodicals.

With the attempts at suppression of samizdat in the 1970s and the defeat of the democratic movement with the emigration of many prominent intellectuals, who had been authors of samizdat, the role of foreign publications (or tamizdat, "published over there") greatly increased. By the early 1980s these publications played a much more important role in the cultural diet of the Soviet intelligentsia than samizdat.

Foreign radio must also be mentioned as a private source of information for millions of Soviet citizens. In 1968, according to our survey of *Pravda* readers (so far the only nonclassified, relatively open study that could include any question about foreign radio), about 10 percent of the respondents avowed that they were regular listeners of foreign radio broadcasts. More recent evidence indicates that as much as one-third of the adult population has listened to foreign radio between 1977 and 1980 (Parta et al., 1982, p. 599). The network of word-of-mouth communication, which provides the majority of Soviet people with information received by their "leaders of communication" from foreign radio or other sources, is an important element of news dissemination.

A specialized branch of underground culture as well as of the economy is the production of art. Painters, sculptors, and other artists of varying caliber sell their products—from excellent paintings (some may even be shown at an exhibition in the West) to vulgar pornographic pictures. Despite the state's attempts to control them, these artists see themselves as independent, free-lance agents.

## Vacations: Contradictory Trends

The role of private initiative in the vacation industry is enormous, though development in this sphere has not been as uniform as in entertainment or the health service, where privatization is a predominant trend.

As vacationers, Soviet people are not as devoted to private forms of life as in other spheres. The majority of them clearly prefer to spend their vacation in public resorts, sanatoriums, rest homes, and other public institutions administered by the state which provide meals, medical services, and entertainment. According to one survey, in 1983 20 million Soviet people, only 10 percent of all vacationers in the country, spent their vacation in public resorts (Perevedentsev, 1985a and 1985b). To a great extent this predilection for public forms of vacation can be attributed to the lack of state-owned facilities that would allow people to have a vacation on their own, either by themselves or with their families. Hotels are accessible only to apparatchiks or wheeler-dealers (for a description of these people on vacation, see Edlis's novel *Intermission* [1986], which describes Sochi, a capital of Black Sea resorts). Restaurants and cafeterias in public resorts are always overcrowded, and the feeding of so-called "wild vacationers"—those who spend vacations outside state resorts—presents a harrowing problem. Public vacations present many other difficulties including getting return tickets. According to Perevedentsev's data, there are three times as many "wild vacationers" at the Black Sea beaches as "normal" ones (those with vacation packages) (Perevedentsev, 1985a, p. 22).

Certainly, for quite a few people public resorts are the ideal place for romance and love affairs, both licit and illicit, which in some cases end in marriage. This aspect of Soviet life is described in numerous novels (see, for instance, Edlis, 1986; Gerasimov, 1983) and movies (see Gubenko's "From the Life of Vacationers," *Nedelia*, 1986, #25, p. 4).

The lack of state facilities for vacationers has spawned feverish activity on the part of hundreds of thousands of Soviet people, who rent rooms, basements, attics, and even the space in gardens because they want to spend their vacation outside their city or village. The private vacation industry involves billions of rubles changing hands and has withstood many assaults on the part of the government. It constitutes a perennial theme in the Soviet press, which has exhorted state organizations for decades to expand their activity in this sector and build more state-owned resorts, but to no avail (see, for instance, *Pravda*'s article "Will Rent a Country House," January 18, 1987, p. 6).

## Political Activity in Illegal Civil Society

The distance between the political private and behavior in illegal civil society in socialist states is usually quite large. Only during periods of liberalization does this distance shrink, and in these periods people do not distinguish between public situations and private contacts.

It is possible to single out three types of political activity in illegal civil society. They differ from each other in the degree to which they challenge the official political order. Let me describe this activity briefly, referring mostly to the 1960s and 1970s.

## *The First Type—Semilegal Activity*

The most important element of political activity in illegal civil society in the Soviet Union involves the use of legal organizations against official policy and ideology.

The most prominent example is the bard movement, which involved thousands of people. Along with this movement, the intelligentsia managed to create centers of political activity for promotion of liberal ideas in various scientific institutions, a new phenomenon in post-Stalin Soviet history.

Another type of semilegal activity involves direct challenges to the political leadership, the KGB, and the Soviet political order in general, even if this challenge is only on legal grounds, i.e., formally permitted by law. People have begun to openly support their freinds and colleagues accused of political crimes. Using all legal means, some individual party meetings have confronted the Soviet political leadership, in some cases even face to face.

## *The Second Type—Illegal Activity in Soviet Institutions*

The most important elements of the second basic type of political activity in illegal civil society involve the emergence of movements totally outside official control, thus challenging the monopoly of the state. Examples include protest letters, and samizdat. In each case rather structurally weak organizations were created spontaneously. Having works published abroad, the refusal of some Soviet lawyers to follow standard instructions during political trials, participation in funerals of stigmatized persons, contacts with foreign correspondents, and holding scientific and other gatherings with some political purposes without official permission, are also examples of this second type.

## *The Third Type—Highly Illegal Activity*

The third type of political behavior—organized actions that directly challenge the Soviet political order and its main bodies, including the KGB—can be considered as having played a leading role in the late 1960s.

Among the major forms of illegal activity are the publication of illegal opposition magazines, attendance at political trials against the will of the authorities, organizing material help to political prisoners, contacts with foreign communist parties, unofficial international seminars, attending or organizing opposition political gatherings and demonstrations, and observing various religious activities prohibited by the state.

# CHAPTER 9

# Illegal Life inside the State: Corruption

So far I have discussed production activity in the second society even in cases where the private producers use raw materials, equipment, and labor belonging to the official public society for their own purposes. However, most of the Soviet people's private activity is not related to the production of any goods such as T-shirts or copies of foreign videocassettes, or services such as car repairs or tutoring, but to redistributing the wealth and other valuable resources belonging to the state in direct violation of rules established by the state. This redistribution, like private production, takes various forms, from the almost invisible trespassing of rules to blatant criminality.

The numerous types of corruption in official Soviet life are mostly determined by the participants' official positions. Usually those involved in illegal public life use as capital in bargaining their ability to use the state for private interests. The process of privatization to a great extent manifests itself in this deflection of public resources to satisfy individual needs over the interests of the state.

The most important condition for developing corruption in public life is the mutual trust to those involved. For this reason, family and friends form the base of most enterprises in unofficial spheres. The vanguard role played by the Caucasian and Central Asian republics in the nation's unofficial life is accountable primarily by the fact that people from these parts of the Soviet Union have developed such close ties of kinship among people belonging to the same tribe or coming to the city from the same village. Writers from these republics, such as

Chingiz Guseinov (see his novels *Mahomed, Mamed and Mamish*, 1977; *Family Secrets*, 1986) and Rustam Ibragimbekov (see his collection of plays, 1983), managed to capture the scope, even if not quite always the depth, of unofficial public life in these regions, which have almost mastered the makeover of officials into servants of the commanders of local organized criminal groups, or mafias (a term widely used in the Soviet Union).

Since Gorbachev, the denunciation of corruption in these national republics has become a leading part of the national cleansing of corrupt officialdom. Thus Uzbekistan, Kazakhstan, and other republics had the limelight of public attention turned on them. In Uzbekistan, more than half the superiors of all ranks were dismissed within the first year under Gorbachev (*XXVII S'ezd*, 1986, vol. 1, p. 210). The new leaders in Uzbekistan and the other republics did not spare their predecessors from criticism, presenting their regional governments as having completely overstepped all laws and rules and as controlled by people who absolutely disregarded the interests of the Soviet state (see, for instance, the twenty-seventh party congress speeches of Inamzhom Usmankhodzhaiev, the Uzbekistan party secretary [*Pravda*, February 28, March 2, 1986], Victor Niiazov, the Turkmenistan party secretary [*Pravda*, March 2, 1986], and others).

Corruption was not only deeply rooted in the national republics but to a lesser degree in other regions of the country, including Moscow. Fragments of this society were portrayed by some writers, filmmakers, and playwrights (see, for instance, Anatolii Kurchatkin's story "The New Glacial Period" in his book *The Stories about Different Places* [1986], or the movies *The Blond Around the Corner* [1985] and *We Who Signed . . .*" [1981]).

## Use of One's Position in the Hierarchy as Capital

Soviet officals who abuse their position most conspicuously are those who keep their job or make a career out of deceiving the state with statistical reports, hide the real production potential of their enterprise, thus diminishing the planned targets, support projects detrimental to the national interest, waste resources, slowdown technological progress, and allow the quality of products to deteriorate in order to fulfill plans.[1]

The system of control in Soviet society is almost helpless to check the private interests of bureaucrats who, colluding with their superiors and subordinates, are normally unassailable from outside forces. Privatization in the behavior of officials takes a clearly illegal or semilegal form when they use the material and labor resources of their office or enterprise for personal purposes (building apartments and country houses at the expense of the state, sexual exploitation, use of subordinates to ghostwrite publications, etc.).

Not only the apparatchiks but the rank and file as well actively use state resources for their personal goals. Soviet citizens devise millions of tricks that allow them to exploit the state for their private interests. In the countryside, for instance, it is a widespread practice to mix one's own cattle in the state herds belonging to collective farms, thus avoiding any expenditures on private animal husbandry (*XXVII S'ezd*, 1986, vol. 1, p. 209; *Pravda*, July 24, 1986).

A typical example of this was the Pskov experiment staged by the Ministry of Communication. It was decided to test the reaction of citizens in this city to the introduction of payment for the use of private telephones, depending on the length of conversations. Anatolii Rubinov, a famous journalist, related that city residents immediately increased use of their business telephones by many times, significantly impairing work productivity (*Literaturnaia Gazeta*, September 17, 1986, p. 12).

## *The Creation of "Mafias" inside the Official Structure*

An important element of illegal activity inside the public sector is the establishment of connections between apparatchiks for mutual support. Such networks flourished under Brezhnev and were widespread throughout nearly the entire country.

Solidarity among officials greatly increases the strength of each one individually, expanding their potential to exploit their position for their own private goals with bribes as their main source of enrichment. Local Soviet mafias can virtually paralyze the system of justice by replacing official law with what is called "telephone law" (by making a phone call the local party secretary can force a judge to pass any sentence the secretary wants). This reduces judges and prosecutors to the role of servants (about it, see Olga Chaikovskaia's and Arkadii Vaksberg's articles in *Literaturnaia Gazeta*, October 22 and December 17, 1986).

The scope of this phenomenon, as well as of nepotism in office and other forms of illegal privatization, started to clear up, even if only partially, after Brezhnev's death, particularly in 1985–86, when Gorbachev proclaimed his policy of *glasnost*. The Soviet mass media started to publish revelatory articles about gangs of party and state apparatchiks who, with their almost impregnable defenses against any attempt to undermine the status of any member of these mafias, had felt themselves absolutely safe for decades. This subject was rather vehemently discussed at the twenty-seventh party congress, especially in the speeches of Boris El'tsin, the new Moscow party secretary (*Pravda*, February 28, 1986) by Egor Ligachev, the Central Committee party secretary responsible for cadres (see *Pravda*, February 28, 1986), and by some other speakers (see also *XXVII S'ezd*, 1986, vol 1, pp. 307, 352–53, 437–38).

For over two years, *Pravda*, as well as other national newspapers, criticizing practically every region in the country, described how the local mafias of the government, headed by the first secretary of the party committee, administered justice and inflicted punishment like feudal barons in the times of medieval fragmentation. Along with the national republics of the Central Asian Caucasus, and Moldavia, Krasnodar, and Rostov, which became national symbols of corruption, the press brought out ample evidence of the existence of mafias in the Moscow region (see Vaksberg, 1987; see also *Literaturnaia Gazeta*, April 9, 1986; *Novoye Ruskoye Slovo*, August 1, 1986; *Pravda*, December 1, 1985).[2] These networks were found in many central ministries in Moscow (such as internal affairs, foreign trade, fisheries, nonferrous metals, communication, and even in the office of the procurator of the Soviet Union) (*Komsomol'skaia Pravda*, November 18, 1987; *Moskovskiie Novosti*, September 29, 1987; *Pravda*, August 10, 1985; *Sotsialisticheskaia Industriia*, May 13 and 30, 1987, June 12, 1987).

Furthermore, mafia activity also embraced the highest level of the Soviet hierarchy. The Soviet press in 1985–87 brought forth a great deal of data on involvement in criminal activity by such people as Shchelokov, minister of internal affairs (he committed suicide, presumably in 1984), his first deputy, Churbanov (Brezhnev's son-in-law), and Rekunov, the procurator of the Soviet Union. Arkadii Vaksberg, who published a revealing article about corrpution at the top of the Soviet system, directly hints that "the threads of criminal activity lead to people who held much higher positions" than the minister of internal affairs—this could only be Brezhnev or other members of the Politburo (Vaksberg, 1987, p. 13; see also *Sotsialisticheskaia Industriia*, June 12, 1987).

These informal relations guaranteeing mutual support at the expense of the state became dominant, not only among apparatchiks, but also between people in all domains of Soviet life—for instance, in cultural affairs, between playwrights and theater directors, and between writers and editors; in science, between scholars and graduate students, and between scholars and administrators; in health service, between doctors and nurses; and so on (see *Sovietskaia* Kul'tura, June 6 and December 6, 1986; *Pravda*, October 17, 1986; *Moskovskiie Novosti*, October 4, 1987).

Culture became one of the areas where the expolitation of official position took on especially absurd forms. Officials in writers' unions could publish the most talentless novelists in the 1970s, whereas some really gifted authors lost all hope having their works published. The ministers of culture in many republics (Tadzhikistan, Moldavia, Turkmenistan, and others) produced horrendous plays and without any compunction ordered dreadful scripts to be staged in theaters or turned into movies (*Literaturnaia Gazeta*, January 14 and June 17, 1987; *Sovietskaia Kul'tura*, May 8 and 29, 1986).

Soviet writers (Veniamin Kaverin in *Two Hours Walk*, Vladimir Tenderiakov in *Eclipse*, Ruslan Kireev in *The Victor*, I. Edlis in *Intermission*, and others) vividly described this new type of energetic and immoral apparatchik in various positions in the hierarchy, absorbed with enrichment and consumerism, and fully indifferent to official ideology and state interests.

## *Nepotism*

Nepotism, the protection of close family members, relatives, and friends at the expense of the state and its goals, is one of the most important phenomena in illegal public society. The promotion of children, wives, mistresses, relatives, people from one's village or province, friends, and friends of friends to various positions in the state and party apparatus as well as in science, management, culture, and all other spheres where they can enjoy privileges, prestige, and easy work, means the submission of state interests in the most sensitive area of the Soviet political system—cadres controlling appointments to all important positions—to the egotistical interests of millions of Soviet apparatchiks who can, with little hesitation, ignore talent, skill, and moral qualities as the criteria for the selection of cadres (for more about the expansion of nepotism, see Piskotin, *Soviet Manager*, 1986).

Nepotism flourishes in even more blatant form in selecting students for the most prestigious universities and institutes in the country. Protectionism, the admission of people to higher schools and their appointment to various positions "after a telephone call" (those who are protected, or favored, in this way got the name "aftercallnik" or "pozvonochniki," which is a pun in Russian), became extremely widespread under Brezhnev. Muckrakers in the first few years of the Gorbachev regime have managed to cast some light on the scope of nepotism.[3]

It became publicly recognized that the Moscow Institute of International Relations, which trains future diplomats, recruited almost 100 percent of its students from the children of the Soviet political elite who had formerly been officials in the Ministry of Foreign Affairs (*Pravda*, October 2, 1986).

Nepotism reached gigantic proportions in the national republics of Central Asia and the Causasus where, as was mentioned, old traditions of kinship created an especially propitious atmosphere for it. Even in 1986, after the great Gorbachev purge, *Pravda* informed readers that 194 professors and students in the Fergana Pedagogical Institute were related to each other (*Pravda*, October 7, 1986; about the role of nepotism in Ksazakhstan, see *Pravda*, October 11, 1986, and January 7, 1987).

## *Privileges and Corruption*

Corruption is generally based on the exploitation of a position in an organization for private interests at the expense of the organization or the consumers of its services. Any access to additional benefits is regarded by the holder of a position as an advantage. Many Soviet people make decisions about jobs keeping in mind these semilegal or illegal sources of income, as well as other bonuses.

At the same time, the Soviet system, which is supposed to reward citizens for their contribution to the prosperity of the country with an appropriate salary, provides many groups of the population, primarily the commanding class, the Nomenclature, with numerous privileges (access to special stores, hospitals, rest houses, hunting houses, permission to travel to the West, and others). These privileges, as Tatiana

Zaslavskaia put it, introduced "the inequality of rubles, because a ruble got by an apparatchik is much more valuable than a ruble at the disposal of an ordinary citizen" (Zaslavskaia, 1986b, pp. 69, 72). These privileges, as they are bestowed by the state, can be considered legal. However, they are concealed from the public (especially those given to apparatchiks), and as secret and therefore "private," have the flavor of illegality.

Under Stalin, so-called "packages," envelopes containing additional money above the official salary, were given to apparatchiks in a way different from the way regular pay envelopes were distributed, and their receivers, contrary to usual practice, were not required to sign for those envelopes, which only highlighted the secret character of the transaction.

Khrushchev's decision to abolish this custom served to underscore the illegal nature of this additional income. However, he as well as Brezhnev preserved and even expanded the network of special institutions that catered to the dominant class and continued to hide it from the public.

An attack against illegal, as well as hidden, even if seemingly legal, privileges of the party apparatus was proclaimed by Gorbachev soon after the new regime was installed. This culminated on the eve of the twenty-seventh party congress with the famous article in *Pravda* (February 13, 1985; see also February 10, 1986), El'tsin's speech at this congress (*XXVII S'ezd*, 1986), and at the later meeting with Moscow party activists (see *Strana i Mir*, 1986, 9, pp. 27–35). Gorbachev inveighed against apparatchiks absorbed with the preservation of their privileges a number of times in 1986, especially in his speech in Krasnodar (*Pravda*, September 19, 1986).

Whatever the real consequences of Gorbachev's policy against party privileges are, it undermined their legitimacy in Soviet society and as a result blurred the borders between these "legal" privileges and the illegal or semilegal abuse of power, and confirmed that all benefits accruing to any position besides official salary and prestige are illegal and corrupt.

## The Self-Serving Sectors

Private interests regularly interfere with the duties not only of the apparatchiks but of almost all Soviet people, whatever their occupation. Whoever has access to some resources will use them to satisfy their own needs first.

During 1985–86 numerous publications revealed that a considerable part of the spare goods in the food and light industries is appropriated by the workers in these industries for their private consumption (see, for instance, Rubinov's article on the confectionery industry, *Literaturnaia Gazeta*, July 16, 1986). The same is true of commerce and restaurants, where almost 10 million workers are the first to obtain goods which they are supposed to sell to the average customer. Shtemler vividly described this as the "right of first access" to consumer goods (see his *Supermarket*, 1984).

The self-serving sectors of the Soviet economy are also found in cultural institutions, where apparatchiks, actors, and administrators of theaters and concert halls get the majority of tickets if their supply exceeds demand;[4] in hospitals, which give doctors, nurses, as well as their relatives priority as patients; in sanatoriums and vacation resorts, which are available first to the relatives and family members of those who work there; in educational institutions, where children of employees are accepted first; and in local government bodies in charge of housing that first provide their own officials with apartments. Librarians and bookstore salespeople or members of their families and friends have the first chance to get interesting books or magazines to read or buy. Employees in public transportation are the first to get tickets. The list could go on and on (see *Pravda*, August 16, 1984; *Sovietskaia Kul'tura*, October 14, 1986).

## The Exchange of Goods and Services and the Speculation with Them

Able to utilize the lion's share of scarce goods for their own use, those who have direct access to them exploit a significant part of them to exchange for equivalent goods or services (Alexander Shokhin names this activity as belonging to the "gray market," Shokhin, 1986, p. 49). This was mentioned before in connection with medical services but it is also true in all other spheres of Soviet life.

The heroine of the Soviet movie, *The Blonde Around the Corner* (1985), an important person in a Moscow supermarket, presents her acquaintances to her fiancé by giving the name as she whispers what services the friend is able to provide—tickets to shows, resorts on the Black Sea, airline and railway tickets, and so on. She is so convinced of her power that she asked a prominent scholar, one of her private clients, what food (caviar, perhaps) the members of the Nobel prize committee would need in order to encourage them to vote for her husband, who in her opinion had made a sensational discovery. The most remarkable trait of this influential female is her deep conviction that these private exchanges of goods and services are the most natural things in a socialist society whose ideology she seemingly does not reject. Another Soviet movie with much less impact describes how a car mechanic can control influential people in the capital, who are ready to give a lot, including their favor as officials, in order to get their car repaired by him.

Private exchanges of services involve the whole intelligentsia, including the most elevated. For example, awarding scientific degrees to someone able to render some vulgar service, such as a vacation package to the Black Sea or a box of Georgian wine to the members of the Scientific Council, became commonplace in the 1970s (see Simis, 1982).

## The Black Market

The black market is a direct outgrowth of the process of privatization inside the state because the better part of the goods circulated on this market are offered by those who in one or another way have exploited their official positions (on Soviet color markets see Katsenelinboigen, 1977).

The authors of a unique Soviet study on the black market, Galina Belikova and Alexander Shokhin (1987), single out three categories of sellers on this market: filchers (*nesuny*, who pilfer from their own workplace), fences (*vezuny*, who sell goods acquired on trips abroad), and appropriators (workers in commerce who hold the best items under the counter for special clients).

Filchers provide the black market with goods stolen from state factories, farms, offices, institutes, and all other Soviet institutions. Pilfering, which satisfies various needs of the Soviet people—not only the need for cash—is discussed below. Here I will concentrate on the latter two categories of black market dealers.

As Belikova and Shokhin state, fences are not of the greatest economic significance. Those who live off of the domestic black market live much better than those who can buy foreign goods abroad. Still, all groups of people who travel—diplomats, actors, sailors, sportsmen, scholars, managers, and others—take part in the illegal import of foreign goods. These authors write that there is even a sort of division of labor among fences. Sailors and railway men usually bring in goods of small size such as silver chains, and watches, while actors and officials bring in electronic goods such as VCRs and tape recorders.

A considerable amount of the goods in the country are removed from open sales and sold under the counter at much higher prices. Parts for private cars is a typical example. According to a special study, no less than one-half of all automobile parts are bought by private car owners from speculators, whose prices often exceed official ones by eight times (see *Eko*, 1985, 5, p. 114). All other scarce goods are sold the same way.

A special case of illegal economic activity is the exploitation of state equipment and raw materials to render services to citizens for money. Among these services the use or cars, buses, and trucks, is the most frequent followed by the exploitation of equipment for the building or repair of apartments and country houses (see for instance, *Literaturnaia Gazeta*, July 31, 1985, p. 11; Zaslavskaia, 1985, p. 11). According to a special investigation conducted by economists 40 percent of all country houses were built with the illegal use of state equipment (*Literaturnaia Gazeta*, August 21, 1986).

The role of the black market is revealed in the fact that 83 percent of the Soviet population, being unable to get what they want in state stores, resort to paying much more than the official price for various goods and services (Belikova and Shokhin, 1987, p. 7). The black market is especially important for young people, where they buy 40 percent of all their goods (mostly of foreign origin) (Shchekochikhin, 1987, p. 13).

The black market has become a fixture of everyday life and is closely intertwined with all spheres of Soviet society. People from all walks of life are among its actors—from the daughter of a general secretary (it is well-known that Galina Brezhneva was deeply involved in black market activity) to people in the most humble position.

## Bribery

The next level of corruption is bribery. In one way or another probably the majority of Soviet people end up as givers and takers of bribes each year. The class division of Soviet society into superiors and subordinates, bosses and rank and file, is useful in analyzing this aspect of the second society.

It is possible to discern three types of bribery relationships: (1) among superiors; (2) between superiors and subordinates; and (3) between subordinates. The first type comprises mostly bribes inside the party and state apparatus. Bribes are given by superiors at lower levels of the hierarchy to those who hold a higher position, mostly to gain leeway in pursuing egotistical goals at the expense of the state and consumers. The 1985–86 trials in Moscow revealed the widely developed system of bribe taking by superiors from their subordinates in the Moscow Ministry of Internal Affairs as well as in the ministries of fisheries and foreign trade. The same system existed in Georgia and other national republics, where each position in the party and state apparatus had its price (*XXVII S'ezd*, 1986, vol. 1; *Strana i Mir*, 1986, 6, pp. 36–42; *Literaturnaia Gazeta*, September 10, 1986, p. 11).

Bribery extends to the relations between local party secretaries and the directors of local enterprises, especially in the countryside. Under Brezhnev, practically all local party bosses taxed the managers in their regions (see *XXVII S'ezd*, v. 1, 1986, p. 104, 106).

There are two kinds of relations between superiors and ordinary people: (1) relations "inside" an enterprise or office between supervisor and employee; and (2) relations between superiors and ordinary people who are not their subordinates.

In the first case, millions of Soviet workers and farmers can survive on the job only if they regularly pay their bosses. Such practices are found among taxi drivers, salespeople, builders, plant operators, workers on state farms, and many other categories. They pay to get rewarding assignments, good cars and equipment, permission to grow vegetables that are in high demand, and to have their supervisor ignore any violation of labor discipline or even stealing from the enterprise. Bribery to disregard an infraction of the law created the basis for the transformation of the Soviet collective from an agent of the state into a system which exploited the state for the private interests of managers and workers (see, for instance, *Nedelia*, 1986, #42, p. 14). The minister of culture, Ekaterian Furtseva, for instance, unabashedly took bribes from Soviet actors and musicians whom he allowed to go abroad (see Simis, 1982; Vishnevskaia, 1984; prosecutor Vladimir Kalinchenko's article in *Nedelia*, 1986, #40, pp. 12–13).

In the second case, ordinary Soviet people confront party bosses in the role of clients, not as subordinates. Soviet people must apply to superiors outside their jobs for a myriad of reasons: to get permission to live in a given city, to change apartments, to get into college or the hospital, to be allowed to go abroad as tourists, and so on. All these requests provide officials in the state and party apparatus with opportunities to extract various forms of bribes—from money to sexual favors.

The third form of bribery—that which takes place among subordinates—involves the interaction of millions of Soviet consumers and those in service jobs who work in supermarkets, railway stations, repair shops, beauty salons, hospitals, theater booking offices, police stations, and cemeteries. These workers have the power to satisfy citizens' requests or ignore them unless they receive a special reward, bribe, or "gift" (see *Rabotnitsa*, 1986–87, pp. 24–25).

The Soviet salesperson can hide goods under the counter which the customer badly needs, an orderly in a hospital can refuse a patient medicine prescribed by the doctor or not allow relatives to visit, a teller in a booking office can deny tickets requested by a client, and waitresses can ignore your presence in a restaurant. This army of people who serve others possess influence and wield tremendous clout over the Soviet people. The fact that the same people who extract additional money or other bonuses from customers are at the same time consumers who are daily mishandled by others, changes nothing. Arkadii Raikin, the famous Soviet satirical actor, has highlighted this in his brillant sketches many times (about this type of bribery, see Simis, 1982; *Literaturnaia Gazeta*, January 22, 1984; *Pravda*, June 4, 1985).

## Pilfering

Soviet people are very tolerant toward the theft of state property. Of course, they are especially tolerant toward their own participation in this process. A special study of theft in Ivanovo textile plants established that workers of both sexes, of all ages, and of various educational backgrounds, take the same active part in pilfering (Gudilina, 1985, p. 34).

There is much evidence to suggest pilfering from Soviet enterprises and offices has become a sort of national sport. As Gorbachev mentioned in his report to the twenty-seventh party congress, people grab everything they find at their disposal (Gorbachev, 1986). The mass character of pilfering has been fully recognized by the Soviet mass media in 1985–86 (see, for instance, *Pravda*, March 31, 1986; *Rabotnitsa*, 1986, 7, p. 24; Olga Soroka, deputy procurator (an equivalent of a deputy of the attorney general in the United States) of the Soviet Union, "Income, Legal and Illegal" in the magazine *Chelovek i Zakon* ("The Individual and the Law"), 1986, 9, p. 7). According to the data of Chistiakov, a Soviet procurator, presented in a lecture in Moscow (September 10, 1985), 2 million people were arrainged by the courts for pilfering (*Strana i Mir*, 1986, 6, p. 37).

Pilfering flourishes primarily where consumer goods are produced or distributed, which is the main reason for the radical deterioration in the quality of goods. The food and light industries, their outlets, cafeterias and restaurants, hospitals, kindergartens, rest homes, as well as the industries producing electrical appliances, watches, car parts, and of course, the building industry that provides raw materials and parts for the construction of country houses, garages, and apartment improvements, are champions as places where embezzlement occurs (on pilfering building materials, see *Pravda*, December 12 and 19, 1984, March 31, 1986; pilfering in hospitals, see *Moskovskiie Novosti*, July 12, 1987).[5]

*Literaturnaia Gazeta* reported that of 1.6 million car parts produced by WAZ, the car plant on the Volga River, 1.1 million were pilfered (*Literaturnaia Gazeta*, September 12, 1984, p. 11). Agriculture competes with the food industry and the building industry in the amount of pilfering. Practically everything produced or used in this branch of the economy is stolen—grain, milk, cattle, etc. Stores, transportation services, the postal service, gas stations, and any other sector of the economy that deals with anything that can be used at home (about pilfering gas, see *Pravda*, December 10, 1984; *Rabotnitsa*, 1986, 7, p. 24) follow the other branches of industry in pilferage. Thefts in Soviet post offices, a phenomenon which was almost unknown until the 1970s, became a sharp national issue (see *Pravda*, March 18, 1985).

A reader of *Literaturnaia Gazeta* colorfully depicts his colleagues, in a plant far removed from food production or the textile industry, as literally stealing everything that they can take home (*Literaturnaia Gazeta*, September 16, 1984, p. 12). A *Pravda* journalist tells about the mass theft of parts from computerized machinery and even robots in the famous "Uralmash," a machine-building plant in the Ural,

(*Pravda*, March 30, 1986; see also *Sovietskaia Rossia*, January 30, 1986). Another *Pravda* journalist recounts a situation where all families in a small city became possessors of a new product not sold in state stores (*Pravda*, January 15, 1986; see also *Pravda*, April 1, 1986; *Nedelia*, 1986, #33, p. 17; *Pravda*, February 11, 1986; January 14, 1986).

CHAPTER
10

# Privatization and the New Social Differentiation

## The Attitudes of Soviet People toward the Emergence of a New Class Structure

Soviet society has definitely polarized in its attitudes toward privatization in the general sense and individually. Two variables can be used to guage Soviet views—the attitudes toward the right of people to exploit their official position for their personal interests and attitudes toward private labor activity.

The division of Soviet society into two classes—superiors and subordinates—is in many ways the best key for understanding the behavior and mentality of the Soviet people, a view shared by many students of Soviet society as well as by myself (see, for instance, Shlapentokh, 1984, 1986). However, attitudes toward privatization do not correlate with position in this class structure, mostly because privatization has been changing the nature of Soviet society, leading to a new class division, which to some extent determines and reflects the attitudes toward this process.

Certainly, a majority of the people, at least verbally, treat the exploitation of position in the state for individual interests and especially corruption, its highest form, as a negative phenomenon and greet any draconian measures against corrupt officials and ordinary workers with enthusiasm. At the same time, a significant part of the population strongly believes that the use of ones' standing in society for individual goals is unavoidable. This makes people value their jobs, which is especially important for bosses of all ranks. What is more, according to the views of these people, in the end the moderate exploitation of power for individual interests improves the quality of life at the expense of the state. People who feel that abuse of power should be recognized as a "normal phenomenon," even if disliked, point out that any campaign against corruption only increases the price of illegal services.

The Soviet people are also strongly divided in the evaluation of private labor activity. A significant number of people oppose any regular work outside social production and even regard moonlighting with suspicion. But even more people are sure that without expanding the private sector there is no chance for economic progress in the country (see Gennadii Batygin's article, "Virtue against Interest," in *Sotsiologicheskie Issledovaniia*, 1987).

Attitudes toward private activity are usually strongly correlated with attitudes toward decentralization of economic management in a socialist society. Defenders of private activity, as a rule, strongly support decentralization and marketization in the Soviet economy. However, the reverse statement is not always true; in a few cases, those who demand autonomy of the socialist enterprise from the central authorities are lukewarm or even hostile toward private activity.

The combination of variables for these two attitudes allows one to distinguish four major types of Soviet people: (1) the foes of any form of privatization, including corruption and private labor activity (let me call them "ideologues" or "zealots"); (2) the advocates of private activity as well as the foes of corruption ("liberals"); (3) the defenders of private activity and, with reservations, in some cases corruption ("materialists"); and (4) the foes of private activity and the supporters of moderate exploitation of power for individual interests ("conservative apparatchiks").

The first group consists mostly of older people with poor education, low social status, and low income. It is a strong advocate of equality among all groups and opposes the higher well-being of any group. A rather tiny core of apparatchiks who would like to see the resurrection of Soviet society based on genuine socialist principles also belongs to this first group. These people are impervious to any opposing argument in favor of inequality based on contribution. They do not recognize the right of intellectuals and managers to gain more than they can, using the same logic which rejects the so-called socialist principle "from each according to ability, each ability—according to its contribution." They, for instance, demand the egalitarian distribution of apartments and are strongly against inequality in this area (see the survey of letters to *Pravda*, February 10, 1986).

They do not acknowledge moral grounds for moonlighters, are fierce enemies of "shabashniks" (free-lance builders), and are against middlemen in the market earning big money even if their services are badly needed by people. Representing such views, Vladimir Kuz'mishchev, while acknowledging that shabashniks are hard workers and are regarded as "saviors" in the countryside where official building is miserable, nevertheless condemns them (*Pravda*, May 15, 1983; *Trud*, March 29, 1983; see also for the same attitudes toward private labor activity *Pravda*, June 6 and July 7, 1986; for a typical article signed by a worker *Pravda*, April 23, 1984; for the survey of readers *Pravda*, June 13, 1986).

In their perceptions of the economic world these people do not recognize the positive role of the supply and demand mechanism, price fluctuation, and the division of labor; nor the necessity to take into account overhead cost, personal skills, any sacrifice made by a person (such as renting a room in one's apartment), in rewarding human performance.

In fact, this group of people wants to eliminate any form of private economic activity and even demands the liquidation of collective farm markets in the country, or at least wants to forbid farmers to set their own prices (see Prelatov's survey of *Pravda* readers' letters, *Pravda*, February 1, 1986). Mikhail Vasin, a Pravda journalist with liberal tendencies, quotes letters that "demand that the private selling of flowers be forbidden immediately because it diverts people from the production of fruit and vegetables," "require the liquidation of private gardens and kitchen gardens because they divert owners from social production," and simply demand closing all markets (*Pravda*, September 10, 1983). Similar letters came to other newspapers (*Literaturnaia Gazeta*, November 23, 1983 and June 10, 1987).

From time to time, Soviet journalists, watching consistent antagonists of any form of privatization, depict its foes as honest individuals who in no way want to relinquish the ideals of socialism or communism as they were inculcated into them in their youth (see, for instance, Larisa Kuznetsova's article about agricultural specialist Lidia Kostenko, a good, honest person who considered the free market a personal insult, *Literaturnaia Gazeta*, December 12, 1984). A theoretician of this group is Vadim Rogovin (1984) and to some degree Alexander Shokhin (1986) who both emphasize "social justice" while almost completely ignoring the affects their egalitarian recommendations (abolishing interest for ordinary savings accounts, increasing taxes on private plots, strong constraints on inheritance, and others) would have on economic efficiency (see Vadim Rogovin's article in *Komsomol'skaia Pravda*, November 12, 1985; Andrei Nuikin in *Moskovskiie Novosti*, June 21, 1987; see also *Pravda*, August 28, 1980).

The ideologues are mainly opposed by the liberals, who also hate corruption and the hidden privileges of apparatchiks, but who recognize, unlike the ideologues, the right of people to a higher income. They feel that efficiency should be the major criterion in the evaluation of economic phenomena and are convinced of the superiority of private business over social production. Whereas the ideologues and conservatives have for decades avoided any comparison of the efficiency of the public and private sectors in agriculture as well as in other branches of the economy, since the 1960s liberals have taken any opportunity to show the people the real state of affairs. In the 1970s, they had to skirt censorship in various ways, but after 1982 they had ample opportunity to air their views (see, for instance, Zaslavskaia, 1986a and 1986b; Nikolai Petrakov's article in *Nedelia*, 1987, #45, p. 3) the articles of Alexander Nikitin, Anatolii Streliannyi, and Gennadii Lisichkin, three of the best Soviet economic journalists, in *Literaturnaia Gazeta*, February 19, November 12, December 3 and 10, 1986, respectively; Leonid Zhukhovistskii and Viacheslaw Kondratiev, prominent writers, in *Literaturnaia Gazeta*, October 15, 1986; *Nedelia*, 1987, #46; see also the discussion between the sociologists G. Batygin (who defended private activity) and L. Ionin in *Nedelia*, 1987, #40, pp. 13–14, and 1987, #42, p. 7).[1]

The liberals insist on the necessity of expanding private initiative in the nation. Of course, they range from very moderate advocates of private activity to the committed admirers of a pure market economy.[2] All liberals support the idea of family farms and family businesses in textile and food industries as well as in service and commerce. They believe in all forms of private activity in education, culture, health service, entertainment, and the vacation industry. Composed mostly of the socially active part of the Soviet population—professionals, the intelligentsia, skilled workers and farmers, as well as liberal apparatchiks—this group has much more realistic views on the functioning of the economic mechanism, rejects the notion of equality of results, and is against a legal limit on income.

Liberals in contrast to ideologues and conservative apparatchiks, accept as normal high prices at free markets and see an increase in supply as the only way to force prices down (as an example of such an approach to prices, see *Nedelia*, 1984, 137, pp. 6–7). They favor high income if it is earned by honest work and determined by real prices (see Gennadii Lisichkin, "Welfare at Other's Expense," *Literaturnaia Gazeta*, February 19, 1986; see also Nikitin, "The Offense of the Tsar—Operator or It Is Possible To Earn Too Much," *Literaturnaia Gazeta*, April 3, 1985, p. 10). Members of this group insist that private activity is compatible with Soviet political and social order and should be encouraged (see, for instance, Anatolii Makarov, "Private Worker?" in *Nedelia*, 1986, #46, p. 5; see also *Moskovskiie Novosti*, November 8, 1987).[3]

From 1983 to 1986, the Soviet mass media reflected the views of this group of the population less intensively than those of the first group, but much more so than in the past (see, for instance, *Pravda*, February 1, June 4, 1986).[4] Intellectuals, as the mouthpiece of the liberals, openly admire the Hungarian and Chinese economic reforms (see Fedor Burlatskii's article on China in *Literaturnaia Gazeta*, June 11, 1986, p. 7).

The third group, materialists, believes only in individual, personal interests and dismisses the possibility of the socialist state being able to check up on them. There are many young people in this group as well as members of the intelligentsia, Westernizers, and those who believe only democracy and political pluralism can help overcome Soviet problems.

The fourth group—conservative apparatchiks—view the expansion of private activity as well as the decentralization of the state economy as a direct danger to their position in society. They indirectly advocate the right of those in power to moderately exploit their position for their own interests as a form of reward for their arduous and responsible work. They justify this position, following Stalin's example, as being necessary to make apparatchiks devoted to the regime and conscientious executors of its will.

This group was dominant in the nation during Brezhnev's regime and became the main enemies of the economic and political course set by Gorbachev in 1985–86 (see Gorbachev, 1986, and especially his speech in Krasnodar, *Pravda*, September 19, 1986). Feeling that efficiency should be the main criterion in the decision-making process, they disregard the economic advantages of private activity and prefer the old economic model. Fedor Burlatskii's article "A Candid Conversation," describing the views of a Brezhnev and a Gorbachev apparatchik, is of special interest in this regard. Whereas a new type of apparatchik asks whether the state should burden itself with all handling of retail "trade and service," the old one points to the enrichment of new businessmen as a dangerous prospect (*Literaturnaia Gazeta*, October 1, 1986, p. 101; the economic views of such apparatchiks are expressed by Mikhail Rutkevich, 1985); see also Nikitin's article "How We Sold Apples," *Literaturnaia Gazeta*, October 13, 1986).

In fact, behind the four types described here lie two latent variables: equality and efficiency. Liberals, assuming an antagonism between equality in results and the efficiency of a socialist economy, clearly prefer the second to the first; ideologues manifest their indifference to efficiency if it comes into conflict with equality; conservative apparatchiks, unwilling to face reality, suppose that both goals can be achieved in a socialist society; and materialists believe that neither can be attained in such a society.

These groups also differ in their attitudes toward the capacity of the Soviet state to solve the problems it faces. On a scale that measures the different views on the capacity of the state to achieve the desirable goals of efficiency and equality, the ideologues, who believe in the might of the state to eliminate the second economy and corruption, are at the top. In the middle are the liberals and conservative apparatchiks, who also believe in the high potential of the state, but much less than the ideologues. The materialists, convinced that the state is in fact helpless in combating both private activity and corruption, are at the bottom.

What is the size of each group? As with other typologies of the Soviet population, it is not an easy question to answer, even approximately. Nobody in the Soviet Union ever conducted a survey about the expansion of private activity in the country. Only materials published in *Literaturnaia Gazeta*, *Pravda*, and other newspapers in the last three years, particularly the surveys of letters sent to these newspapers, can serve as sources of some information on this subject. Certainly, these letters, and especially those particularly mentioned in the newspaper surveys, are not representative of the Soviet population. However, with all these flaws, they give us a unique glimpse into the mentality of the Soviet people.

The discussion about high earnings revealed that readers of *Literaturnaia Gazeta* (who represent the most educated part of the population) are polarized on this subject and a considerable number of them manifested their loathing of a high income even if earned "honestly" (*Literaturnaia Gazeta*, August 21, 1985, p. 12; see also another survey of readers in *Literaturnaia Gazeta*, February 19, 1986). The survey of *Sovietskaia Kul'tura*'s readers about people with high incomes revealed the same belief (*Sovietskaia Kul'tura*, January 25, 1986), as did readers' letters to *Kommunist* in response to T. Zaslavskaia's article in this magazine (*Kommunist*, 1986, #17, pp. 61–68). At the same time as can be seen from other evidence, a considerable part, perhaps even more than half, of the population supports private activity in the economy (see *Pravda*, September 10, 1985; *Literaturnaia Gazeta*, April 23, 1986, p. 12).

## The New Stratification

So far I have discussed the attitudes toward privatization. Typing the Soviet people based on their real involvement with private activity only partially overlaps the typing based on their attitudes toward this activity.

The class of people involved in private activity are in opposition to the class of people engaged only in work in the public sector. Each class consists of two clearly different strata: the hard workers—private fanatics—who channel their energy and inventiveness into the production of goods and services, and the exploiters of their official position in the Soviet state at various levels in the hierarchy. Certainly, these two strata are not mutually exclusive. Quite a few workaholics are corrupt, a situation reminiscent of the early bourgeois class that contained the captains of industry (to use Marx's expression), numerous speculators, and merchants embroiled in the corruption of the bureaucracy.

Soviet propaganda and even honest intellectuals identified a whole new class of private Soviet businessmen as wheeler-dealers, nouveaux riches who, closely allied with the bureaucracy, emerged from behind the scenes in the 1970s and started to publicly display their well-being and connections. To some degree, official propaganda managed to obscure the issue from the public by confusing these people with those honest workers who cannot tolerate the slow pace of social production and the low income linked to it.

Of course, those who benefit from corruption are more influential and visible than "pure" producers of goods and services in the private sector. The last type is even portrayed as worse than a wheeler-dealer and for good reason—Soviet authors can much easier flagellate crooks than an individual who works eighteen hours a day. For this reason, the Soviet mass media is ambivalent toward *shabashniks*, free-lance builders reknown in the country for their extreme conscientiousness and diligence.

However, most members of both strata are inclined to demonstrate their opulence and well-being simply because only the satisfaction from conspicuous consumption, as well as its comfort, provides the incentives to work outside the legal work system.[5]

The emergence of the new class significantly changed the social atmosphere in the country. Often flaunting their "high life," luxury goods (practically all of foreign origin), and their ability to hobnob with those in power (unlike the new class, apparatchiks must conceal the quality of their lives and their liaisons), the new nouveau rich class ("they are boisterous, conceited, and often aggressive" generalizes a *Pravda* journalist, *Pravda*, July 6, 1986, p. 3) set up norms for the rest of the population, especially for young people. A prominent Soviet journalist wrote in early 1986 that "present millionaires are not at all embarrassed about their riches" (*Nedelia*, 1986, 8, p. 13). B. Kravtsov, minister of justice, concurs with this journalist, complaining that these people "are not embarrassed to acquire expensive things, luxuries" (*Pravda*, June 6, 1986). Ultimately, the example of the new class has depreciated the legal income and pushed people into looking for various sorts of income outside their legally authorized work.

In a survey of readers' letters to *Sovietskaia Kul'tura*, a journalist cites many who are full of hatred for "those crooks, businessmen, and twisters who brazenly look condescendingly and with irony at honest workers who cannot live so lavishly as they." Another reader recounted how she, a scholar, found herself in the company of salespeople who felt contempt for her because each of them could earn more in one day than a scholar in a year (*Sovietskaia Kul'tura*, January 25, 1986; see also Dubko, 1985, pp. 50–51).

A prominent Soviet writer, Boris Vasiliev, describes his perception of the triumph of materialism and nouveaux riches in his country: "[I] look with hatred at those who devote their lives to heinous accumulation, who see the single joy only in grabbing as much as possible, to fetch more and more things into their apartment. Such people are able to commit any mean act, they do not even have an idea of what is permissible, they do not believe in other styles of life besides the all-embracing desire 'to not be worse than others.' Oh, these modern kulaks, with what contempt they look at those who do not have foreign rags and appliances. And the most terrible thing is that you can meet such people under the roof of a research institute or in the rest home for writers, in the new quarters of big cities or in the home of a very good artisan" (*Literaturnaia Gazeta*, August 15, 1984).

Oblivious of the great hatred the new class has engendered for itself, it has begun to establish its own lifestyle, competing in this respect with intellectuals. Being a product of the drive for conspicuous consumption, this class has very much strengthened that process.

The desire to satisfy all these material needs pushes millions of Soviet people toward various illegal or semilegal activities, mostly in the legal state economy or in the second, civil, society. As *Pravda*'s journalists wrote about these people, "their life goal—personal prosperity at any price," They are possessed by the devastating craving for getting consumer goods without hard work, and they want it all at once: apartment, car, fashionable clothes, and "prestigious gold" jewelry (*Pravda*, July 23, 1986; see also Bestuzhev-Lada, "The Individual among Things," *Literaturnaia Gazeta*, November 23, 1983; *Motiashov*, *The Power of Things and the Power of Man*, 1985).

Privatization is both fueled by and stimulates negative attitudes toward occupations of vital importance to the country. Privatization coupled with consumerism has fanned envy, which has become a leading psychological feature of Soviet life, in direct contrast to the past. More and more often the Soviet press addresses envy generated by conspicuous consumption as an acute social problem (see, for instance, L. Mikhailova's article "Who Has To Hide Eyes?", *Pravda*, June 6, 1985, p. 3).

Privatization has led to a decline in the prestige of higher education as well as the occupations of professor, scholar, and engineer. In the 1970s millions of Soviet professionals left their positions for work in services, commerce, transportation, and even manual labor if the pay was high enough (see *Pravda*, June 23, 1984; May 20, 1985; *Literaturnaia Gazeta*, March 21, 1981, June 4, 1986; *Nedelia*, 1986, #5, p. 6; EKO, 1980, 5, pp. 35–37).

The new social constellation in the country has already been depicted in movies, plays, and numerous literary works. In the famous Soviet movie, Riasanov's *Rail Station for Two* (1983), a market speculator boasts before a musician and another person about his video recorder, a contraption they had never seen before and perhaps had never even heard of. In another Riasanov movie, *Garage* (1980), the director of a market, who is clearly embroiled in numerous illegal activities that bring her big money and even enable her to bribe the deputy director of a research institute (in order to get access to the garage of this institute), could scarcely hide her contempt for scholars and their childlikeness with respect to "real life."

If the wheeler-dealers in these movies were secondary to the main heroes, by the middle of the 1980s a number of movies presented them as the main characters—Alexander Chervinskii's *The Blond Around the Corner*, and Iulii Raizman's *The Times of Desires*. In all these movies the heroes easily dominate honest people, and as the masters of life achieve all their goals. Along with these movies, a growing number of Soviet novels and plays in the early 1980s began to depict the new Soviet bourgeois, who looks down on those who can rely only on their legal income and who have, from their point of view, a miserable life. Vladimir Arro's play, *Look Who Has Come*, and Edward Radzinskii's play, *Sport Scenes* (1981), received special attention for their presentation of impertinent representatives of the new class.

After some hesitation, Soviet social scientists have also approached the subject, however mostly indirectly. Only Tatiana Zaslavskaia, in her famous *Novosibirsk Memo* (1984), dared raise this subject relatively openly.

During the Brezhnev regime the new social stratification of Soviet society was completely ignored by the authorities. Following the dogma about how Soviet society had achieved almost perfect social homogeneity, the ideologues and politicians completely avoided any issues that could undermine this belief (see, for instance, Filippov and Slesarev, 1981; Rutkevich, 1982; Semenov, 1977; Siniavskii, 1982).

Recognition of the growing social inequality in the country was one of the first statements of Andropov's and then of Gorbachev's regime (Andropov, 1983; Gorbachev, 1986). A practically new concept—social justice—was advanced by post-Brezhnev leaders. This concept had three targets—lazy workers getting an "average salary," receivers of "nonlabor income," and apparatchiks, with illegal and even legal privileges—and was generally directed against those who profit from the privatization of Soviet society (see Afanasiev, 1985; Rogovin, 1984; Rogovin and Usanov, 1985; Rutkevich, 1985).

# Conclusion

The withdrawal of human energy, emotions, and interests from activity controlled by the socialist state is one of the most important processes going on in the contemporary world. This process undermines the political and economic system which is dominant in the Soviet Union, China, Poland, and all other socialist countries. It hurts the economy especially, retards technological progress, spreads corruption, demoralizes people, creates a new stratification, and indeed threatens the whole structure of socialist society.

As a matter of fact, privatization is the combination of two processes: one which is connected with the radical decline in the authority of the state in Soviet society, the other with the creation of civil society based on the private activity of the Soviet people.

The Soviet state has lost its prestige, foremost, as a manager. It has become obvious to the majority of the people that the state is unable to run the economy efficiently and produce the goods and services necessary for the populace. State control over the economy is accompanied by gigantic waste of natural and human resources, raw materials, and equipment. The state's civil economy is unable to produce most goods at the level of world standards, and the Soviet people, especially the youth, consistently hunt for all sorts of foreign goods. Moreover, the state economy has proven inept even at sustaining the previous high rate of economic growth based on low-quality goods or of guaranteeing the reproduction of assets. An increasing number of school, hospital, and other institutional buildings are becoming decrepit, while Soviet factories are replete with obsolete equipment. Even more remarkable is the fact that the Soviet state on its seventieth anniversary cannot provide the people with a sufficient amount of food and must import grain, meat, butter, and fruit from abroad.

The state has also been incapable of promoting science, and despite tremendous expenditures, Soviet scholars are in most areas far behind their foreign colleagues—which explains why technological progress in the country is extremely slow and is sustained mostly by imitation of Western achievements.

The low quality of the state medical services accounts for the systematic deterioration of the health of the people. The death rate is climbing, particularly among males and infants.

The Soviet state has also demonstrated its ineptitude at satisfying the cultural needs of its people, who again have looked to the West for interesting movies, novels, and music.

There is only one sphere of state activity which has gained genuine recognition by the majority of the population: foreign policy and defense. The Soviet state has been successful in persuading the average individual to believe that it protects the interests of the country in the best possible way. Only the Afghan war has to some degree destroyed consensus on this issue.

However, no matter how strong the patriotic feelings of the people are (Russians above all), in a period of peace with no direct threat to the country the material needs of the people dictate most of their behavior and attitudes in their everyday lives.

The people do not respect the domestic political activity of the state either. Being a member of various organizations, the average individual in no way considers them—from the party to trade unions—to represent his or her interests but rather looks at them as branches of the state which uses them for its own purposes. The people have only contempt for the phoney elections of governmental bodies as well as the state-controlled mass media that provides them with only incomplete or even distorted information about domestic and international developments.

The people identify the state with apparatchiks, Soviet bureaucrats. During this period of *glasnost*, when the people are relatively free to reveal their feelings and thoughts, they express just how deep their hatred of their superiors is. They see them as totally corrupted individuals who have covered the country with a network of mafias and who are ready to do anything in order to defend their legal and illegal privileges.

In general, the people consider their society unable to evaluate human effort, skill, and initiative correctly and to reward individuals' contributions to the common cause correspondingly. They strongly believe that efficient performance has little or even an adverse influence on promotion and that only conformism and compliance with one's superiors are the conditions for prosperity in the Soviet Union.

Even as they confront various deficiencies of the state machine in their everyday lives, many people are far from questioning the fundamentals of the Soviet system. The state, though inefficient in most of its activities, is strong enough to severely punish (even if not by resorting to Stalin's measures) anyone who challenges its political monopoly. Therefore, the people manage to adjust to the state by developing a mythological level in their thinking, which accepts most official dogmas and at the same time in no way affects their material behavior (mostly directed against the interests of the state). To a considerable degree *glasnost* has destroyed this subtle balance between mythology and behavior, forcing people to reconsider many of their general views on the nature of their society.

The growing alienation from the state and the loss of belief in the state's fairness strongly accelerated the process of privatization in Soviet society. It began with the decline of people's interest in working efficiently for the state. This gave rise to the gradually increasing importance of family, friends, and other private institutions to the lives of even the most energetic and ambitious.

The process of privatization got a strong impetus from bureaucrats who gradually decreased their identification with the state after Stalin's death and who began more and more brazenly to exploit their positions in the state machine for their own private interests. Corrupted superiors could only stimulate their subordinates to ignore the interests of the state and to take any opportunity—from show work to pilfering—to satisfy their own needs.

With the withdrawal of their energy and emotions from the state, the people gradually expanded the level of their private activity in all spheres of society—the economy, culture, education, the health service, and even politics. With more frequent interaction among people acting as private individuals, a genuine civil society is playing an increasing role in the country. The coexistence of the first (official) and second (unofficial, civil) societies has become the most important feature of the Soviet Union as well as of almost all socialist countries which have left behind the period of mass terror.

Privatization along with the expansion of civil society has evolved in Poland and Hungary much further than in the Soviet Union. In China, Vietnam and East Germany, where privatization has reached a high level in the economy, civil society in other societal spheres is making only its first inroads.

It is only natural in the Soviet Union as well as in other socialist countries, for the state sooner or later to react to the expansion of the illegal civil society which persistently undermines the tenets of the state's political and economic systems. In fact, there are only two ways to react to privatization. One, the Stalinist way, uses draconian methods to stop corruption and reduce the illegal civil society to a minimum, particularly the second economy, and it replaces the old cadres with new ones, more devoted to the state. The other way assumes instead that politics should encourage private initiative and will legalize many activities in civil society, trying to exploit it for the benefit of the state, while still combating the illegal abuse of power.

The main problem with the second option is its incompatibility with the existing political order, and in particular, with the political monopoly of the party. The expansion of legal civil society inescapably makes some political liberalization of the regime necessary, a serious price for the acceleration of economic growth and technological progress.

The political elite in each socialist country contains factions which support one of these options. Neither can claim that their policy will guarantee the survival of the existing political and social order, since there are too many variables that affect the implementation of any policy. In the Soviet Union, for example, among those variables of special importance are relations with the United States and the multiethnic character of the country.

The necessity of having at least military parity with the United States is a powerful impetus to implement any reforms that might help overcome the technological gap with the West. But the same reforms encourage the liberal movement in the country and the drive for democratization. And democratization can only exacerbate ethnic conflicts in the country, allowing ethnic minorities to be more active in their yearning for autonomy and even independence.

Gorbachev turned out to be a leader who, in contrast to Brezhnev, decided to challenge the problems engendered by privatization, which flourished in the 1970s. Starting with a rather neo-Stalinist program focusing on "negative action"—the purge of corrupt apparatchiks, the strengthening of labor ethics, and the reduction of the second economy—he gradually moved in the opposite direction, placing more emphasis on positive stimuli, in particular liberalization and the expansion of the legal civil society.

It is impossible to predict what faction in the Soviet political establishment will gain the upper hand in the next historical period, whether the liberal wing of the political elite is strong enough to implement its reforms or will yield to neo-Stalinists who believe that radical administrative measures against negative trends are more fit for the nature of Soviet society. Nor is it possible to rule out that the Kremlin will return to Brezhnev's policy of consistent conservatism and unwillingness to make any serious changes in the Soviet structure for fear that its whole edifice will crumble.

However, in my opinion, the process of privatization is unavoidable for socialist societies of the Soviet type, even if there are attempts to halt it and to react with even more draconian means. The Soviet Union, as well as China and Poland, will continue in the last part of this century to evolve into a complex mixture of state, private, and semiprivate institutions, producing in the coming decades a new society that will be different not only from the Stalinist one but also from the Soviet society we now know. Whether this society will be stronger or weaker than at present, whether the quality of life will be lower or higher, whether the Soviet empire will even survive all future mutations produced by privatization are questions that cannot be answered today. Too many other variables—domestic and international—join privatization in changing the face of Soviet society.

# Notes

## Introduction

1. Some authors also use the public-private paradigm very broadly to define any activity outside the family as public (see, for instance, the literature on women's issues: Elshtain's *Public Man, Private Woman*, 1981; see also Gamarnikov et al., 1983; Saraceno, 1984; Siltanen and Stanworth, 1984; Tiano, 1984).

2. Since the nineteenth century the term "civil society" has been used by historians analyzing the transformation of absolutist monarchies into bourgeois societies (the term "bourgeois" was used practically as a synonym for "civil"). Of recent publications, see for instance, Koselleck's *State and Society in Prussia 1815–1848* (1962) and Antony Black's *Guilds and Civil Society in European Political Thought from the Twelfth Century to the Present* (1984). See also Brucker, 1977; Sperber, 1985, and others.

3. The terms "civic" and "civil" societies are often used in the literature as synonyms. However, in common with many authors (for instance, Cohen, 1983; Giner, 1985; Pierson, 1984; Rodger, 1985, and others), I prefer to use the latter term to characterize an activity or institution different from one directed by the state, and the former term for denoting activity important for the whole of society, as when we speak of "civic culture" or "civic duties." The terms "civic world" or "civic sociology" are used equivalently to "civil society" (see Brucker's *The Civic World of Early Renaissance Florence*, 1977; see also Ross, 1932; Ross and McCaull, 1926).

4. Alexis de Tocqueville did not use the term "civil society" in his works. But in *Democracy in America* (1835) and *The Old Regime and the French Revolution* (1856) he analyzed social processes strictly in terms of the public-private dichotomy. Both terms—public and private—and usually in opposition to each other, appear on practically every page of both his major works. In speaking about the role of political associations, as well as of many other institutions in America, he in fact opposes civil society to government and presents it as a main custodial force for freedom. In his view the conflict between the private citizen and the French monarchy was one of the major factors which led to the Revolution.

5. Discussing the role of the welfare state Mark Lillas, an editor of *The Public Interest*, in the article "What is the Civic Interest," strongly opposes "public" to "civic" in the understanding of "public interests." He describes two traditions; the first is social democratic, traditional, and paternalistic in substance, regarding individuals in both public and private spheres only as consumers. Another tradition, which Lillas links to the New Deal, sees individuals as citizens who have duties as well as rights with regard to society.

Following Daniel Bell's *The Cultural Contradictions of Capitalism*, Lillas wants to separate public and private needs and refuses to reduce the former to the latter as do those who, disregarding the real public goods—public transportation, libraries, parks, and so on—tend to redistribute all public funds among individuals. As a result of the mixture of public and civic elements, American society now experiences "public affluence and civic squalor" (Lillas, 1985).

It is curious that the emphasis on social, public needs, as well as on the civic duties of the individual, are typical of Soviet ideology. See, for instance, Fedoseev's textbook *Scientific Communism* (1985), which uses the same phraseology about the superiority of public interests over private ones as a legitimization of the existing political order.

6. In this connection the debate among official Soviet political scientists and legal scholars about the relationship between the Soviet state and the party is noteworthy. Some of them insist on the old postulate about the party as being "above the state" and as having the highest moral and political authority (see, for example, Shevtsov, 1979). At the same time others, feeling uncomfortable with such a position that is incompatible with the claim of the democratic character of Soviet society and with the direct involvement of party committees in state activity, try to persuade the authorities that it is more convenient to speak about the party as an element of the state (using this term in a broad sense) (Burlatskii, 1977; Shakhnazarov and Burlatskii, 1980, pp. 10–23; see also Brown, 1981).

7. Instead of privatization, some authors use the term "privatism" to denote the indifference of the average citizen to public affairs, primarily political (Kinder and Sears, 1985, pp. 660–61; Turkel, 1980).

## Chapter 1

1. The inspection by political police of the library card of a person suspected by the KGB of engaging in undesirable activity should not be surprising. As Andrei Siniavskii recounts in his autobiographical novel *Good Night*, when the KGB got on his track as a person who published anti-Soviet stories in the West under the pseudonym "Abram Terz" his card in the Lenin library, as a woman librarian indirectly told him, was also studied (Terz, 1984).

2. The Society of Sobriety was created in 1985 as part of the campaign against alcoholism initiated by Gorbachev. As is usual in such cases, the party committees wanted to make the local branches of this society as large as possible and proclaimed membership in it as a sign of party loyalty. But even *Pravda* was forced to take a stance against the artificial growth of the local antialcoholic organization. (See *Pravda*'s article "'Embraced . . ." April 27, 1986.)

3. In this respect the famous Seattle–Leningrad TV exchange, the citizens' summit carried out in late 1986 by Phil Donahue and Vladimir Pozner, was especially interesting. Practically all Soviet participants, unlike Americans, backed their country's official views on all subjects raised during the debates, even if they were forced to tell blatant lies, such as that Soviet people are always in agreement with their government and that if they were not, they could reelect different politicians. It is very likely that a considerable number of the Soviet participants were aware of these and other mendacities but had no compunctions about their behavior and were not ashamed of their lies

before relatives and friends. These people were, as can be judged from other sources, convinced that they performed their patriotic duty, where all means are acceptable in confrontation with the enemy. Of course, a significant number of other participants, even if carefully selected by Soviet officials, would have spoken differently if fear of the consequences was not present.

4. Since the early 1980s the family is more and more often considered a production unit, particularly in agriculture. A family farm as a part of a collective or state farm is a concept that became inceasingly popular in the Soviet Union and was even praised by Gorbachev at the twnety-seventh party congress (see Gorbachev, 1986; Shlapentokh, 1984a).

## Chapter 2

1. Like Klopov and Shkaratan, two other leading Soviet industrial sociologists, Aitov reflected closely the convoluted development of the Soviet political system in his books. Starting in the 1960s with relatively objective studies (see, for instance, Aitov, 1968) he, as the two others, excelled in lauding the high labor ethics and productivity of the Soviet workers (1981). But soon thereafter, even more quickly than Shkaratan and Klopov, once the new regime was installed he left (probably with pleasure) the exercises in apology and again started to publish more sober books, including one with the provocative title of *Good and Bad Workers* (1983; see also 1985).

2. Definitions of professional creativity, apparently very different, all assume diversity as the essential feature of creative activity (see, for instance, Maier, 1970; Parnes et al., 1977; Stan, 1974; Vernon, 1970). All the authors compare this activity to routine, monotonous work, using as synonyms or correlates such terms as initiative, novelty, and originality. This stance is especially characteristic of sociologists dealing with work attitudes (Iadov et al., 1967; Iadov, 1979, p. 127; Kohn, 1969, pp. 35–37).

3. As could be expected, gender is a very strong factor influencing attitudes toward work as such. Women much more often indicate their readiness to leave work if they can get the same amount of money without it. In one study 24 percent of male Armenians would quit work as opposed to 53 percent of women who would do the same (Kuregian, 1979, p. 99). Family size is another important factor on work attitudes.

4. The survey used by Valentina Alekseeva (Kharcheva) is an exception. Being asked about their main life goals, 40 percent of 400 young workers (1974–75) put "success in work" in first place followed by "the respect of colleagues" (Alekseeva, 1983, p. 130).

5. The respondents in Changli's surveys were ready to answer the most ludicrous questions and were eager to choose the most absurd of the options offered as their own opinion. For instance, when answering "what do you feel when you are declared as the victor in socialistic emulation," 90 percent picked the choices "very strong" and "strong enough" in reflecting their feelings toward "the necessity to help rivals" (Changli, 1979b, p. 179). At the same time, respondents almost unanimously rejected the idea that their success is important because of the "glory" which accompanies it (Ibid., p. 182).

6. Patrushev and Razmolova asked the workers of the famous Kirov plant in Leningrad (1983) about "the moral responsibility of the workers for the use of working time of others." Eighty-seven percent of the respondents answered positively to this

highly loaded question, which in 1983 must be viewed in the context of the height of Andopov's crusade against poor discipline. However, even in answering this question young people differed significantly in comparison with older ones. Among people below thirty-five 81 percent supported the statement while 96 percent of those above fifty supported it (Patrushev and Razmolova, 1984, p. 100).

7. Gennadii Osipov and his colleagues stood out even among the most conspicuous ideological sociologists in their desire to produce data pleasing to the authorities. Without qualification they described the evolution of labor attitudes in Gorki workers as having made enormous progress: "In 1979, in comparison with 1969, the proportion of workers with an orientation toward diversity in work increased by 1.5 times; toward autonomy, 9 times; on responsibility, 4.5 times; and general orientation toward creativity, 3 times" (Osipov et al., 1982, p. 18).

These data are in such discrepancy with Soviet reality that Iadov, in an unprecedented move for a Soviet sociologist (public criticism is almost unknown in this field), expressed, albeit mildly, doubt on the validity of Osipov's figures (see Iadov, 1983, p. 59).

8. It is interesting to compare two of Iadov's publications (1982 and 1983) on the results of his longitudinal studies. Between publication of the articles was a change in regime. The first work is almost entirely lacking in figures and completely ignores negative tendencies. The second article, published in the Soviet sociological magazine (July–August–September 1983) with a quotation from Andropov demanding "the sober approach" to Soviet reality, is filled with much interesting data and discusses—indirectly—some negative trends in the attitudes of young workers (Iadov, 1982, 1983).

The article about the same study published by Iadov's colleagues in the next issue of the magazine (October–November–December 1983) heralded a new step in Soviet sociology. New data from the Leningrad study was released, and this time the authors could speak openly of negative developments (Golofast et al., 1983).

9. A specific indicator of the deterioration of labor ethics during Brezhnev's era is the increase in the number of people satisfied with their work. If data of Osipov and his colleagues (Osipov et al., 1982, p. 21) that the number of satisfied workers in Gorki in 1975 reached the level of 72 percent and the number of workers not satisfied with work decreased between 1965 and 1979 by 2.6 times are correct, it can only suggest that the standard of workers' behavior in this period had become significantly more lax.

10. Contrary to the usual tendency of Soviet sociologists to glorify the positive effect of the rise of education on productivity, Shkaratan's study in Leningrad (1970 and 1976–77) concluded that highly educated workers (graduation from a secondary school or technical college) show small improvement in productivity over those with only an elementary school education. Shkaratan's data, consisting of scores on a five-point scale (with one as minimal), reveal almost no difference in the fulfillment of production norms (2.50 and 2.48), the quality of work (2.53 and 2.55), discipline (2.54 and 2.59), initiative (2.15 and 2.19), and in inventive activity (1.59 and 1.53) (Shkaratan, 1985, p. 109).

11. Only 38 percent of all workers questioned in Moscow and Perm in 1970 thought that their income corresponded to their work contribution (Komozin, 1983, p. 113).

12. This figure aroused some amazement because it is so low. According to other data the number of those who are satisfied with their salary is much higher—about 40–50 percent (see Klopov, 1985, p. 117).

13. At the same time, a considerable number of people are ready to work hard in order to improve their living conditions. According to studies in Siberia (1982 and

1984), up to 29 percent of workers willingly work overtime. Seventeen percent of the residents of Siberian cities have additional part-time jobs, and 27 percent wanted them (Zaslavskaia et al., 1986). However, as L. Goldin, a social scientist, asserts, the number of those who wanted to work overtime at their legal job in the 1960s was two times higher (*Literaturnaia Gazeta*, March 27, 1985, p. 10).

14. According to Shubkin's data, in the Novosibirsk region the willingness of girls to work after secondary school declined, from 8 percent in 1963 to 3 percent in 1983, whereas the respective data for boys was 7 and 16 (Shubkin and Babushkina, 1986, p. 38).

15. In evaluating these data it is necessary to take into account that, as some investigations show (see for instance, Chernovolenko et al., 1979; Kriagzhde, 1981; Rubina, 1981; Zuzin, 1978), the attraction of an occupation depends very much on the chances of people to get into it. In other words, all other things being equal, the better the chances, the more desirable the occupation will be. Therefore, the attitudes of Soviet youth toward the occupation of worker are even worse, because many of them know they will be compelled to become workers and so, to some degree, they even overestimate the workers' occupation (those who work in an unpopular occupation evaluate it much higher than the public opinion in general) (Cherednichenko and Shubkin, 1985, p. 67; Shubkin, 1984, p. 83).

16. Even such a brilliant and shrewd sociologist as Vladimir Shubkin, and his coauthor, cannot avoid some clichés imposed by ideology. After finding exhaustive data demonstrating the almost total reluctance of young people to become manual laborers, Shubkin shifts some responsibility to the fathers, especially if they are workers themselves. He found them "as navigators in professional orientation . . . unequal to the occasion," leading to the sad fact that such a "low percent of children from workers' families want to choose the occupation of their fathers." Paternal reprimands to indolent children, such as "If you do not stop dawdling you will be as me, a worker," are also responsible for the wrong professional disposition of young people (Cherednichenko and Shubkin, 1985, p. 68).

17. The study of the labor motivation of highly educated people or of children from educated families is especially difficult. These people are much more receptive to the dominant values in their milieu, mostly because the role of prestige grows with the rise of education and general culture. Secondary education can be considered the turning point in this respect. The absorption with what others think about oneself (as Erving Goffmann described it in *Presentation of Self in Everyday Life*) is already very strong in high school seniors.

First starting to conduct mass surveys in the late 1950s, Soviet sociologists were not aware of this phenomenon. Western textbooks, the main source of methodological knowledge during this period, were not helpful because practically all of them ignored this subject (see Shlapentokh, 1985a). Adding to the confusion, in this period creativity, science, education, and culture were at the peak of their prestige, and it was legal for intellectuals to praise them (Soviet ideology highly lauds these values too). But this indirectly opposed several Soviet dogmas: for instance, "the leading role of the working class in socialist society."

Leading Soviet sociologists accepted without criticism the data in Shubkin's study of high school graduates, where only 2 percent of his respondents claimed high salary was the motive in their choice of a profession (Shubkin, 1966, p. 188). Other Soviet sociologists also accepted at face value data about the decisive role of creativity and diversity of work as the main determinants of labor attitudes (Iadov et al., 1967).

By the late 1970s Soviet sociologists became much more critical, and in a number of publications they demonstrated their deep understanding of the influence of desirable values on respondents (see, for instance, Boiko, 1980; Popova, 1984; Popova and Moin, 1983). But, a number of sociologists still refused to look at survey data critically. So, for instance, Raphail Filippov and his Bulgarian coauthor cite that 42 percent of students in the Soviet Union and 46 percent in Bulgaria consider "good salary" as of little or no importance in the choice of a job with no qualms about reliability at all (Filippov and Mitev, 1984, p. 104).

In this respect the work of Melvin Kohn and his coauthors deserves special attention. Using sophisticated analysis, they found that content of work and occupational experience have a great influence on the values of respondents, especially on their attitudes toward their job. Unfortunately, they did not explore the influence that dominant values (autonomy among professionals, for instance) have on the verbal information people are willing to give, or the impact of the human tendency to laud what one has (a particular job, for instance) on the same information (see Kohn, 1969, 1978, 1981, 1983; Kohn and Schooler, 1973, 1982).

18. The data demonstrating the number of people who left their jobs because of the character of work also reflect, at least partially, a dissatisfaction with material reward, such as with those who complained about poor prospects for professional growth or about badly organized work, which accounts for low salaries.

19. Of course, those who finished so-called special schools (English, mathematical, and others) and whose parents in almost all cases belonged to the political or cultural elite, or at least to the intelligentsia, became workers only 1.8 times more often (Kozyrev et al., 1975, p. 57).

20. One indication of the attractiveness of big cities is that people still want to move to them despite the fact that most newcomers will face a radical deterioration in their housing conditions. Among workers who came to Moscow (1979 survey), 71 percent had previously lived in their own home, 12 percent in individual apartments, only 6 percent in dormitories and the rest with relatives or in communal apartments. Now in Moscow, 87 percent live in dormitories, only 2 percent in individual apartments, and none in their own home. The chances of these people getting their own apartment in Moscow in the next five to seven years are very slim, but despite this young people strive to live in the capital (Moiseenko 1983, p. 21).

21. If the value of the "budget basket of goods," i.e., goods necessary for the sustenance of the family, in the Russian republic is taken as 1, its value in the Ural region will be 1.1, and in the Far East 1.8 (Aitov, 1985, p. 69). Also, the cultural facilities in the remote regions are much worse than in the European part of the country. Movie theaters in the European part of the country are often empty, yet only 4 percent of residents in remote cities can go to them as often as they wish (Borshchevskii, 1983, p. 44).

## Chapter 3

1. In 1986, under the new Gorbachev regime, the ruling elite for the first time in Soviet history yielded to the pressure of the intelligentsia and—publicly—cancelled two decisions adopted by the previous regime. One was related to the rerouting of Siberian

rivers toward the south and the other was the building of a monument in Moscow in honor of the victory over Hitler. The decision of the Politburo to annul these projects in deference to public opinion was published in the Soviet press (*Pravda*, August 16, 1986).

2. It is noticeable that some Soviet sociologists, contrary to the data, assert that on the average 20–40 percent of people who received questionnaires in the mail in a general survey (i.e., not addressed to the contingent of people to the issues involved) sent them back without being prompted with a special reward to do so (see Osipov, 1983, p. 410; Rukavishnikov et al., 1984, p. 110). In numerous studies that I conducted in the Soviet Union over a period of ten years, the return rate was always 5–6 percent (only in the *Pravda* survey of 1977 did the return rate reach 10 percent). This was the case in the mail surveys of *Izvestia* readers (1966 and 1968), *Literaturnaia Gazeta* readers (1967 and 1970), and others. The use of special means (rewards or reminders) in the Soviet Union has only increased the return rate up to 10–15 percent. It is easy to explain why some sociologists exaggerate the rate of return: it is considered a significant indicator of political activity in the country.

3. The authors of the letters are much more socially active in all other respects: they take the floor often in meetings (up to 80 percent) and are much more visible in voluntary social work (up to 60–70 percent) (see Prokhorov, 1981, p. 217; Tokarovskii, 1976, pp. 119, 125; Verkhovskaia, 1972, pp. 152–53; see also Davydchenkov, 1970, p. 152). Even among the authors of the letters to *Komsomol'skaia Pravda*, the newspaper of the Young Communist League, education is strongly correlated with this activity—45 percent had a higher education (Verkhovskaia, 1972, p. 99).

4. Another sociologist, Sergei Plaksii, did not include in his survey any response option that directly suggested that the public good is the purpose of social work. All his alternatives implied personal, even selfish, interests in doing social work, including a response he regarded as the most desirable ideologically—"Social work enhances your authority in the collective, makes you close to it, and helps you to influence its life." This alternative, however, was chosen by only 75 percent; many (including those who picked this alternative) chose even more personal alternatives—about two-thirds said "social work enlarges their vision of the world," 6 percent said it "allows you to be visible," and 8 percent "because I was forced to do it" (Plaksii, 1982, p. 104).

5. The results would have been even more striking had the sociologists asked the respondents to pick only one alternative (instead of as many as the respondent wished), which prompted many to seemingly resort to a "basket of alternatives" that contained those that reflected their real concerns and those used as a response to ideological pressure.

6. The number of women superiors in social work exceeded that of men—54 percent as compared to 47 (Klopov, 1985, p. 215).

## Chapter 4

1. As Valentin Ratnikov writes in his book *Collective as Social Community* (1978), when it is said that the personality is the highest value in socialist society, it is supposed that for such a personality the interests of the collective are higher than its egotistical interests. Otherwise this personality cannot claim to be socialist and thereby be the highest value in society (Ratnikov, 1978, p. 150).

## Chapter 5

1. The results of this survey, in which the author participated as head of the sample design group, have not been fully published in the Soviet Union (about this survey, see Chernakova, 1979; Muchnik et al., 1980; Petrenko and Iaroshenko, 1979; Shlapentokh, 1976).

2. In this respect, comparing American and Soviet movies is of some interest. It is difficult to find a Soviet movie which in one way or another does not touch upon life in the West. Western clothes and music, foreign literature and languages, travels to the West, and Western lifestyle are mentioned or demonstrated in numerous ways, are discussed by heroes, are hailed or rejected, but are always omnipresent.

Let me cite some of the best Soviet movies of the last decade. The hero of Riasanov's *Office Romance*, the deputy director of a Soviet statistical office, arrived in the Soviet Union from Switzerland and tries to get favors from various people by handing them imported gifts. His apartment is full of various foreign-made gadgets as well as foreign records.

In Gubenko's movie *From the Life of Vacationers*, the heroes discuss the life in the West and their tourist travels often. In a movie *Married for the First Time*, a daughter accuses her mother of not teaching her English in her childhood, which could have opened up job opportunities abroad for her. The daughter of another heroine in Todorovskii's movie *The Beloved Woman of Mechanic Gavrilov* also upbraids her mother, but this time for her ignorance of the latest John Updike novel. In Riasanov's *Rail Station for Two* the West is represented by a foreign-made video recorder, an absolute novelty in the Soviet Union, is in the possession of a speculator.

In another Raisanov movie, *Garage*, it is imputed that a main character gets a trip to Paris as a privilege which she managed to extort using dishonest means, while another person, the son of a high official, lightly boasted of a jacket bought in Hong Kong. In Danelia's movie *Autumn Marathon*, the West is present in the person of a Dutch literary translator who attracts the attention of many of the movie's heroes. The main male hero in Mikailian's movie *Fell in Love at Own Request* is a manual laborer, but not an ordinary one. Previously a sportsman (bicyclist) he traveled a lot abroad and could return to this life if he agreed to serve his former corrupt boss.

3. It is noteworthy that readers of *Trud*, mostly people with low education (1967), answered the question "in what field they wanted to enlarge their knowledge." International relations led all other issues—33 percent as compared to 22 percent of respondents who indicated technology, and 19 percent literature and art (Shlapentokh, 1969a, p. 55).

4. It is worth noticing that party members and nonparty members in the Leningrad study expressed nearly as much interest in international information—92 and 82 percent, respectively. However, the difference increases if we move to internal political information—90 and 76 percent, respectively, and especially to economic information—73 and 50 (Losenkov, 1983, p. 54).

5. It is quite indicative of the uneasiness of some Soviet ideologues over this interest in Western affairs that an author such as Boris Firsov, in the period of political reaction, wanted to refute "the untrue statements by many people about the preference for international to domestic information." In order to prove his point, he lumped together all rubrics pertaining to domestic life and compared it to all news from abroad. However, even in this case, his data showed that city dwellers (85 percent of all respon-

dents) viewed national developments with no greater interest than international (84 percent). Only rural residents, generally less well educated, are not as eager to get international news from TV (Firsov, 1981, pp. 107–09).

6. *Literaturnaia Gazeta* readers clearly prefer authentic articles on Western cultural life, undistorted by ideological commentary, to Soviet critical analysis of its developments. Sixty-one percent of *Literaturnaia Gazeta* readers followed "information on the news in Western culture," and 50 percent read about "the life of figures in Western culture," but only 39 percent do the same with ideologically loaded articles on "polemics with foreign theoreticians of Western culture" (Fomicheva, 1978, p. 64).

7. The sociologists also studied the demand on sixty literary works in the libraries included in the study. Among other things, they focused on books which, because of intensive demand, could be read only in the reading rooms of libraries. It turned out that 86 percent of all such books were written by foreign authors (Frolova, 1976, pp. 35–59).

8. The interest in foreign literature is a strong indicator of Westernization and of attitudes toward the existing political system. It is hardly accidental that among rural residents with a higher education in national republics exposed to Western influence there are a considerable number of people who said that "they read only foreign literature." In Lithuania it was 53 percent, Moldavia, 17, the Ukraine, 13, and only 1 percent in Kazakhstan (Dobrynina, 1978, p. 35).

9. A special insight into the role of foreign authors in the life of the average Soviet individual is provided by the experience in fifty Soviet cities where books in high demand would be given for mackle paper. Since in this case the authorities had to behave strictly according to the principle of supply and demand (nobody would volunteer to collect mackle paper for the sake of uninteresting or nonprestigious books), they had to include popular works in the list of 100 books offered to the enthusiasts of collecting recycled paper. The list was dominated by such Western authors as Alexander Dumas (only in 1985 was *Queen Margo* published, with 3 million copies), Maurice Druon (3.8 million copies printed in 1980 of his two books), Arthur Conan Doyle, Jules Verne, Stendhal, Wilkie Collins (*The Woman in White* and *The Moonstone)*, and others (about this experiment, see Levinson's brilliant article [1985]). Of eleven best-sellers on the book black market in Ikutsk, four were by foreign authors (Agatha Christie, Robert Musil, Marcel Proust, and Boleslav Prus (*Komsomol'skaia Pravda*, January 15, 1987).

10. Describing with relative objectivity life at a Soviet supermarket (the novel was received positively in the Soviet Union) Il'a Shtemler showed that the activity of the whole commercial enterprise and all human relations inside it as well as all connections of its workers with the outside, revolved around one thing—imported clothes (Shtemler, 1984). The heroes of the brilliant Soviet movie, *The Most Attractive* (1985), are divided into those who have and those who do not have Western garments. The last category is named in this comedy as "the most backward stratum of the population . . . the people from the Urals."

11. Only toward the mid-1980s did the mania for Western and sheepskin coats subside a little. This is because, after two decades of effort, Soviet industry, with the help of a foreign license, managed to produce their own jeans that some people were ready to buy.

12. In their book *On the Eve of Civic Maturity* (devoted almost completely to the denunciation of the West), Svetlana Ikonnikova and Vladimir Lisovskii cited an episode that occurred in Vorkuta, a city in the north of the European part of the Soviet Union. One day rumors were spread in the city that foreign jeans were being sold. People left

their workplaces and ran to the shopping center. Being certain that some machinations would take place in connection with the sale of these jeans, the public, on their own initiative, created a special commission for the control of the sale. In the end, the local authorities decided to solve the problem in a different fashion: the jeans were distributed not through commerce but directly in enterprises, and only shock workers were entitled to them. In recounting this case, the authors were outraged about the decline of morals (Ikonnikova and Lisovskii, 1982, pp. 139–40).

13. The obsession with Western goods has influenced the judgments of Soviet youth in a variety of ways. Blue jeans or T-shirts made in the United States have come to be labeled as "firm's" goods, i.e., made by American firms. Gaidar Aliev, a Politburo member, recognized this when he complained that "it is no secret that so far buyers prefer a foreign thing to a native one, with a 'firm's' label" (*Pravda*, June 8, 1986, p. 3). This term is taken to indicate a quality product and is a status symbol. Now, as *Komsomol'skaia Pravda* (July 27, 1984) indicates, even a prestigious Soviet university is labeled a firm, "firmennyi."

## Chapter 6

1. Having lost confidence in the sense justice of their direct superiors, as well as in their capacity to make decisions in the interest of the state, Soviet people found themselves involved in a highly typical Soviet activity—sending thousands of anonymous letters to the Central Committee and Moscow newspapers with various denunciations of their bosses. Along with those which genuinely wanted to help the authorities deal with the illegal or semilegal activities of some managers, the anonymous letters also served as an effective means of squaring accounts with colleagues and neighbors.

Inundated with these letters, the Soviet authorities were not able to take a clear stance regarding them for many decades. On the one hand, they condemned the authors of anonymous letters for lacking civic courage, but on the other hand, they could not deny that by refusing to take these letters into account they would deprive themselves of an important source of exclusive information (debates on the significance of anonymous letters emerge from time to time in the Soviet press without any conclusive decisions. See one of the last discussions on this subject in *Literaturnaia Gazeta*, August 22, 1984, p. 11; September 4, 1985, p. 6; see also *Nedelia*, 1984, #50; *Chelovek i Zakon*, 1986, 5, p. 53).

## Chapter 7

1. Valentine Rasputin's novel *Live and Remember* (1980) is a hallmark of the evolution of Soviet public opinion on the relations between the state and the family. The appearance of such a novel would probably have been impossible even a few years earlier. This novel takes place during World War II. Through a series of various events, Andrei Gus'kov, a young peasant, becomes a deserter, committing one of the most despicable crimes in Russia. He hides close to his native Siberian village, where his wife, Nastena, discovers him. Moved by conflicting feelings—love for her husband and

horror toward his cowardly action—she helps her husband survive and conceals him from others, including his father. Finding herself pregnant after a secret meeting with Andrei, Nastena explains her condition as a result of a love affair and staunchly endures her shame in the village, but does not betray her husband.

For the first time in Soviet literature, family ties are placed above the state. This case, which reminds one of the famous Antigone, is diametrically opposed to the glorification of Pavlik Morozov, the thirteen-year-old boy who reported on his father during the collectivization of the 1930s, as well as other cases from this period when family members denounced each other as enemies of the state.

2. It is obvious that many Soviets who are polled, unsophisticated in the subtleties of Soviet ideology, straightforwardly identify "friendship," "comradeship," and "collectivism" as synonymous concepts, a circumstance important to keep in mind when dealing with Soviet sociological data.

3. Grigorii Kvasov, an official in the Central Committee known for his ideological aggressiveness, published the results of a rather curious survey by Soviet ideological standards. The survey was carried out in a Moldavian cloth factory between 1974 and 1979. When asked about attitudes toward certain values, the majority of respondents (mostly women) clearly demonstrated that they assessed human relations much higher than official values. When asked about their priorities, love ranked first (73 percent), respect for other people (67 percent) was mentioned second most often, followed by "to be useful to other people" and "friendship" (both mentioned by 64 percent) Kvasov, 1982, p. 189).

4. Although Soviet public opinion favors an increase in privacy, there is a realization that under the guise of privacy a growing number of people have become wild egotists, violating elementary rules in their domestic life. The public, from time to time and in contrast with the main trend, demands the state intervention into the private life of moral nihilists (see Irina Ovchinnikova's article "With Whole Community," in *Nedelia*, 1986, #8).

5. The decrease in the role of public cultural institutions is also revealed by the steady decline in their economic efficiency. In 1975–80 the ratio between income and expenditures in Soviet theaters dropped from 64 to 53 percent. Even circuses, which, because of their popularity are nondeficient enterprises, saw their profits fall by almost half in this period (Zinin and Diskin, 1985, pp. 86–87).

6. Groups and the parties they organize play an extremely great role in the life of people living in dormitories. According to some data, young dormitory residents spend almost 20–25 percent of their salary on parties (Pavlov, 1975, p. 116).

## Chapter 9

1. A survey of young people in Byelorussia and Estonia (1981–84) found that working males felt the most serious forms of antisocial behavior are embezzlement and fraud in statistical reporting. Violation of labor discipline was ranked fourth. Working women put hooliganism first, followed by rudeness, obsequiousness, and indifference (Babosov et al., 1985, p. 116).

2. For information about corruption in Moldavia see *Literaturnaia Gazeta*, April 9, 1986, the Ukraine (*Pravda*, February 10, 1985; August 24, 1986; *Sovietskaia*

*Kul'tura*, August 12, 1986), Latvia (*Pravda*, June 27, 1986), Tumen (*Pravda*, August 13, 1986), Vladivostok (*Pravda*, August 19, 1986), Saratov (*Pravda*, August 8, 1986; *Sovietskaia Rossia*, June 25, 1986), Kirov (*Pravda*, July 24, 1986), Leningrad (*Pravda*, July 8, 1986), Komi (*Pravda*, August 12, 1986), Orenburg (*Pravda*, December 12, 1985), Novosibirsk (*Pravda*, March 29, 1986), and Pskov (*Pravda*, June 13, 1986).

3. Corruption in connection with admittance to Soviet medical schools was so great that even the head of the department of medical education of the Ministry of Health was implicated. Gorbachev had him fired and excluded from the party (*Pravda*, September 15, 1986).

4. Oleg Tabakov, then director of the popular Moscow theater "Sovremennik" told me that only 20–30 percent of all tickets went into "free sale." The rest are appropriated by Moscow party and governmental bodies and by the staff of the theater. In addition, the tickets which presumably had to be accessible to the man on the street are mostly used by managers in booking offices as a resource to exchange for scarce goods and services. According to a special investigation, of the 3,406 tickets to the Bolshoi Theater to be sold to the general public, only 1593 were. This means that 53 percent of all tickets were sold under the counter or exchanged by box office personnel for services. (About the distribution of theater tickets in Moscow, see *Nedelia*, 1985, #248, p. 14; *Komsomol'skaia Pravda*, January 3, 1988.)

It is interesting how some actors use the tickets which are at their disposal. As *Sovietskaia Rossia*, a Moscow newspaper, revealed in 1984, they invite their admirers or other people simply anxious to get into the theater to form a personal claque to "organize" the enthusiastic reception of their performance (*Novoye Russkoye Slovo*, February 14, 1984).

5. In a relatively small Georgian confectionery with hardly more than 12,000 workers, 260 cases of theft were discovered during a year-and-a-half, which means two to three cases of theft discovered for each 100 workers. The same magnitude of theft is found in other branches of food and other light industries despite the significant strengthening of control since Brezhnev (*Pravda*, August 12, 1986).

## Chapter 10

1. Alexander Gel'man, a leading dramaturge, defended the views of this group: "Intellect, abilities, physical strength, and conscience are and forever will be in an unalienated individual, the private property of the individual" (Gel'man, 1986, p. 10).

2. Those Russophile authors who admire pre-Soviet Russia, despite their radical differences with the liberal intelligentsia, share practically the same views on privatization in the economy and other spheres of Soviet society. Being highly cautious on describing what economic program they desire, they only revealed their negative attitudes toward collective farms when they described agricultural collectivization as well as life in the countryside in the postwar period. In this respect Belov's *On the Eve* (1976) or Mozhaev's *From the Life of Ivan Kuzkin* (1981) are of special significance (see also Zalygin's *On the Irtysh River*, 1966).

Yet these writers are much less active in advocating private economic behavior as might be expected in view of their respect for pre-revolutionary Russian society and their praise of the Russian peasants. Ivan Vasiliev's article (1986) in the magazine *Nash*

*Sovremennik* ("Our Contemporary"), known for its blatant Russophile tendencies, is remarkable in this respect. The author avows, supporting the ideas of Rasputin's *Fire* (1985b), that "people lost the ability to work in the collective," that "the individual principle of reward takes the upper hand over the stimulation of work in brigades," and that peasants are now incapable of undertaking any action favoring the village. Fiercely attacking the party apparatus and the managers as responsible for the decline of agriculture and collective work, the author, however, comes to the defense of collectivism in rural life and appeals for its resurrection.

3. It is peculiar that it was Soviet theater directors who turned out to be the most eloquent and outspoken advocates of decentralization and private activity among Soviet intellectuals. In 1985–86 many of them (primarily Mark Zakharov, also Oleg Efremov, Georgii Tovstonogov, and others) demanded autonomy for the theater in repertoire, cadre policy, and in setting actors' salaries and ticket prices, as well as the right to create new theaters, even for noncertified (without an official diploma) actors (for example, see *Literaturnaia Gazeta*, December 25, 1985, p. 8; *Pravda*, February 21, 1986; *Sovietskaia Kul'tura*, November 29, 1986, p. 3).

4. What is more, Iulian Semenov, an author openly acknowledging his connection with the KGB, praises privatization and kindred institutions in all his work. In the screenplay for the TV movie *The Confrontation* (summer 1985), he had a police officer give a long lament in favor of private business in service.

5. A study in Georgia found that 40 percent of the owners of foreign cars, an extremely expensive and prestigious item in the Soviet Union, are service workers and one-third are professional drivers (Shokhin, 1986, p. 53).

# References

Abramov, F. 1982. *Trava-Murava. Povesti i Rasskazy*. Moscow: Sovremennik.

Abramov, F. 1973. *Brat'ia i Sestry: Dve Zimy i Tri Leta*. Moscow: Sovetskii Pisatel'.

Afanasiev, V. 1985. "Ob uskorenii sotsial'no-ekonomicheskogo razvitiia." *Pravda*, September 10.

Aganbegian, A. 1987. "Chelovek: Ekonomika." *Ogoniok* 17:12–15.

Ageev, V. 1984. *Ekonomicheskiie Interesy i Stimuly pri Sotsialisme*. Moscow: Sovietskaia Rossia.

Agranovskii, A. 1982. *Detali i Glavnoie. Ocherki*. Moscow: Sovietskii Pisatel'.

Aitmatov, C. 1986. "Plakha." *Novy Mir* 6, 8, 9.

Aitov, N. 1985. *Sotsial'noie Razvitiie Regionov*. Moscow: Mysl'.

Aitov, N. 1983. *Rabochiie Khoroshiie i Plokhiie*. Moscow: Sovietskaia Rossia.

Aitov, N. 1981. *Sovietskii Rabochii*. Moscow: Politizdat.

Aitov, A. 1968. "Obrazovaniie i Zhizn'." *Oktiabr'* 7.

Akhlibininskii, B., and V. Surin (eds.). 1980. *Dialektika Vzaimosviazi Lichnogo i Sotsial'nogo v Usloviakh Razvitogo Sotsialisma*. Leningrad: Leningradskii Universitet.

Alekseev, A. 1970. "Opyt sopostavitell'nogo analiza rezul'tatov raznykh issledovanii massovoi kommunikatsii." In *Problemy Sotsiologii Pechati*, vol. 2, edited by V. Shlapentokh, pp. 178–97. Novosibirsk: Nauka.

Alekseeva, L. 1984. *Istoriia Inakomysliia v SSSR. Noveishii Period*. Benson, Va.: Khronika Press.

Alekseeva, L., and V. Chalidze. 1985. *Mass Rioting in the USSR*. Silver Springs, Md: Foundation for Soviet Studies.

Alekseeva, V. 1983. *Molodoi Rabochii*. Moscow: Mysl'.

Alexandrov, A. 1986. "Rech' na XXVII S'ezde KPSS." In *Materially XXVII S"ezda KPSS*. Moscow: Politizdat.

Alford, R., and R. Friedland. 1985. *Powers of Theory: Capitalism, State, and Democracy*. Cambridge: Cambridge University Press.

Alliluieva, S. 1969. *Tol'ko Odin God*. New York: Harper & Row.

Alliluieva, S. 1967. *Dvadtsat' Pisem Drugu*. New York: Harper & Row.

Almond, G., and S. Verba. 1965. *The Civic Culture*. Boston: Little, Brown.

Altman, I. 1975. *The Environment and Social Behavior*. Monterey, Cal.: Brooks/Cole.

Amalrik, A. 1982. *Notes of a Revolutionary*. New York: Knopf.

Andreieva, G. 1980. *Sotsial'naia Psikhologiia*. Moscow: Izdatel'stvo Moskovskogo Universiteta.

Andropov, Iu. 1983. *Izbrannyie Rechi i Stat'i*. Moscow: Politizdat.

Antosenkov, E. 1974. *Dvizheniie Rabochikh Kadrov na Promyshlennykh Predpriatiiakh*. Moscow: Ekonomika.

Antosenkov, E. 1969. *Opyt Issledovaniia Peremeny Truda v Promyshlennosti*. Novosibirsk: Nauka.

Antosenkov, E., and V. Kalmyk (eds.). 1970. *Otnoshenie k Trudu i Tekuchest' Kadrov*. Novosibirsk: Institut Ekonomiki i Organizatsii Promyshlennogo Proizvodstva.

Antosenkov, E., and Z. Kupriianova (eds.). 1985. *Dvizheniie Kadrov v Sibirskom Gorode*. Novosibirsk: Nauka.

Anufriev, B. 1984. *Sotsial'nyi Status i Aktivnost' Lichnosti*. Moscow: Izdatel'stvo Moskovskogo Universiteta.

Artemov, V., and V. Patrushev (eds.). 1973. *Budzhet Vremeni Zhitelei g. Pskova*. Novosibirsk: Institut Ekonomiki.

Arutiunian, Iu. 1980a. "Natsional 'no-regional' noie mnogobraziie Sovietskoi derevni." *Sotsiologicheskiie Issledovaniia* 3:73–81.

Arutiunian, Iu. (ed.). 1980b. *Opyt Etnosotsiologicheskogo Issledovaniia Obraza Zhizni*. Moscow: Nauka.

Arutiunian, Iu. 1972. "Sotsial'no-kulturnyi aspekty razvitiia i sblizheniia natsii." *Sovietskaia Etnografiia* 3:3–25.

Aseiev, V., L. Gorchakov, and N. Kogan. 1981. "Kakim ty pridesh v rabochii klass." In *Sovietskaia Molodezh*, edited by E. Vasil'ieva, pp. 52–65. Moscow: Finansy i Statistika.

Ashkenazy, V. 1985. *Beyond Frontiers*. London: Collins.

Astafiev, V. 1986. "Pechal'nyi detektiv." *Oktiabr'* 1:1–80.

Astafiev, V. 1984a. *Tsar-Ryba. Povestvovaniie v Raskazakh*. Moscow: Molodaia Gvardiia.

Astafiev, V. 1984b. *Rasskazy*. Moscow: Sovietskaia Rossia.

Babosov, E. 1985. *Nravstvennaiia Kul'tura Lichnosti'*. Minsk: Nauka i Tekhnika.

Babosov, E., G. Sokolova, and A. Sokolova. 1983. *Sovietskii Rabochii: Sotsial'nyi i Dukhovnyi Oblik*. Minsk: Nauka i Tekhnika.

Babosov, E., et al. 1985. *Nravstvennyi Oblik Sovietskoi Molodezhi*. Minsk: Nauka i Tekhnika.

Bagdasarov, A., and E. Pervushin. 1983. "Proizvoditel'nost', Truda: teoriia, praktika, reservy rosta." *Kommunist* 2:10–20.

Balandin, A. 1979. "Udovletvorennost' trudom i razvitie lichnosti." In *Vospitaniie Vsestroronne Ravitoi Lichnosti v Trudovom Kollektive*, edited by N. Mansurov, pp. 21–22. Moscow: Institut Sotsiologicheskikh Issledovanii.

Barandeev, A. (ed.). 1984. *Novoie v Partiinoi Rabote*. Moscow: Moskovskii Rabochii.

Baranov, A. 1981. *Sotsial'no-Demograficheskoie Razvitiie Krupnogo Goroda*. Moscow: Finansy i Statistika.

Barron, J. 1982. *Letchik Miga*. Frankfurt: Posev.

Baturin, F. 1984. *Sotsial'naia Aktivnosti' Trudiashchikhsia. Sushchnost' i Upravleniie*. Novosibirsk: Nauka.

Batygin, G. 1987. "Dobrodetel' protiv interesa." *Sotsiologicheskiie Issledovaniia* 3:24–36.

Baumeister, R., J. Hamilton, and D. Tice. 1985. "Public Versus Private Expectancy of Success." *Journal of Personality and Social Psychology*, 48, 6:1447–52.

Belikova, G., and A. Shokhin. 1987. "Chernyi Rynok: Liudi, Veshchi, fakty." *Ogoniok* 36: 6–8.

Belkin, E., and F. Sheregi. 1985. *Formirovanilae Naseleniia v Zone BAMA*. Moscow: Mysl'.

Bell. D. 1976. *The Cultural Contradictions of Capitalism*. New York: Basic Books.

Bellah, R., R. Madsen, W. Sullivan, A. Swidler, and S. Tipton. 1985. *Habits of the Heart*. Berkeley: University of California Press.

Belov, V. 1976. *Kanuny*. Moscow: Sovremennik.

Benn. S., and G. Gaus. 1983. *Public and Private in Social Life*. New York: St. Martin's Press.

Berberova, N. 1983. *Kursiv Moi: Abtobiografiia* (vols. 1 and 2). New York: Russica.

Berg, R. 1984. "Varvary na oblommkakh zivilizatsii." *Kontinent* 41:219–52.

Berlin, I. 1969. *Four Essays on Liberty*. London: Oxford University Press.

Bigulov, V., O. Kryshtanovskii, and O. Michurin. 1984. "Material'noie Blagosostoianiie i sotsial'noie blagopoluchiie." *Sotsiologicheskiie Issledovaniia* 4:88–93.

Bikkenin, N. 1983. *Sotsialisticheskaia Ideologiia*. Moscow: Gospolitizdat.

Bindiukov, N. 1983. "Sotsiol'nyie faktory povysheniia kachestva produktsii." *Sotsiologicheskiie Issledovaniia* 1:134–35.

Black, A. 1984. *Guilds and Civil Society in European Political Thought from the Twelfth Century to the Present*. London: Methuen.

Blinov, N. 1979. *Trudoviaia Deiatal'nost' kak Osnova Sotsialisticheskogo Obraza Zhizni*. Moscow: Nauka.

Blinov, N., and M. Titma. 1985. "Nravstvennyie orientatsii sovietskoi molodezhi." *Sotsiologicheskiie Issledovaniia* 1:9–17.

Bogdanova, O, and O. Kalinina (eds.). 1984. *Osnovy Kommunishcheskoi Morali. Posobiie dlia uchitelia.* Moscow: Prosveshcheniie.

Bogdanova, O., B. Slavin, N. Demidova, et al. 1987. *Kommunisticheskoe Vospitaniie na Urokakh Literatury.* Moscow: Prosveshchenie.

Boiko, V. 1980. *Molodezhnaia Sem'ia.* Moscow: Statistika.

Bokarev, N. 1979. "Problemy povysheniia deistvennosti partiinykh sobranii." In *Voprosy Sovershenstvovaniia Deiatel' nosti Obshchestvennykh Organizatsii*, edited by N. Bokarev and A. Beliakov, pp. 108–31. Moscow: Institut Sotsiologicheskikh Issledovanii.

Bokarev, N. 1979b. *Rasshireniie Uchastiia Trudiashhchikhsia v Upravlenii Proizvodstvom.* Moscow: Nauka.

Bondarev, Y. 1985. *Igra.* Moscow: Sovietskii Pisatel'.

Bondarev, Y. 1980. *Vybor.* Moscow: Sovietskii Pisatel'.

Borshchevskii, M. 1983. "Zhiteli severnykh gorodov i ikh dosug." *Sotsiologicheskiie Issledovaniia* 3:39–46.

Bozhkov, O., and V. Golofast. 1985. "Otsenka naseleniiem uslovii zhizni v krupnykh gorodakh." *Sotsiologicheskiie Issledovaniia* 3:95–101.

Breev, B. 1977. *Podvizhnost' Naseleniia i Trudovykh Resursov.* Moscow: Statistika.

Brezhnev, L. 1981. *Otchetnyi Doklad Tsentral'nogo Komiteta KPSS XXVI S'edzu Kommunisticheskoi Partii Sovietskogo Souza i Ocherednyie Zadachi Partii v Oblasti Vnutrennei i Vneshnei Politiki.* Moscow: Politizdat.

Brezhnev, L. 1976. *Otchet Zentral'nogo Komiteta KPSS i Ocherednyie Zadachi Partii v Oblasti Vnutrennei i Vneshnei Politiki.* Moscow: Politizdat.

Brown, A. 1981. "Political Power and the Soviet State: Western and Soviet Perspectives." In *The State in Socialist Society*, edited by N. Harding. Albany: State University of New York Press.

Brucker, G. 1977. *The Civic World of Early Renaissance Florence.* Princeton: Princeton University Press.

Bueiva, L. 1983. *Sotisial'naia Struktura Sotsialisticheskogo Obshchestva i Vsestoronnie Razvitiie Lichnosti.* Moscow: Nauka.

Bueiva, L., and V. Alekseeva. 1982. "Obshcheniie kak faktor razvitiia." *Sotsiologicheskiie Issledovaniia* 2:31–42.

Bukovskii, V. 1979. *I Vozvrashchaietsia Veter.* New York: Khronika.

Bunich, P. 1986. *Glavnoie—Zainteresovat'.* Moscow: Ekonomika.

Burlatskii, F. 1977. "Politicheskaiia sistema razvitogo sotsialisma." *Voprosy Filosofii* 8:10–20.

Campbell, A., P. Converse, and W. Rogers. 1976. *The Quality of American Life: Perceptions, Evaluations, and Satisfactions.* New York: Russell Sage Foundation.

Campbell, D., and D. Fiske. 1959. "Convergent and Discriminant Validation by the Multitrait-Multimethod Matrix." *Psychological Bulletin* 56:27–39.

Chaikovskaia, O. 1986. "Slovo o Cheste." *Literaturnaia Gazeta*, April 16, 1986.

Changli, I. 1979a. "Trud kak osnova sotsiaisticheskogo obraza zhizni." In *Trud kak Osnova Sotsialisticheskogo Obraza Zhizni*, edited by V. Staroverov. Moscow: Institut Sotsiologicheskikh Issledovanii.

Changli, I. (ed.). 1979b. *Sotsialisticheskii Trud: Prava, Obiazannosti, Svobody*. Moscow: Institut Sotsiologicheskikh Issledovanii.

Changli, I. (ed.). 1978. *Sotsialisticheskoie Sorevnovaniie: Voprosy Teorii, Praktiki I Organizatsii*. Moscow: Nauka.

Changli, I. (ed.). 1976. *Sotsial'nye Problemy Truda i Sorevnovaniia*. Moscow: Institut Sotsiologicheskikh Issledovanii.

Changli, I. 1973. *Trud*. Moscow: Nauka.

Cherednichenko, G., and V. Shubkin. 1985. *Molodezh Vstupaiet v Zhizn'*. Moscow: Mysl'.

Chernakova, N. 1979. "Informatsionnyie potrebnosti auditorii gazet, radio i televideniia." In *Sotsiologicheskiie Problemy Obshchestvennogo Mneniia i Deiatel'nosti Sredstv Massovoi Informatsii*, edited by V. Korabeinikov, pp. 15–25. Moscow: Institut Sotsiologicheskikh Issledovanii.

Chernovolenko, V., V. Ossovski, and V. Paniotto. 1979. *Prestizh Professii i Problemy Sotsialno-professional'noi Orientatsii Molodezhi*. Kiev: Naukova Dumka.

Chukovskaia, L. 1981. *Opustelyi Dom*. Paris: Alagante.

Chukovskaia, L. 1976, 1980. *Zapiski ob Anne Akhmatova* (Vols. 1 and 2). Paris: Ymka Press.

Churbanov, E. 1986. *Kul'tura i Sotsial'no-Ekonomicheskii Progress*. Moscow: Znaniie.

Cohen, F. 1983. *Class and Civil Society: The Limits of Marxian Critical Theory*. Oxford: Martin Robertson.

Cook, C. 1984. "Participation in Public Interest—Group Membership Motivation." *American Political Quarterly*, October, 409–30.

Davydchenkov, N. 1970. "Organizatsiia sotsiologicheskogo obsledovaniia i vnedreniie poluchennykh resul'tatov v zentral'noi gazete." In *Sotsiologiia Pechati*, edited by V. Shlapentokh, vol. 2, pp. 147–77. Novosibirsk: Nauka.

Degtiarova, R. 1985. *O Deiatel'nosti KPSS po Fozmirovaniiu Politicheskoi Kul'tury Nauchno-Technicheskoi Intelligentsii v Usloviakh Razvitogo Sotsialisma*. Leningrad: Izdatel'stvo Leningradskogo Universitet.

Djilas, M. 1970. *Razgovory so Stalinym*. Frankfurt: Posev.

Dmitrenko, T., and I. Kornakovskii. 1984. "Sotsial'nyi portret sovremennogo peredovogo rabochego." In *Problemy Sotsialisticheskogo Sorevnovannia*, edited by L. Rogachevskaia, pp. 264–84. Moscow: Nauka.

Dobrynina, N. 1978. "Internatsiolizatsiia chteniia na sele." In *Kniga i Chteniie v Zhizni Sovietskogo Sela: Problemy i Tendentsii*, edited by N. Solovieva, pp. 19–46. Moscow: Kniga.

Dontsov, A. 1984. *Psikhologiia Kollektiva. Methodologicheskiie Problemy Issledovaniia*. Moscow: Izdatel'stvo Moskovskogo Universiteta.

Druckner, P. 1985. *Innovation and Entrepeneurship: Practice and Principles*. New York: Harper & Row Publishers, Inc.

Dubko, E. 1985. *Priroda Moral'nogo Konflikta*. Moscow: Znaniie.

Dumnov, D., V. Ruthaiser, and A. Shmarov. 1984. *Budzhet Vremeni Naseleniia*. Moscow: Finansy i Statistika.

Edlis, I. 1986. "Antrakt." *Novy Mir*, 4:6–77 and 5:84–151.

Eglite, P. 1985. "Osobiennosti reproduktivnogo povedeniia v usloviiakh vysokoi vneseemeinoi aktivnosti naseleniia." *Sotsiologicheskiie Issledovaniia* 4:59–65.

Eglite, P., Z. Gosha, and I. Farinsh. 1984. *Faktory i Motivy Demograficheskogo povedeniia*. Riga: Zinatne.

Elshtain, B. 1981. *Public Man, Private Woman*. Princeton: Princeton University Press.

Elstsin, B. 1986. "Rech' na XXVII S"ezde KPSS." In *XXVII S'ezd KPSS*, Vol. 1, pp. 140–45. Moscow: Politizdat.

Emanuel', N. 1982. "Sotsialisticheskoie Sorevnovaniie i povysheniie effektivnosti nauchnykh issledovanii." In *Problemy Sorevnovaniia v Nauchnykn Kollektivakh*, edited by Rudolf Ianovskii, pp. 149–52. Moscow: Vysshaia Shkola.

Erme, I. 1977. "Izucheniie orientatsii starsheklassinikov v sfere svobodnogo vremeni." In *Sotsial'naia i Professional'naia Orientatsiia Molodezhi i Problemy Kommunisticheskogo Vospitaniia*, edited by M. Titma, pp. 115–27. Tallin: Akademiia Nauk Estonskoi SSR.

Ermolaiev, I. 1979. "Khudozhestvennaiia literatura kak faktor nravstvennogo formirovanniia lichnosti molodogo rabochego." In *Vospitatel'noie Vozdeistviie na Lichnost' Sredstv Massovoi Informatsii i Uchrezhdenii Kul'tury*, edited by N. Mansurov, pp. 68–70. Moscow: Institut Sotsiologicheskikh Issledovanii.

Evladov, B., A. Pokrovskii, and V. Shlapentokh. 1969. "Chetyre tysiachi i odno interviu." *Zhurnalist* 10:34–37.

Evtushenko, E. 1986. "Iz novykh stikhov." *Pravda*, June 8, p. 3.

Fadeev, A. 1985. *Aktual'nyie Voprosy Razvitiia Dvizheniia za Kommunisticheskoiie Otnosheniie k Trudu*. Moscow: Znaniie.

Fainburg, Z. (ed.). 1982. *Sotsiologiia Sotsialisticheskogo Proizvodstvennogo Kollektiva*. Moscow: Profizdat.

Fainburg, Z. 1977. "Problema emotsional'nykh faktorov formirovaniia sem'i." In *Izmeneniie Polozheniia Zhenshchiny i Sem'ia*, edited by A. Kharchev, pp. 133–38. Moscow: Nauka.

Fainburg, Z. 1969. "Tsennostnyie orientatsii lichnosti v nekotorykh sotsial-'nykh gruppakh sotsialisticheskogo obshchestva." In *Lichnost' i Ieie Tsennostnie Orientatsii*, vol. 2, edited by V. Iadov and I. Kon. Moscow: Institut Konkretnykh Sotsial'nykh Issledovanii.

Faisulin, F. 1978. "Osobennosti sotsial'nykh peremeshchenii v gorode." In *Ludi v Gorodakh i na Sele*, edited by D. Valentei. Moscow: Statistika.

Farrell, M., and S. Rosenberg. 1981. *Men At Midlife*. Boston: Auburn House.

Fedoseev, P. (ed.). 1985. *Nauchnyi Kommunism. Uchebnik*. Moscow: Politizdat.

Fenigstein, A., et al. 1975. "Public and Private Self-Counsciousness: Assessment and Theory." *Journal of Consulting and Clinical Psychology* 43:522–25.

Filippov, F. 1976. *Vseobshcheie Sredneie Obrazovaniie v SSSR*. Moscow: Mysl'.

Filippov, F., and P. Mitev. 1984. *Molodezh i Vyssheie Obrazovaniie v Sotsialisticheskikh Stranakh*. Moscow: Nauka.

Filippov, F., and G. Slesarev (eds.). 1981. *Formirovaniie Sotsial'noi Odnorodnosti Sotsialisticheskogo Obshchestva*. Moscow: Nauka.

Firsov, B. (ed.). 1981. *Massovaia Kommunikatsiia v Usloviiakh Nauchno-Technicheskoi Revolutsii*. Leningrad: Nauka.

Foddy, W., and W. Finnigan. 1978. "The Concept of Privacy From Symbolic Interaction Perspective." *Journal of Theory and Social Behavior* 10:1–17.

Fomicheva, I. (ed). 1978. *Literaturnaia Gazeta i Ieie Auditoriia*. Moscow: Izdatel'stvo MGU.

Fomicheva, I. 1976. *Zhurnalistika i Auditoriia*. Moscow: Moskovskii Universitet.

Friedhut, T. 1977. *Political Participation in the USSR*. Princeton: Princeton University Press.

Frolova, T. (ed.). 1976. *Dinamika Chteniia i Chitatel'skogo Sprosa v Massovykh Bibliotekakh*. Moscow: Gosudarstvennaia Biblioteka imeni Lenina.

Gamarnikov, E., D. Morgan, J. Purvis, and D. Taylorson (eds.). 1983. *The Public and the Private*. London: Heinemann.

Gavison, B., 1983. "Information Control: Availability or Exclusion." In *Public and Private in Social Life*, edited by S. Benn and G. Gaus. New York: St. Martin Press.

Gel'man, A. 1986. "Chto snachala, chto potom." *Literaturnaia Gazeta*, September 10, 1986, p. 10.

Gerasimov, I. 1985. *Semeinyi Roman*. Moscow: Sovietskii Pisatel'.

Gerasimov, I. 1983. "Probel v kalendarie." *Novy Mir* 3:6–143.

Gimpelson, V., and S. Shpilko. 1987. "Khorosho li Organizovan Otpusk Moskvichei." *Sotsiologicheski Issledovaniia* 4:50–59.

Giner, S. 1985. "The Withering Away of Civic Society." *Praxis International* 5:247–61.

Ginsburg, E. 1985. *Krutoi Marshrut* (vol. 1). New York: Posev.

Goffman, E. 1959. *The Presentation of Self in Everyday Life*. Garden City, N.Y.: Doubleday.

Golod, S. 1977. "Sotsial'no-psykhologicheskiie i nravstvennyie tsennosti sem'i." In *Molodaia Sem'ia*, edited by D. Valentei. Moscow: Statistika.

Golod, S., and E. Sokolov. 1977. *Dosug i Kul'tura Molodogo Rabochego*. Leningrad: Obschchestvo Znaniie.

Golofast, B., L. Kesel'man, and T. Protasenko. 1983. "Effektivnost' truda i struktura potrebleniia u promyshlennykh rabochikh." *Sotsiologicheskiie Issledovaniia 4*:57–64.

Golyakhovsky, V. 1984. *Russian Doctor*. New York: St. Martin's Press.

Gorbachev, M. 1987. *Izbrannye Rechi i Stat'i*. Moscow: Politizdat.

Gorbachev, M. 1987. "Oktiabr' i Perestroika: Revoliutsiia Prodolzhaetsia." *Kommunist* 17:3–40.

Gorbachev, M. 1987. "O Perestroike i Kadrovoi Politike Partii." *Kommunist* 3:55–52.

Gorbachev, M. 1987. "O Zadachakh Partii po Korennoi Perestroike Upravleniia Ekonomiki." *Kommunist* 10:5–46.

Gorbachev, M. 1987. *Pravda*, November 2.

Gorbachev, M. 1986. "Politicheskii Doklad Zentral'nogo Komiteta KPSS XXVII S'ezdy Kommunisticheskoi Partii Sovietskogo Souza." *Pravda*, February 26, 1986, pp. 2–10.

Gorbachev, M. 1985. *Izbrannyie Rechi i Stat'i*. Moscow: Gospolitizdat.

Gordon, L., and E. Klopov. 1972. *Chelovek Posle Raboty*. Moscow: Nauka.

Goriachev, M., M. Syroiseshkina, and V. Sdobnov. 1978. "Nekotoryie voprosy povysheniia effektivnosti ideino-politicheskogo i nravstvennogo vospitaniia uchashcheisia molodezhi." In *Sotsiologicheskiie Problemy Kommunisticheskogo Vospitaniia*, edited by N. Mansurov, pp. 31–75. Moscow: Institut Sotsiologicheskikh Issledovanii.

Grechin, A. 1983. "Opyt sotsiologicheskogo izucheniia pravosoznaniia." *Sotsiologicheskiie Issledovaniia* 2:121–28.

Grekova, I. 1983. *Kafedra*. Moscow: Sovietskii Pisatel'.

Grigorenko, P. 1982. *Memoirs*. New York: Norton.

Grossman, G. 1982. "The 'Shadow Economy' in the Socialist Sector of the USSR." In *NATO: Economics and Information Directorates, The CMEA Five-Year Plans (1981–1985) in a New Perspective*.

Grossman, G. 1977. "The 'Second Economy' of the USSR." *Problems of Communism* 26, 5: September–October.

Grossman, V. 1980. *Zhisn' i Sud'ba*. Lausanne: L'âge d'homme.

Grossman, V. 1974. *Vse Techet*. Frankfurt: Posev.

Grushin, B. 1967. *Mir Mnenii i Mneniia o Mire*. Moscow: Politizdat.

Grushin, B., and L. Onikov (eds.). 1980). *Massovaia Informatsiia v Sovetskom Promyshlennon Gorode.* Moscow: Politizdat.

Gudilina, E. 1985. *Bor'ba s Nravstvennymi Porokami i Pozitsiia Lichnosti.* Moscow: Znaniie.

Guseinov, C. 1986. *Semeinyie Tainy.* Moscow: Sovietskil Pisatel'.

Guseinov, C. 1977. *Mahomed, Mamed, Mamish.* Moscow: Sovietskii Pisatel'.

Gvozdev, N. 1985. *Stimuly Sotsialisticheskoi Ekonomiki.* Moscow: Ekonomika.

Habermass, Y. 1975. *The Legitimization Crisis.* Boston: Beacon Press.

Hegel, G. 1945. *The Philosophy of Law.* Oxford, U.K.: Clarendon Press.

Hough, J. 1979. *How the Soviet Union is Governed.* Cambridge, Mass. Harvard University Press.

Hough, J. 1977. *The Soviet Union and Social Science Theory.* Cambridge, Mass.: Harvard University Press.

Iablokov, I. 1979. *Sotsiologiia Religii.* Moscow: Mysl'.

Iadov, V. 1983. "Otnosheniie k Trudu: Konzeptual'naia model' i real'nyie Tendentsii." *Sotsiologicheskiie Issledovaniia* 3:50–63.

Iadov, V. 1982. "Motivatsiia truda: Problemy i puti razvitiia issledovanii." In *Sovietskaia Sotsiologiia*, edited by T. Riabushkin and G. Osipov, vol. 2, pp. 29–38. Moscow: Nauka.

Iadov, V. (ed.). 1979. *Samoregulatsia i Prognozirovanie Sotsial' nogo Povedieniia Lichnosti.* Leningrad: Nauka.

Iadov, V. (ed.). 1977. *Sotsial'no-Psikhologicheskii Portret Inzhenera.* Moscow: Mysl'.

Iadov, V., and A. Kissel'. 1974. "Udovletvorennost' rabotoi: Analyz empiricheskikh otnoshenii i popytka ikh teoreticheskogo analiza." *Sotsiologicheskiie Issledovaniia* 1:76–88.

Iadov, V., V. Rozhin, and A. Zdravomyslov. 1967. *Chelovek i Iego Rabota.* Moscow: Mysl'.

Iadov, V., and A. Zdravomyslov (eds.). 1970. *Man and His Work.* White Plains: International Arts and Science Press.

Iakovlev, A. 1984. *Effektivnost' Ideologicheskoi Raboty.* Moscow: Politizdat.

Iakovlev, B. (ed.). 1977. *Monolog Sovremennika.* Moscow: Politizdat.

Iakovleva, Z. (ed.). 1986. *Pravovaia Statistika.* Moscow: Iuridicheskaia Literatura.

Iakuba, E., and A. Andrushchenko. 1976. "Orientatsiia lichnosti kak vazhneishaiia cherta sotsialisticheskogo tipa lichnosti." In *Aktivnost' Lichnosti v Sotsialisticheskom Obshchestve*, edited by T. Iaroshevskii and N. Mansurov, pp. 157–71. Moscow: Nauka.

Iakunin, G. 1979. "O Sovremennom polozhenii russkoi pravoslavnoi tserkvi i perspektivakh religioznogo vozrozhdeniia rossii." *Volno'ie Slovo* 35–36:5–138.

Iankova, Z. 1979. *Gorodskaia Sem'ia.* Moscow: Nauka.

Ianovskii, R. (ed.). 1982. *Problemy Sorevnovaniia Nauchnykh Kollektivov.* Moscow: Vysshaia Shkola.

Ianovskii, R. 1979a. *Formirovaniie Lichnosti Uchenogo v Usloviakh Razvitogo Sotsialisma.* Novosibirsk: Nauka.

Ianovskii, R. 1979b. "Sotsial'nyie i politicheskie problemy vospitania lichnosti uchenogo." In *Nauka, Organizatsia, i Upravlenie*, edited by A. Okladnikov. Novosibirsk: Nauka.

Ibragimbekov, B. 1984. *Izbrannoie.* Moscow: Iskusstvo.

Ibragimbekov, R. 1983. *P'esy.* Moscow: Sovetskii Pisatel'.

Ikonnikova, S., and V. Lisovskii. 1982. *Na Poroge Grazhdanskoi Zrelosti.* Leningrad: Leninzdat.

Ikonnikova, S., and V. Lisovskii. 1969. *Molodezh o Sebe, Svoikh Sverstnikakh.* Leningrad: Leninzdat.

Il'ichev, L., and P. Fedoseev (eds.). 1983. *Filosofskii Enziklopedicheskii Slovar'.* Moscow: Sovietskaia Enziklopediia.

Inkeles, A. 1980. "Modernization and Family Patterns: A Test of Convergence Theory." In *Conspectus of History*, edited by D. Hoover and J. Koumouldies.

Inkeles, A., and R. Bauer. 1968. *The Soviet Citizen: Daily Life in a Totalitarian Society.* New York: Atheneum.

Inkeles, A., and D. Smith. 1974. *Becoming Modern.* Cambridge, Mass.: Harvard University Press.

Ivanov, O., and V. Patrushev. 1976. "Vliianiie uslovii truda na udovletvorennost' trudom rabotnikov sel'skogo khoziastva." *Sotsialogicheskiie Issledovaniia* 3:35–46.

Ivanova, V., and I. Stoliarova. 1979. "Motivatsiia truda u Sovetskikh rabochikh." In *Trud kak Osnova Sotsialisticheskogo Obraza Zhizni*, edited by V. Staroverov, pp. 31–46. Moscow: Institut Sotsiologicheskikh Issledovanii.

Jackman, M. 1978. "General and Applied Tolerance: Does Education Increase Commitment to Racial Integration?" *American Journal of Political Science* 22:302–24.

Janowitz, M. 1978. *The Last Half-Century: Change and Politics in America.* Chicago: University of Chicago Press.

Jones, W. 1984. "Public Role, Private Role and Differential Moral Assessments of Role Performance." *Ethics*, July, 94 (4):603–20.

Kamaieva, N. 1977. "Sokrashchenie tekuchesti kak rezerv trudovoi aktivnosti rabochikh." In *Sotsial'nyie Problemy Sokrashcheniia Tekuchesti Kadrov i Formirovanie Stabil'nykh Proizvodstvennykh Kollektivov*, edited by B. Kononuik, pp. 99–106. Moscow: Institut Sotsiologicheskikh Issledovanii.

Kaminskaia, D. 1984. *Zapiski Advokata.* Benson, Va.: Khronika Press.

Kapelush, I., V. Sazonov, and L. Fedotova. 1985. *Uchrezhdeniia Kul'tury v Nebol'shom Gorode i Naseleniie.* Moscow: Mysl'.

Kapustin, E. 1984. "Osnovnyie teoreticheskiie problemy dal'neishego razvitiia dvizheniia za kommunisticheskoie otnosheniie k trudy." In

*Kommunisticheskoie Otnosheniie k Trudy: Opyt, Problemy*, edited by V. Smol'kov and M. Valitov. Moscow: Profizdat.

Karpukhin, O., and V. Kutsenko. 1983. *Student Segodnia-Specialist Zavtra*. Moscow: Molodaia Gvardiia.

Kataiev, S. 1986. "Muzykal'nyie Vkusy molodezhi." *Sotsiologicheskiie Issledovaniia* 1:105–08.

Katseneliboigen, A. 1978. *Studies in Soviet Economic Planning*. White Plains: M. E. Sharpe.

Keane, J. 1984. *Public Life and Late Capitalism: Toward Socialist Theory of Democracy*. London: Cambridge University Press.

Kelle, V., S. Kugel', and N. Makeshin. 1978. "Sotsiologicheskie aspekty organizatsii truda nauchnykh rabotnikov." In *Sotsiologicheskie Problemy Nauchnoi Deiatel'nosti*, edited by V. Kelle. Moscow: Nauka.

Kerimov, D., and Zh. Toshchenko. 1978. "Konstitutsiia SSSR i razvitiie Sotsial'no-politicheskoi aktivnosti trudiashchikhsiia." *Sotsiologicheskiie Issledovaniia* 1:1–15.

Kerimov, D., et al. 1985. *Gosudarstvennaia Disziplina i Sotsialisticheskii Pravoporiadok*. Moscow: Politizdat.

Kesel'man, E. 1981. "Sotsial'no-demograficheskiie faktory professional'no-proizvodstvennoi deiatel'nosti Rabochikh." In *Rabochii Klass SSSR na Rubezhe/80 kh Godov*. Moscow: Nauka.

Khabibullin, K. (ed.). 1980. *Razvitie Dukhovnykh Potrebnostei v Sisteme Sotsialishcheskogo Obraza Zhizni*. Leningrad: Pedagogicheskii Institut imeni Gerzena.

Khaikin, S. 1979. "Sotsial'no-psikhologicheskii aspekt formirovaniia otnosheniia k trudu v sel'skokhosiastvennom kollektive." In *Trud kak Osnova Sotsialisticheskogo Obraza Zhizni*, edited by V. Staroverov, pp. 59–72. Moscow: Institut Sotsiologicheskikh Issledovanii.

Kharchev, A. (ed.). 1982. *Sem'ia i Obshchestvo*. Moscow: Nauka.

Kharchev, A. 1979. *Brak i Sem'ia v SSSR*. Moscow: Mysl'.

Kharchev, A. (ed.). 1976. *Moral' Razvitogo Sotsializma*. (*Aktual'nyie problemy teorii*). Moscow: Mysl'.

Kharchev, A., and S. Golod. 1971. *Professional'naia Rabota Zhenshchin i Sem'ia*. Leningrad: Nauka.

Kharchev, A., and M. Matskovskii. 1978. *Sovremenaia Sem'ia i Ieie Problemy*. Moscow: Statistika.

Kharchev, A., and G. Odintsov (eds.). 1977. *Sotsiologicheskoi Sorevnovanie i Vospitanie Molodykh Rabochikh*. Moscow: Znaniie.

Khorev, B. 1981. *Territorial'naia Organisatsiia Obshchestva*. Moscow: Mysl'.

Khrushchev, N. 1961. "Otchet Zentral'nogo Komiteta Kommunisticheskoi Partii Sovietskogo Souza XXII S'ezdu KPSS." In *Materialy XXII S'edz KPSS*. Moscow: Gospolitizdat.

Kinder, D., and D. Sears. 1985. "Public Opinion and Political Action." In

*Handbook of Social Psychology*, edited by G. Lindsey and E. Tronson, vol. 2, pp. 659–742. New York: Random House.

Kinsburskii, S. 1984. "Vseobshcheie Professional'noie Obrazovaniie Molodezhi: Mneniia, Otsenki." *Sotsiologicheskiie Issledovaniia* 4:101–04.

Kupriianov, A., and L. Kuznetsova (eds.). 1986. *Trudovoi Kollektv i Aktivnaia Zhiznennaia Pozitsiia Lichnosti.* Leningrad: Izdatel'stvo Leningradskogo Universiteta.

Klementiev, D. 1984. *Lichnost' Razvitogo Sotsialisticheskogo Obshchestva.* Moscow: Moskovskii Universitet.

Klopov, E. 1985. *Rabochii Klass SSSR* (*Tendentsii Razvitiia v 60*–70 gg). Moscow: Mysl'.

Knizhnaia Palata. 1984. *Pechat' SSSR v 1983 Godu. Statistichesikii Sbornik.* Moscow: Finansy i Statiskika.

Kocherga, A., and A. Mazaraki. 1981. *Narodnokhosiastvennyi Kompleks i Sotsial'nyie Problemy.* Moscow: Ekonomika.

Kogan, L. (ed.). 1983. *Sotsial' no-Kul'turnyie Predposylki Samorealizatsii Lichnosti v .Sotsialisticheskom Obshchestve.* Sverdlovsk: Ural'skii Nauchnyi Zentr.

Kogan, L. (ed.). 1981. *Kul'turnaia Deiatel'nost: Opyt Sotsiologicheskogo Issledovaniia.* Moscow: Nauka.

Kogan, L. 1975. "Kniga i sovremennoie televideniie." In *Problemy Sotsiologii i Psikhologii Chteniia*, edited by E. Khrastetskii, pp. 103–17. Moscow: Kniga.

Kogan, L. 1970. *Iskusstvo i My.* Moscow: Iskusstvo.

Kogan, L., and A. Merenkov. 1983. "Kompleksnye brigady: Mneniia, otsenki, opyt vnedreniia." *Sotsiologicheskie Issledovaniia* 1:86–90.

Kohn, M. 1983. *Work and Personality: An Inquiry into the Impact of Social Stratification.* Norwood, N.J.: Ablex.

Kohn, M. 1981. "Personality, Occupation and Social Stratification: A Frame of Reference." In *Research in Social Stratification and Mobility*, edited by D. Treiman and R. Robinson, pp. 167–97. Geenwich: JAI Press.

Kohn, M. 1978. "The Reciprocal Effects of the Substantive Complexity of Work and Intellectual Flexibility: A Longitudinal Assessment." *American Journal of Sociology* 84:24–52.

Kohn, M. 1969. *Class and Conformity: A Study of Values.* Homewood, Ill.: Dorsey Press.

Kohn, M., and C. Schooler. 1982. "Job Conditions and Personality: A Longitudinal Assessment of their Reciprocal Effects." *American Journal of Sociology* 87:1257–86.

Kohn, M., and C. Schooler. 1973. "Occupational Experience and Psychological Functioning: An Assessment of Reciprocal Effects." *American Sociological Review* 38:97–118.

Kolbanovskii, V. (ed.). 1970. *Kollektiv Kolkhoznikov: Sotsial'no-Psikhologicheskoe Issledovaniie.* Moscow: Mysl'.

Kolker, Iu. 1985. "Ostrova blazhennykh." *Strana i Mir* 1-2:104-14.
Kol'man, E. 1982. *My Tak Ne Dolzhny Byli Zhit'.* New York: Chaldize.
Kolodizh, B. 1978. "Prestizh predpriiatiia v obshchestvennom mnenii zhitelei goroda." *Sotsiologicheskiie Issledovaniia* 3:110-77.
Kolpakov, B., and V. Patrushev (eds.). 1971. *Budzhet Vremeni Gorodskogo Naseleniia.* Moscow: Statistika.
Komozin, A. 1984. "Otsenka rabochimi razlichnykh storon brigadnogo metoda." *Sotsiologicheskiie Issledovaniia* 3:64-66.
Kon, I. (ed.). 1983. *Slovar' po Etike.* Moscow: Politizdat.
Kon, I. 1980. *Druzhba.* Moscow: Politizdat.
Konchanin, T. 1975. *Adaptatsiia Molodezhi k Trudu v Usloviiakh Zaversheniia Perekhoda ko Vseobshchemy Srednemu Obrazovaniiu.* Avtoreferat Kandidatskoi Dissertatsii. Moscow: Institut Sotsiologicheskikh Issledovanii.
Kononiuk, B. 1977. "Tekuchest' kadrov i sozdaniie stabil'nykh proizvodstvennykh kollektivov." In *Sotsial'nye Problemy Sokrashcheniia Tekuchesti Kadrov i Formirovanie Stabil'nkyk Proizvodstvennykh Kollektivov,* edited by B. Kononiuk, pp. 26-42. Moscow: Institut Sotsiologicheskikh Issledovanii.
Konstantinovskii, D. 1977. *Dinamika Professional'nykh Orientatsii Molodezhi Sibiri.* Novosibirsk: Nauka.
Konstantinovskii, D., and V. Shubkin. 1977. *Molodezh i Obrazovaniie.* Moscow: Nauka.
Konstitutsiia SSSR. 1977. Moscow: Politizdat.
Kontorovich, V., and V. Shlapentokh. 1986. *Organizational Innovation. Hidden Reserves in the Soviet Economy.* Pittsburgh: Center for Russian and East European Studies, University of Pittsburgh.
Kopelev, L. 1978. *I Sotvori Sebe Kumira.* Ann Arbor, Mich: Ardis.
Kopelev, L. 1975. *Khranit' Vechno.* Ann Arbor, Mich.: Ardis.
Koselleck, R. 1962. "Staat und Gesellschaft in Preussen 1815-1848." In *Staat und Gesellschaft im Deutschen Vorma'rz 1815-1848,* edited by W. Gonze. Stuttgart: E. Klatt.
Kosolapov, V., V. Vasilenko, and V. Volovich. 1982. *NTR i Formirovaniie Dukhovnogo Oblika Sovietskogo Rabochego.* Kiev: Izdatel'stvo Politichykoi Literatury Ukrainy.
Kostiuk, V., M. Traskunova, and D. Konstantinovskii. 1980. *Molodezh Sibiri: Obrazovanie i Vybor Professii.* Novosibirsk: Nauka.
Kotliar, A. (ed.). 1982. *Dvizheniie Rabochei Sily v Krupnom Corode'.* Moscow: Finansy i Statistika.
Kotliar, A., and V. Trubin. 1978. *Problemy Regulirovaniia Pereraspredeleniia Rabochei Sily.* Moscow: Ekonomika.
Kovalev, A. 1975. *Kollektiv i Sotsial'no-psikhologicheskiie Problemy Rukovodstva.* Moscow: Gospolitizdat.
Kozhevnikova, N. 1985. "Migratsionnyie prozessy i ikh vzaimosviaz' s sotzi-

al'no-demograficheskim razvitiiem territorii." In *Sovremennyie Problemy Migratsii*, edited by L. Rybakovskii, pp. 82–100. Moscow: Mysl'.

Kozlov, A., and A. Lisovskii. 1986. *Molodoi Chelovek: Stanovleniie Obraza Zhizni.* Moscow: Politizdat.

Kozlov, V., and D. Khlevniuk. 1985. "Chelovecheskii faktor v razvitii ekonomiki: Uroki 30kh godov." *Kommunist* 2:55–64.

Kozlova, T. 1983. *Vozrastnyie Gruppy v Nauchnom Kollektive.* Moscow: Nauka.

Kozlova, T., and C. Subbotina. 1976. "Tvorcheskaiia aktivnost' nauchnykh rabotnikov." In *Aktivnost' Lichnosti v Sotsialisticheskom Obshchestve*, edited by T. Iaroshevskii and N. Mansurov, pp. 185–99. Moscow: Nauka.

Kozyrev, Iu., and R. Nikiforov. 1975. "Vybor professii: prognozy i real'nost'." In *Sotsiologichesikiie Issledovaniia Orientatsii Molodezhi*, edited by Iu. Kozyrev, pp. 42–58. Moscow: Institut Sotsiologicheskikh Issledovanii.

Kriagzhde, S. 1981. *Psikhologiia Formirovaniia Professional'nykh Interesov.* Vil'nius: Mokslas.

Krupin, V. 1985. *Vo Vsiu Ivanovskuiu.* Moscow: Sovietskii Pisatel'.

Krutova, O. 1985. *Chelovek kak Tvorets Morali.* Moscow: Znaniie.

Kugel, S., and O. Nikandrov. 1971. *Molodyie Inzhenery.* Moscow: Nauka.

Kupriianova, Z., and Pushkarev, V. (eds.). 1982. *Formirovaniie i Stabilizatsiia Kvalifizirovannykh Kadrov Promyshlennosti i Stroitel'stva.* Novosibirsk: Nauka.

Kurchatkin, A. 1986. *Istorii Raznykh Mest.* Moscow: Sovremennik.

Kuregian, E. 1983. "Otnosheniie k trudu i distsiplina promyshlennykn rabochikh." *Sotsiologicheskiie Issledovaniia* 2:129–30.

Kuregian, E. 1979. "Opyt empiricheskogo issledovaniia faktorov stanovleniia kommunisticheskogo otnosheniia k trudy." In *Sotsialishicheskii Trud*, edited by I. Changli, pp. 86–102. Moscow: Institut Sotsiologicheskikh Issledovanii.

Kurman, M. 1971. *Dvizheniie Rabochiksi Kadrov promyshlennogo predpriiatiia.* Moscow: Statistika.

Kuzmin, A. 1985. "V prodolzhenii vazhnogo razgovora." *Nash Sovremennik* 3:182–90.

Kvasov, G. 1982. "Kollektivism kak obraz zhizni: Analiz stanovleniia moral'nykh tsennostei." In *Sovietskaia Sotsiologiia*, edited by T. Riabushkin, vol. 1, pp. 181–89. Moscow: Nauka.

Lapidus, G. 1978. *Women in Soviet Society.* Berkeley: University of California Press.

Lebidinskii, V., and T. Mal'kovskaia (eds.). 1984. *Metodika Vospitatel'noi Raboty s Pionerami i Oktiabriatami.* Moscow: Prosveshchenie.

Lehman, H. 1953. *Age and Achievement.* Princeton: Yale University Press.

Lerner, D. 1968. "Modernization: Social Aspects." In *International Encyclopedia of the Social Sciences*, edited by D. Sills, vol. 10. New York: Macmillan and Free Press.

Levin, B., and M. Petrovich. 1984. *Ekonomicheskiie Funktsii Sem'i*. Moscow: Finansy i Statistika.

Levinson, A. 1985. "Makulatura i Knigi." In *Chteniie: Problemy i Razrabotki*, edited by V. Stelmakh, pp. 63–88. Moscow: Biblioteka imeni Lenina.

Levykin, I. 1984. "K voprosy ob integral'nykh pokazateliakh sotsialisticheskogo obraza zhizni." *Sotsiologicheskiie Issledovaniia* 2:90–97.

Lillas, M. 1985. "What is the Civic Interest?" *The Public Interest* 81:64–81.

Lipkin, S. 1983. *Dekada*. New York: Chalidze.

Litvinov, P. 1976. "O dvizhenii za prava cheloveka." In *Samosoznaniie. Sbornik Statei*, edited by P. Litvinov, M. Meerson-Aksenov, and B. Shragin. New York: Khronika.

Lobanov, N., and G. Cherkasov (eds.). 1981. *Sotsial'nyie Faktory Povysheniia Effectivnosti Truda*. Leningrad: Nauka.

Loiberg, M. 1982. *Stabilizatsiia Proizvodstvennykh Kollektivov v Lesnoi i Derevoobratyvaushchei Promyshlennosti*. Moscow: Lesnaia Promyshlennost'.

Lopata, P., and V. Petukhov. 1986. *Sozidatel'naia Sila Sotsialisticheskogo Samoupravleniia Naroda*. Moscow: Znaniie.

Losenkov, V. 1983. *Sotsial'naia Informatsiia v Zhizni Gorodskogo Naseleniia*. Leningrad: Nauka.

Lysenko, V 1982. *Poslednii Reis*. Frankfurt: Posev.

Magun, V. 1983a. *Potrebnosti i Psikhologiia Sotsial'noi Deiatel'nosti Lichnosti*. Leningrad: Nauka.

Magun, V. 1983b. "Dva tipa sootnosheniia produktivnosti truda i udovletvorennost'iu rabotoi," *Sotsiologicheskiie Issledovaniia* 4:64–71.

Makanin, V. 1984. *Gde Skhodilos' nebo s Kholmami*. Moscow: Sovremennik.

Mangutov, I. 1980. *Inzhener*. Moscow: Sovietskaia Rossia.

Mansurov, N. 1979. "Sistemnyi podkhod k izucheniiu sredstv massovoi informatsii i uchrezhdenii kul'tury." In *Massovaia Kommunikatsiia v Sotsialistcheskom Obshchestve*, edited by A. Dmitriev, N. Mansurov, and P. Tamash, pp. 112–30. Leningrad: Nauka.

Mansurov, N. 1978. "Kompleksnyi podkhod k vospitaniiu." In *Sotsiologicheskiie Problemy Kommunisticheskogo Vospitaniia*, edited by N. Mansurov, pp. 7–30. Moscow: Institut Sotsiologicheskikh Issledovanii.

Markus, M. 1982. "Overt and Covert Modes of Legitimization in East European Societies." In *Political Legitimization in Communist States*, edited by T. Rigby and F. Feher, pp. 82–93. London: The Macmillan Press.

*Materially XXVII S"ezda Kommunisticheskoi Partii Sovietskogo Soiuza*, 1986. Moscow: Politizdat.

McClosky, H., and F. Turner. 1960. *The Soviet Dictatorship*. New York: McGraw-Hill.

Melentiev, Iu. 1986. *Glazami Naroda*. Moscow: Sovremennik.

Merton, R. 1957. *Social Theory and Social Structure*. Glencoe, Ill: Free Press.

Metchenko, A., and S. Petrov (eds.). 1983. *Istoriia Russkoi Sovietskoi Literatury (1917–1970)*. Moscow: Prosveshcheniie.

Mickiewicz, E. 1981. *Media and the Russian Public*. New York: Praeger.

Mikoian, A. 1975. *V Nachale Dvadsatykh*. Moscow: Gospolitizdat.

Mints, C., and T. Nepomniashchii. 1979. "Tendentsii izmeneniia budzheta vremeni rabotaiushchego naseleniia gorodov Latviiskoi SSSR." In *Tendentsii Izmeneniia Budzheta Vremeni Trudiashchikhsia*, edited by V. Patrushev, pp. 33–43. Moscow: Institut Sotsiologicheskikh Issledovanii.

Moiseenko, V. 1985. "Migratsiia naseleniia." In *Demograficheskii Entsiklopedicheskii Slovar'*, edited by D. Valentei, pp. 251–55. Moscow: Sovietskaia Entsiklopediia.

Moiseenko, V. 1983. "Migranty v krupneishem gorode." In *Na Novom Meste*, edited by E. Vasilieva, pp. 12–22. Moscow: Finansy i Statistka.

Moor, B. 1985. "Privacy." *Society* 22, 4:17–27.

Moor, B. 1984. *Privacy: Studies in Social and Cultural History*. Armonk, N.Y.: M. E. Sharpe.

Morozov, B. (ed.). 1984. *Sredstva Massovoi Informatsii i Propagandy*. Moscow: Politizdat.

Morozov, B., V. Fadeiev, and V. Shinkarenko. 1984. *Planirovaniie Ideologicheskoi Politiko-vospitatel'noi Raboty*. Moscow: Mysl'.

Morozova, G. 1985. "Territorial'naia differentsiatsiia prizhivaemosti novoselov." In *Sovremennyie Problemy Migratzii*, edited by L. Rybakovsikii, pp. 17–28.

Mosher, R. 1980. *Moral Education*. New York: Praeger.

Motiashov, V. 1985. *Vlast' Veshchei i Vlast' Cheloveka*. Moscow: Molodaia Gvardiia.

Mozhaev, B. 1981. *Minuvshiie Gody*. Moscow: Sovietskii Pisatel'.

Mozyreva, T. 1982. "Faktory formirovaniia stabil'nykh kadrov ITR." In *Formirovaniie i Stabilizatsiia Kvalifizirovanykh Kadrov Promyshlennosti i Stroitel'stva*, edited by Z. Kupriianova and V. Pushkarev, pp. 177–96. Novosibirsk: Nauka.

Muchnik. I., E. Petrenko, E. Sinitsyn, and T. Iaroshenko. 1980. *Territorial'naia Vyborka v Sotsiologicheskikh Issledovaniiakh*. Moscow: Nauka.

Mus'ko, N. 1979. "K Voprosu o formirovanii ekonomicheskogo myshleniia proizvodstvennikov." In *Trud kak Osnova Sotsialisticheskogo Obraza Zhizni*, edited by V. Staroverov, pp. 109–16. Moscow: Institut Sotsiologicheskikh Issledovanii.

Natalushko, S. 1981. "Povyshenie urovnia sotsial'nogo rasvitiia trudovogo kollektiva kak faktora rosta effektivnosti truda." In *Planirovanie i Upravlenie v Nauchnykh Kollektivakh*. Moscow: Institut Sotsoiologicheskikh Issledovanii.

Nesterov, F. 1984. *Sviaz' Vremen* (2nd ed.). Moscow: Molodaia Gvardiia.

Nikitenko, V., and V. Ossovskii. 1981. "Obrazovaniie i proforientatsiia molodezhi (na primere USSR)." In *Sovietskaia Molodezh. Demograficheskii Aspekt*, edited by E. Vasilieva, pp. 32–43. Moscow: Finansy i Statistika.

Nikitin, A. 1986. "Ne robei khosiain." *Literaturnaia Gazeta*, August 6, p. 10.

Norkin, C. 1982. "Sotsiol'naia aktivnost' trudiashchikhsia v sfere kontrolia Za disciplinoi truda." In *Sotsiol'naia Aktivnost' Rabochego Klassa V Usloviiakh Razvitogo Sotsialisma*, edited by D. Mutagirov and S. Lazuka, pp. 86–97. Leningrad: Izdatel'stvo Leningradskogo Universiteta.

Nove, A. 1980. "Socialism, Centralized Planning and One-Party State." In *Authority, Power and Policy in the USSR*, edited by T. Rigby, A. Brown, and P. Reddaway, pp. 77–97. London: Macmillan.

Novoselov, V. 1985. *Uchastiie Grazhdan v Upravleniie Gosudarstvennymi i Obshchestvennymi Delami*. Moscow: Znaniie.

Odintsov, V. 1976. "Klubnoie obsluzhivaniie naseleniia." *Sotsiologicheskiie Issledovaniia* 1:124–25.

Olson, M. 1965. *The Logic of Collective Action: Public Goods and the Theory of Groups*. Cambridge, Mass.: Harvard University Press.

Orlova, R. 1982. "Frida Vigdorova." *Vnutrenniie Protivorechiia* 3:300–26.

Osipov, G. (ed.). 1983. *Rabochaia Kniga Sotsiologa*. Moscow: Nauka.

Osipov, G., and V. Andreenkov. 1982. "Rabochii klass i inzhenerno-tekhnicheskaia intelligentsiia: Pokazateli sotsial'nogo razvitia." In *Sovietskaia Sotsiologiia*, vol. 2, edited by T. Riabushkin and G. Osipov. Moscow: Nauka.

Osipov, G., and E. Andreev (Eds.). 1981. *Standartizatsiia Pokazatelei v Sotsiologicheskom Issledovanii*. Moscow: Nauka.

Osipov, V. 1978. *Tri Otnosheniia k Rodine*. Frankfurt: Posev.

Panov, V. (ed.). 1985. *Ezhegodnik Bol'shoi Sovietskoi Entsiklopedii*. Moscow: Sovietskaia Entsiklopediia.

Panova, V. 1975. *O Moiei Zhizni, Knigakh i Chitateliakh*. Leningrad: Leninzdat.

Parta, E., F. Klensin, and I. de Sola Pool. 1982. "The shortwave audience in the USSR—methods for improving the estimates." *Communication Resources* 9 (October):581–601.

Parygin, B. 1981. *Sotsial'no-Psikhologicheskii Klimat Kollektiva*. Leningrad: Nauka.

Pashkov, S. (ed.). 1983. "Trud i sotsial'noie razvitiie sotsialisticheskogo Obshchestsa." *Chelovek i Obshchestvo*. v XVIII. Leningrad: Izdatel'stvo Leningradskogo Universitet.

Patrushev, V. 1979. "Tendentsii izmeneniia budzheta vremeni trudiashchikhsia promyshlennosti i sel' skogo khosiastva v period 1960–1970." In *Tendentsii Izmeneniia Budzheta Vremeni Trudiashchikhsia*, edited by

V. Patrushev, pp. 6–32. Moscow: Institut Sotsiologicheskikh Issledovanii.

Patrushev, V., and L. Razmolova. 1984. "Otnosheniie k rabochemu vremeni v Proizvodstvennykh Kollektivakh." *Sotsiologicheskiie Issledovaniia* 3:98–105.

Pavlov, B. 1975. "Razvitiie kollektivisma v bytu rabochei molodezhi." In *Issledovaniie i Planirovaniie Dukhovnoi Kul'tury Trudiashchikhsia Urala*, edited by L. Kogan and A. Sharova, pp. 104–24. Sverdlovsk: Ural'skii Nauchnyi Zentr AN SSSR.

Pazenok, V. (ed.). 1983. *Razvitoi Sotsialism i Lichnost'*. Kiev: Kievskii Universitet.

Perevedentsev, V. 1985a. "Chelovek s putevkoi." *Rabotnitsa* 8:16–17.

Perevedentsev, V. 1985b. "Dikari na Kurorte." *Rabotnitsa* 10:22–23.

Perevedentsev, V. 1979. "Mezhdu derevnei i gorodom." In *Kuda i Zachem Edut Liudi*, edited by D. Valentei, pp. 17–25. Moscow: Statistika.

Perevedentsev, V. 1975. *Metody Izucheniia Migratsii Naseleniia*. Moscow: Nauka.

Petrenko, E., and T. Iaroshenko. 1979. *Sotial'no-demograficheskiie Pokazateli v Sotsiologicheskikh Issledovaniiakh*. Moscow: Statistika.

Pierson, C. 1984. "New Theories of State and Civil Society." *Sociology* 18, 4:563–71.

Piskotin, M. 1986. *Sovietskii Rukovoditel'*. Moscow: Znaniie.

Plaksii, S. 1982. *Tvoi Molodoi Sovremennik*. Moscow: Molodaia Gvardiia.

Plushch, L. 1979. *Na Karnavale Istorii*. London: Overseas Press.

Podmazov, A. 1985. *Sovremennaia Religioznost'*. Riga: Zinatne.

Pogosian, G. 1983. "Forma voprosa i tselevaia ustanovka issledovatelia." *Sotsiologicheskiie Issledovaniia* 3:162–67.

Pogrebin, C. 1986. *Among Friends: Who We Like, Why We Like Them and What We Do With Them*. New York: McGraw-Hill.

Poliakov, Iu. 1986. "Rabota nad oshibkami." *Iunost'* 9:3–43.

Poliakov, Iu. 1985. "ChP raionogo maschtaba." *Iunost"* 1:12–52.

Polikanov, S. 1983. *Razryv*. Frankfurt: Posev.

Ponomarev, L., and Z. Toshchenko (eds.). 1984. *Kommunistetkoie Vospitaniie. Slovar'*. Moscow: Politizdat.

Popov, V. 1979. *Obrazovaniie, Lichnost', Obshchestvo*. Saratov: Oblizdat.

Popova, I. 1984. "Tsenostnye predstavleniia i paradoksy soznaniia." *Sotsiologicheskiie Issledovaniia* 4:29–36.

Popova, I., and V. Moin. 1983. "Zarabotnaia plata kak sotsial' naia tsennost'." *Sotsiologicheskiie Issledovaniia* 2:102–10.

Pozdniakova, M. 1987. "Obespechennost" naseleniia predmetami kul'turnobytovogo naznacheniia." *Sotsiologicheskie Issledovaniia* 3:59–61.

Programma Kommunisticheskoi Partii Sovietskogo Souza. 1986. In *Materially XXVII S"ezda Kommunisticheskoi Partii Sovietskogo Souza*. Moscow: Gospolitizdat.

Prokhorov, E. (ed.). 1981. *Sotsiologiia Zhurnalistiki*. Moscow: Izdatel'stvo Moskovskogo Universiteta.

Prokofiev, M. (ed.). 1985. *Narodnoie Obrazovaniie v SSSR*. Moscow: Pedagogika.

Protasenko, T. 1985. "Osnovnyie kharakteristiki material' nogo blagosostoianiia." *Sotsiologicheskiie Issledovaniia* 3:101–10.

Pruts, Z., B. Sultanova, and M. Talaloi. 1980. *Sozdaniie Postoiannykh Kadrov na Predpriiatiiakh*. Moscow: Profizdat.

Pulatov, T. 1984. *Zhizneopisaniie Stroptivogo Bukhartza*. Moscow: Khudozhestvennaia Literatura.

Raig, I. 1986. "Chto mozhet individual' noie khosiastvo." *Sotsiologicheskiie Issledovaniia* 1:33–41.

Rasputin, V. 1985a *Vek Zhivi-Vek Lubi*. Moscow: Izvestia.

Rasputin, V. 1985b. "Pozhar." *Nash Sovremennik* 7:1–50.

Rasputin, V. 1980. *Povesti*. Moscow: Molodaia Gvardiia.

Ratnikov, V. 1978. *Kollektiv Kak Sotsial'naia Obshchnost'*. Moscow: Izdatel'stvo Moskovskogo Universiteta.

Reznik, S. 1982. *Trudovyie Resursy v Stroitel'stve*. Moscow: Stroiizdat.

Reznik, S., and Yu. Lipovskii. 1981. "Trudovaia distsiplina stroitel'nykh rabochikh." *Sotsiologicheskie Issledovaniia* 1:135–45.

Riabushkin, T. (ed.). 1978a. *Sotsial'nai Structura Sovietskogo Obshchestva i Sotsialisticheskii Obraz Zhizni* (Vol. 1). Moscow: Naska.

Riabushkin, T. (ed.). 1978b. *Demograficheskiie Problemy Sem'i*. Moscow: Nauka.

Riabushkin, T., and L. Rybakovskii (eds.). 1981. *Demograficheskiie Prozessy v Sotsialisticheskom Obshchestve*. Moscow: Finansy i Statistika.

Rigby, T. H. 1980. "A Conceptual Approach to Authority, Power, and Policy in the Soviet Union." In *Authority, Power, and Policy in the USSR*, edited by T. H. Rigby, A. Brown, and P. Reddaway. London: Macmillan.

Rigby, T. H. 1976. "Politics in the Mono-organizational Society." In *Authoritarian Politics in Communist Europe: Uniformity and Diversity in the One-Party State*, edited by A. Janos. Berkeley: University of California International Studies.

Rimashevskaia, N., and S. Karapetian. 1985. *Sem'ia i Narodnoie Blagosostoianiie v Razvitom Sotsialisticheskom Obshchestve*. Moscow: Mysl'.

Rodionov, P. (ed.). 1984. *Voprosy Vnutripartiinogo Razvitiia KPSS v Usloviiakh Zrelogo Sotsialisma*. Moscow: Gospolitizdat.

Roger, F. 1985. "On the Degeneration of the Public Sphere." *Political Studies* 33:203–17.

Rogovin, V. 1984. *Obshchestvo Zrelogo Sotsialisma*. Moscow: Mysl'.

Rogovin, V. 1980. *Sotsial'naia Politika v Razvitom Sotsialisticheskom Obshchestve*. Moscow: Nauka.

Rogovin, V., and V. Usanov. 1985. "Sotsial'naia sfera: Puti i sredstva sovershenstvovaniia." *Pravda*, September 9.

Rokeach, M. 1973. *The Nature of Human Values*. New York: Free Press.

Romashov, O. 1976. "Vliianiie proizvodstvennoi informirovannosti rabochikh na ikh obshchestvenno-politicheskuiu i trudovuiu aktivnost'." *Sotsiologicheskiie Issledovaniia* 4:68–73.

Rosenbaum, V. 1983. "Lichnyi primer rukovoditelia." *Literaturnaia Gazeta*, July 20, 1983, p. 13.

Ross, E. 1932. *Civic Sociology*. New York: World Book Company.

Ross, E., and M. McCaull. 1926. *Readings in Civic Sociology*. New York: World Book company.

Rossels, F. 1979. "Sovershenstvovaniie zaniatosti sotsial' no-neprivlekatel' nymi vidami truda". In *Sotsialisticheskii Trud*, edited by I. Changli, pp. 23–36.

Rotman, D. 1979. ''Nekotoryie problemy sovershenstvovaniia organizatisii Sotsialisticheskogo sorevnovaniia v trudovykh kollektivakh." In *Sotsialisticheskii Trud*, edited by I. Changli, pp. 115–28. Moscow: Institut Sotsialisticheskikh Issledovanii.

Rubin, T. 1983. "One to One: Understanding Personal Relationships." *U.S. News and World Report*, February 11.

Rubina, L. 1981. *Sovietskoie Studenchestvo*. Moscow: Mysl'.

Rubinov, A. 1984. "Avtostrasti pri lune." *Literaturnaia Gazeta*, May 9, 1984.

Rukavishnikov, V., V. Paniotto, and N. Churilov. 1984. *Oprosy Naseleniia*. Moscow: Finansy i Statistika.

Rumiantsev, A. (ed.). 1983. *Nauchnyi Kommunism. Slovar*. Moscow: Politizdat.

Rusetskaia, V. 1984. *Kollektivistskaia Sushchnost' Obshchestvennykh Otnoshenii pri Sotsialisme*. Minsk: Nauka i Tekhnika.

Rutkevich, M. 1985. "Sotsial'noie neravenstvo i spravedlivost." *Sovietskaia Rossia*, March 3.

Rutkevich, M. 1982. *Stanovleniie Sotsial'noi Odnorodnosti. Sotsialism*. Moscow: Gospolitizdat.

Ruzhzhe, V., I. Eliseieva, and T. Kadibur. 1983. *Struktura i Funktsii Semeinykh Grup*. Moscow: Finansy i Statistika.

Ryvkina, R. 1979. *Obraz Zhizni Sel'skogo Naseleniia*. Novosibirsk: Nauka.

Safarov, R. 1975. *Obshchestvennoie Mneniie i Gosudarstvennoie Upravleniie*. Moscow: Iuridicheskaia Literatura.

Samoilova, E. 1978. *Naselenie i Obrazovanie*. Moscow: Statistika.

Saraceno, S. 1984. ''Shifts in Public and Private Boundaries: Women as Mothers and Service Workers." *Feminist Studies*, 10 (1), Spring, 1–29.

Sbytov, V. 1983. *Upravleniie Sotsial'nymi i Ideologicheskimi Prozessami v Period Razvitogo Sotsialisma*. Moscow: Nauka.

Sdobnov, S. 1985. *Sotsialishcheskaiia Sobstvennost' i Sotsial'nyi Progress*. Moscow: Ekonomika.

Semenov, G. 1986. "Um lisitsy." *Novy Mir* 7:6–61.

Semenov, G. 1985a. *Zapakh Sgorevshego Meda*. Moscow: Sovremennik.

Semenov, G. 1985b. *Gorodskoi Peizazh.* Moscow: Sovietskii Pisatel'.
Semenov, I. 1983–84. *Sobraniie sochinenii,* Vol. 1–5. Moscow: Sovremennik.
Semenov, V. 1985. "Kurs na uskorenie Sotsial'no-ekonomicheskogo razvitiia, no sovershenstrovanie obshchestva razvitogo sotsializma." *Voprosy Filosofii* 5:15–34.
Semenov, V. 1977. *Dialektika Razvitiia Sotsial'noi Struktury Sovietskogo Obshchestva.* Moscow: Mysl'.
Semenova, V. 1979. "Trudovoi kollektiv kak faktor, vliiaushchii na nravstvennoie razvitiie lichnosti." In *Trud Kak Osnova Sotsialisticheskogo Obraza Zhizni,* edited by V. Staroverov, pp. 165–80. Moscow: Institut Sotsiologicheskikh Issledovanii.
Sennett, R. 1977. *The Fall of Public Man.* New York: Knopf.
Shafarevich, I. 1977. *Sotsialism kak Iavlenie Mirovoi Istorii.* Paris: Ymka.
Shakhnazarov, G., and F. Burlatskii. 1980. "O razvitii Marksistko—Leninskoi politicheskoi nauku." *Voprosy Filosofii* 12:10–23.
Shalenko, V. 1977. "Nravstvennoie vospitaniie. Trudovoi kollektiv i lichnost'." In *Kompleksnyi Podkhod k Kommunisticheskomy Vospitaniiu,* edited by N. Mansurov, pp. 64–78. Moscow: Institut Sotsiologicheskikh Issledovanii.
Shanov, D., and A. Kuznetsov. 1977. "Opyt sotsiologicheskogo analiza problemy sotsial'nogo planirovaniia v nauchnom kollektive." In *Problemy Sotsial'nogo Planirovaniia v Nauchnom Kollektive,* edited by A. Zworykin. Moscow: Institut Sotsiologicheskikh Issledovanii.
Shapiro, V. 1983. *Sotsial'naia Aktivnost' Pozhilykh Ludei V SSSR.* Moscow: Nauka.
Shapiro, V. 1980. *Chelovek na Pensii.* Moscow: Mysl'.
Shchekochikhin, Iu. 1987. "Pered zerkalom." *Literaturnaia Gazeta,* September 2, 1987, p. 13.
Sheinin, Iu. 1980. "Uslovia nauchnogo truda." In *Nauka v Sotsial'nykh, Gnoseolocheskikh i Tsennostnykh Aspektakh,* edited by L. Bazhenov and A. Akhundov. Moscow: Nauka.
Shevtsov, V. 1979. *Gosudarstvennyi Suverinitet.* Moscow: Politizdat.
Shipler, D. 1983. *Russia: Broken Idols, Solemn Dreams.* New York: Times Books.
Shishkina, L. 1985. "Kharakteristika prozessa tekuchesti kadrov v promyshlennosti Novosibirska." In *Dvizheniie Kadrov v Sibirskom Gorode,* edited by E. Antosenkov and Z. Kupriianova, pp. 90–130. Novosibirsk: Nauka.
Shishov, A. 1983. *Grupkomsorgu.* Moscow: Molodaia Gvardiia.
Shkaratan, O. (ed.). 1985. *Rabochii i Inzhener.* Moscow: Mysl'.
Shkaratan, O. 1982. "Effektivnost' truda i otnoshenie k trudu." *Sotsiologicheskiie Issledovaniia* 1:19–28.
Shkaratan, O. 1978. *Promyshlennoie Predpriiatiie.* Moscow: Mysl'.

Shkaratan, O., O. Staknanova, and O. Filippova. 1977. "Cherty sotsial'nogo rosta Sovietskogo rabochego." *Sotsiologicheskiie Issledovaniia* 4:40–50.

Shlapentokh, V. 1987a. "Evolution in the Soviet Sociology of Work." *Work and Occupation* 3:410–33.

Shlapentokh, V. 1987b. *The Politics of Sociology in the Soviet Union.* Boulder, Colo.: Westview Press.

Shlapentokh, V. 1986. *Public Opinion and Ideology: Pragmatism in Interaction.* New York: Praeger.

Shlapentokh, V. 1985a. *Sociology and Politics: The Soviet Case.* Falls Church, Va.: Delphic Associates.

Shlapentokh, V. 1985b. *Evolution in the Soviet Sociology of Work: From Ideology to Pragmatism.* The Carl Beck Papers in Russian and East European Studies. Pittsburgh: University of Pittsburgh.

Shlapentokh, V. 1985c. "Two Levels of Public Opinion: The Soviet Case." *Public Opinion Quarterly*, Winter: 443–59.

Shlapentokh, V. 1984a. *Love, Marriage and Friendship in the Soviet Union: Ideals and Practices.* New York: Praeger.

Shlapentokh, V. 1984b. "Moscow's War Propaganda and Soviet Public Opinion." *Problems of Communism*, September–October, pp. 88–94.

Shlapentokh, V. 1982. "Human Aspirations as a Cause of the Failure of Soviet Agricultue." *The Rural Sociologist 2:138*–49.

Shlapentokh, V. 1978a. "Methodologicheskie problemy sopostavleniia sotsiologicheskikh pokazatelei." In *Sotsial'nye Issledovaniia: Postroennie i Sravnenie Pokazatelei,* edited by E. Andreev, N. Blinov, and V. Shlapentokh, pp. 130–212. Moscow: Nauka.

Shlapentokh, V. 1978b. "Veshchi: druz'ia ili vragi." In *Vospitaniie Grazhdanina,* edited by D. Gamanina and V. Matveeva, pp. 167–87. Moscow: Pedagogika.

Shlapentokh, V. 1976. *Problemy Representativnosti Sotsiologicheskoi Informatsii.* Moscow: Statistika.

Shlapentokh, V. 1973. *Problemy Dostoverrnosti Statistichekoi Informatsii v Sotsiologicheskikh Issledovaniiakh.* Moscow: Statistika.

Shlapentokh, V. 1970. *Sotsiologiia Dliia Vsekh.* Moscow: Sovietskaia Rossia.

Shlapentokh, V. (ed.). 1969a. *Chitatel' i Gazeta: Chitateli Truda.* Moscow: Institut Konkretnykh Sotsial'nykh Issledovanii.

Shlapentokh, V. (ed.). 1969b. *Chitatel' i Gazeta: Chitateli Izvestii i Literaturnaia Gazeta.* Moscow: Institut Konkretnykh Sotsial'nykn Issledovanii.

Shlapentokh, V. (ed.). 1969c. *Sotsiologiia Pechati,* Vol. 1 Novosibirsk: Statistika.

Shlapentokh, V. 1969d. "Vosrast i zarabotnaia plata kak faktory tekuchesti rabochei sily." In *Opyt Issledovaniia Peremeny Truda v Promyshlennosti,* edited by E. Antosenkov, pp. 115–29. Novosibirsk: Nauka.

Shmelev, G. 1985. *Lichnoie Podsobnoie Khosiastvo.* Moscow: Politizdat.

Shokhin, A. 1986. *Neprimirimost' k Netrudovym Dokhodam*. Moscow: Znaniie.

Shorokhova, E., and O. Zotova (eds.). 1980. *Sotsial'no-Psikhologicheskii Klimat Kollektiva*. Moscow: Nauka.

Shtemler, I. 1986. "Poezd." *Novy Mir*, 8:7–86 and 9:67–129.

Shtemler, I. 1984. *Univermag*. Moscow: Molodaia Gvardiia.

Shubkin, V. (ed.). 1984. *Trudiashchaiasia Molodesh: Obrazovaniie, Professiia, Mobil'nost'*. Moscow: Nauka.

Shubkin, V. 1970. *Sotsiologicheskiie Opyty*. Moscow: Mysl'.

Shubkin, V. 1966. "Kolichestvennyie metody v sotsiologicheskikh issledovaniiakh problem trudoustroistva i vybora professii." In *Kolichestvennyie Metody v Sotsiologii*, edited by V. Shubkin, pp. 168–232. Moscow: Nauka.

Shubkin, V., and T. Babushkina. 1986. "Otsenka professii: obshehee i spezificheskoie." In *Vybor Professii: Motivy i Ikh Realisatsiia*, edited by S. Kuznetsova, pp. 27–53. Moscow: Znaniie.

Shukshin, V. 1984. *Rasskazy*. Moscow: Khudozhestvennaia Literatura.

Shukshin, V. 1982. *Ia Prishel Dat' Vam Volu*. Kishinev: Literatura Artistika.

Shukshin, V. 1970. *Ziemliaki*. Moscow: Khudozhestvennaia Literatura.

Shumakov, A. (ed.). 1983. *Knizhka Partiinogo Aktivista*. Moscow: Gospolitizdat.

Siltanen, F., and M. Stanworth. 1984. "The Politics of Private Woman and Public Man." *Theory and Society* 13, 1:91–118.

Simis, K. 1982. *USSR: The Corrupt Society*. New York: Simon and Schuster.

Simonian, R. 1986. *Kollektiv, Sorevnovaniie, Lichnost'*. Moscow: Sovietskaia Rossia.

Simush, P. (ed.). 1965. *Kolkhoz-Shkola Kommunisma Dlia Krest'ianstva*. Moscow: Mysl'.

Siniavskii, S. 1982. *Sotsial'naia Struktura Sovietskogo Obshchestva v Usloviiakh Razvitogo Sotsialisma (1961–1980gg)*. Moscow: Mysl'.

Sizemskaia, I. 1981. *Chelovek i Trud*. Moscow: Politizdat.

Skvortsov, I. 1968. "Trud glazami Chitatelei." *Zhurnalist* 7:45–50.

Slater, P. 1970. *The Pursuit of Loneliness: American Culture at the Breaking Point*. Boston: Beacon.

Smelser, N. 1981. *Sociology*. Englewood Cliffs, N.J.: Prentice-Hall.

Smirnov, V. 1979. *Sotsial'naia Aktivnost' Sovietskikh Rabochikh*. Moscow: Politizdat.

Smith, H. 1976. *The Russians*. New York: Ballantine.

Sobolev, M. (ed.). 1984. *Partiino-Politicheskaia Rabota v Sovietskoi Armii i Flote*. Moscow: Voenizdat.

Sokirko, V. 1981. "Ekonomika 1990: Chto nas zhdet i est li vykhod." *Posev* 1.

Sokolov, V. 1981. *Nravstvennyi Mir Sovietskogo Cheloveka*. Moscow: Politizdat.

Sokolov, V. 1978. "Problemy nravstvennogo vospitaniia kak ob'ekt sotsiologicheskogo issledovaniia." *Sotsiologicheskiie Issledovaniia* 1:48–52.

Sokolova, G. 1984. *Kul'tura Truda v Sotial'nom Razvitii Rabochego Klassa.* Minsk: Nauka i Tekhnika.

Solovieva, N. (ed.). 1978. *Kniga i Chteniie v Zhizni Sovietskogo Sela.* Moscow: Kniga.

Solovykh, N. 1977. "Orientatsiia shkol'nikov i podgotovka kadrov dlia nauki." In *Opyt Issledovaniia Sotsiologicheskikh Problemy Truda, Obrazovaniia i Vospitaniia Molodezhi Sibiri,* edited by R. Ianovskii, pp. 65–76. Novosibirsk: Institut Istorii, Filologii i Filosofii.

Solzhenitsyn, A. 1984. *One Day in the Life of Ivan Denisovich.* Harmondsworth: Penguin.

Solzhenitsyn, A. 1972. *A Letter to Pimen, Patriarch of All Russia.* Minneapolis: Burgess.

Sonin, M. 1986. *Sotsialisticheskaia Disciplina Truda.* Moscow: Profizdat.

Sonin, M., and A. Dyskin, 1984. *Pozhiloi Chelovek v Sem'ie i Obshchestve.* Moscow: Finansy i Statistika.

Sperber. Y. 1985. "State and Civil Society in Prussia." *Journal of Modern History* 57 (2):278–96.

Staroverov, V. (ed.). 1979. *Trud Kak Osnova Sotsialisticheskogo Obraza Zhizni.* Moscow: Institut Sotiologicheskikh Issledovanii.

Starr, F. 1983. *Red and Hot: The Fate of Jazz in the Soviet Union, 1917–1980.* New York: Oxford University Press.

Stavitskii, A. 1986. "Ulitsa Sholom-Aleikhema, 40." *Teatr* 7:28–51.

Stepanian, Z. (ed.). 1983. *Sovetskaia Intelligentsiia i Ieie Rol' v Stroitel'stve Kommunisma.* Moscow: Nauka.

Stites, R. 1978. *The Women's Liberation Movement in Russia.* Princeton: Princeton University Press.

Strelianyi, A. 1984. *V Gostiakh u Materi: Ocherki.* Moscow: Sovietskii Pisatel'.

Striganov, V. 1981. *Sotsiologiia Kul'tury.* Moscow: Nauchno-Issledovatel'skii Institut Kul'tury.

Strizhov, G. (ed.). 1984. *O Reforme Obshcheobrazovatel'noi i Professional'noi Shkoly.* Moscow: Politizdat.

Sullivan, W. 1982. *Reconstructing Public Philosophy.* Berkeley: University of California Press.

Sundiev, I. 1987. "Neformal'nye molodezhnye ob'edeniia: opyt ekspositsii." *Sotsiologicheskie Issledovaniia* 5:56–62.

Svininnikov, V. 1985. *Sotsialism i Svobodnoie Vremia. Pravo na Otdykh.* Moscow: Vysshaia Shkola.

Sychev, Iu. 1974. *Mikrosreda i Lichnost'.* Moscow: Mysl'.

Tarasov, K., and Iu. Kotunov. 1984. *Vsestoronniie Razvitiie Lichnosti v Usloviiakh Zrelogo Sotsialisma.* Moscow: Mysl'.

Tarasova, V. 1985. "Problemy Povysheniia Migratsionnoi Aktivnoshi Naseleniia." In *Sovremennyie Problemy Migratsii,* edited by L. Rybakovskii, pp. 47–63.

Terz, A. 1984. *Spokoinoi Nochi.* Paris: Syntaksis.

Tiano, S. 1984. "The Public-Private Dichotomy: Theoretical Perspectives on "Women in Development." *The Social Science Journal* 21 (4): October, 11–28.

Tiit, E. 1978. "Faktory vliiaushchiie na stabil'nost braka." In *Sem'i kak Sotsial'naia Problema*, edited by Z. Iankova. Moscow: Institut Sotsiologicheskikh Issledovanii.

Timush, T. 1978. *Slushateli i Chitateli.* Kishinev: Karta Moldoveniaskl.

Titarenko, A. (ed.). 1980. *Marksistkaia Etika.* Moscow: Politizdat.

Titma, M. (ed.). 1982. *Sotsial'nyie Peremeshcheniia v Studentchestve.* Vilnius: Institut Filosofii, Sotsiologii i Prava AN Litovskii SSR.

Titma, M. (ed.). 1981. *Sotsial'no-Professinal'naia Orientatsiia Studentchestva.* Vil'nius: Institut Filosofii, Sotsiologii i Prava AN Litovskii SSR.

Titma, M. (ed.). 1977. *Sotsial'no-professional'nai Orientatsia Molodezhi v Usloviiakh Razvitogo Sotsialisticheskogo Obshchestva.* Tallin: Institut Sotsiologicheskikh Issledovanii.

Titma, M. (ed.). 1973. *Sotsial'no-Professional'nai Orientatsia Molodezhi.* Tartu: Tartuskii Universitet.

Tocqueville, A. 1961. *Democracy in America.* London: Oxford University Press.

Tocqueville, A. 1955. *The Old Regime and the French Revolution.* Garden City, N.J.: Doubleday/Anchor.

Tokarovskii, G. 1976. "Pis'ma Trudiashchikhsia kak kanal vyrazheniia obshchestvennogo mneniia." In *Sotsiologicheskiie Problemy ObshchestVennogo Mneniia i Deiatel'nost' Sredstv Massovoi Informatsii*, edited by V. Korabeinikov, pp. 113–26. Moscow: Institut Sotsiologicheskikh Issledovanii.

Trifonov, Yu. 1983a. *Dom na Naberezhnoi.* Ann Arbor, Mich.: Ardis.

Trifonov, Yu. 1983b. *Izbrannoie.* Minsk: Vyshlishaia Shkola.

Trifonov, Yu. 1980. *Vremia i Mesto.* Postskriptum.

TsSU. 1986. *Narodnoe Khosiastvo SSSR v 1985g.* Moscow: Finansy i Statistika.

TsSU. 1985. *Narodnoie Khosiasatvo SSSR v 1984g.* Moscow: Finansy i Statistika.

TsSU. 1984a. *Chislennost' i Sostav Naseleniia SSSR.* Moscow: Finansy i Statistika.

TsSU. 1984b. *Narodnoie Khosiastvo SSSR v 1983g. Godu.* Moscow: Finansy i Statistika.

TsSU. 1982a. *Narodnoie Khosiastvo SSSR, 1922–1982.* Moscow: Finansy i Statistika.

TsSU. 1982b. *Zhenshchiny v SSSR.* Moscow: Finansy i Statistika.

TsSU. 1981. *Narodnoie Khosicestov SSSR v 1980g.* Moscow: Statistika.

TsSU. 1971. *Narodnoie Khosiastvo SSSR v 1970g.* Moscow: Statistika.

Tukumtsev, B. 1979. "Otnosheniie k trudu kak pokasatel' effektivnosti sotsialishcheskogo sorevnovaniia." In *Sotsiolisticheskii Trud*, edited by

I. Changli, pp. 103–15. Moscow: Institut Sotsiologicheskikh Issledovanii.

Tunnell, C. 1984. "The Discrepancy Between Private and Public Selves: Public Self-Consciousness and Its Correlates." *Journal of Personality Assessment*, 48, 5:549–55.

Turkel, G. 1980. "Privatism and Orientation Toward Political Action." *Urban Life* 9 (2):217–35.

Ulanovskaia, No. and M. Ulanovskaia. 1982. *Istoriia Odnoi Sem'i*. New York: Chaldize Publishers.

Ulybin, K. 1986. *Sovremennoie Ekonomicheskoie Myshleniie*. Moscow: Gospolitizdat.

Vail, B. 1980. *Osobo Opasnyi*. London: Overseas Publications.

Vaksberg, A. 1987. "Sud'ba prokurora." *Literaturnaia Gazeta*, October 28, 1987, p. 13.

Vasiliev, I. 1986. "Orientiry." *Nash Sovremennik* 6:3–27.

Vasilieva, E., I. Eliseeva, D. Kashina, and V. Laptev (eds.). 1980. *Dinamika Naseleniia SSSR 1960–1980 gg*. Moscow: Finansy i Statistika.

Vasilieva, E., A. Kinsburskii, and L. Kokliagina. 1987. "Otnoshenie studentov k obshchestvennym naukam." *Sotsiologicheskie Issledovaniia* 4:20–24.

Verkhovskaia, A. 1972. *Pis'mo v redaktsiiu i chitatel*. Moscow: Izdatel'stvo Moskovskogo Universitetia.

Vishnevskaia, G. 1984. *Galina*. New York: Random House.

Vishnevskii, A. 1982. *Vosproizvodstvo Naseleniia i Obshchestvo*. Moscow: Finansy i Statistika.

Vishnevskii, S., M. Rutkevich, and Z. Toshchenko (eds.). 1984. *Sotsialisticheskii Obraz Zhizni*. Moscow: Politizdat.

Vladimov, G. 1984. *Bol'shaia Ruda*. Frankfurt: Posev.

Vodzinskaia, V. 1967. "K voprosu o sotsial'noi obuslovlennosti professii." In *Chelovek i Obshchestvo* (Vol. 2). Leningrad: Nauka.

Voina, V. 1984. "Drug ili priiatel'." *Nedelia* 16:14.

Voinova, V. 1976. "Sobraniia v trudovykh kollektivakh i formirovaniie obshchestrennogo mneniia." In *Sotsiologicheskii Problemy Obshchestvennogo Mneniia i Deiatel'nost' Sredstv Massovoi Informatsii*, edited by V. Korabeinikov. Moscow: Institut Sotsiologicheskikh Issledovanii.

Voinova, V., and N. Chernakova. 1979. "Rol' sobranii obshchestvennykh organizatsii." In *Voprosy Sovershenstvovaniia Deiatelnosti Obshchestvenykh Organizatsii*, edited by N. Bokarev and A. Beliakov, pp. 61–93. Moscow: Institut Sotsiologicheskikh Issledovanii.

Voinova, V., and V. Korabeinikov. 1984. "Obshchestvennoie mneniie o reforme shkoly-edinstvo i mnogoobraziie." *Sotsiologicheskiie Issledovaniia* 4:97–101.

Voinova, V., and E. Petrov. 1975. "Ob izuchenii roli i mesta sobranii v zhizni trudovykh kollektivov." In *Sotsiologicheskiie Problemy Obshchestven-*

*nogo Mneniia*, edited by V. Korabeinikov, pp. 160–69. Moscow: Institut Sotsiologicheskikh Issledovanii.

Voinovich, V. 1985. *Antisovetskii Sovietskii Souz*. Ann Arbor, Mich.: Ardis.

Voinovich, V. 1963. "Khochu byt' chestnym." *Novy Mir*, 2.

Volgin, T., and K. Sidiakin, 1985. "Kak sokratit' poteri Rabochego Vremeni." *Sotsiologicheskiie Issledovaniia* 4:41–47.

Volkov, A. 1986. *Sem'ia-Ob'ekt Demografii*. Moscow: Finansy i Statistika.

Volkov, A., and G. Kozlova. 1984. "Brachnoie sostoaianiie Naseleniia i sostav semei v SSSR." In *Vsesouznaia Perepis' Naseleniia 1979 Goda*, edited by A. Isupov and N. Shwartzer. Moscow: Finansy i Statistika.

Volkov, F., and L. Novotnyi (Eds.). 1984. *Systema Kommunisticheskogo Vospitaniia Studentov v Uchebnom Prozesse*. Moscow: Moskovskii Universitet.

Volkov, I., and V. Mukhachev. 1976. "Aktivnost' rabochikh v sisteme upravleniia obshchestvennym proizvodstvom." In *Aktivnost' lichnosti v Sotsialisticheskom obshchestve*, edited by T. Iaroshevskii and N. Mansurov, pp. 3–27. Moscow: Nauka.

Volkov, M. (ed.). 1979. *Politicheskaia Economiia Slovar'*. Moscow: Politizdat.

Volkov, S. 1982. "Rok-musika v Sovietskom Souze." In *SSSR: Vnutrenniie Protivorechiia*, edited by V. Chalidze, Vol. 5, pp. 44–50. New York: Chalidze.

Voslenski, M. 1980. *La Nomenclature*. Paris: Pierre Belfon.

Yankelovich, D. 1974. *The New Morality: A Portrait of American Youth in the 70's*. New York: McGraw-Hill.

Young, F. (ed.). 1978. *Privacy*. Chichester, Eng.: John Wiley.

Zaionchkovskaia, Z. 1985. "Zachem i kak prognozirovat' migratsiiu." In *Poisk Vedut Demografy*, edited by E. Vasil'eva, pp. 88–96. Moscow: Mysl'.

Zaionchkovskaia, Z. 1972. *Novosely v Gorodakh*. Moscow: Statistika.

Zalygin, S. 1966. *Tropy Altaia. Na Irtyshe. Rasskazy*. Moscow: Khudozhestvennaia Literatura.

Zaslavskaia, T. 1986a. "Reshaushchiie usloviie uskoreniia sotsial'no-ekonomicheskogo razvitiia." *Eko* 3:3–25.

Zaslavskaia, T. 1986b. "Chelovecheskii faktor razvitiia ekonomiki i sotssila'naia spravedlivost'." *Kommuist* 3:61–73.

Zaslavskaia, T. 1985. "Ekonomika Skvoz' prizmu Sotsiologii." *Eko* 7:3–22.

Zaslavaksia, T. 1984. Paper to a Moscow seminar. *Russia* 9:27–42.

Zaslavskaia, T. (ed.). 1970. *Migratsiia Sel'skogo Naseleniia*. Moscow: Mysl'.

Zaslavskaia, T., and V. Kalmyk. (eds.). 1976. *Sibirskaia Derevnia v Usloviiakh Urbanizatsii*. Novosibirsk: Institut Ekonomiki.

Zaslavskaia, T., and V. Kalmyk (eds.). 1976. *Sotsiologicheskie Issledovaniia Sibirskoi Derevni*. Novosibirsk: Institut Ekonomiki.

Zaslavskaia, T., and V. Kalmyk (eds.). 1975. *Sovremennaia Sibirskaia Derevnia*, vols. 1 and 2. Novosibirsk: Nauka.

Zaslavskaia, T., and V. Kalmyk (eds.). 1972. *Sotsial'no-ekonomicheskoe Razvitie Sela i Migratsiia Naseleniia.* Novosibirsk: Nauka.

Zaslavskaia, T., V. Kalmykh, U. Khakhulina, and A. Khakhulin. 1986. "Problemy sotsial'nogo razvitiia Sibiri i puti ikh resheniia" *Izvestiia Sibirskogo Otdeleniia Akademii Nauk SSSR. Seriia Ekonomiki i Prikladnoi Sotsiologii", 1*, vol. 1. pp. 36–45.

Zaslavskaia, T., and R. Ryvkina (eds.). 1980. *Metodologiia i metodika sistemnogo izucheniia derevni.* Novosibirsk: Nauka.

Zaslavskaia, T., and R. Ryvkina (eds.). 1977. *Metodologicheskie Problemy Sistemnogo Izucheniia Derevni.* Novosibirsk: Nauka.

Zaslavskaia, T., and R. Ryvkina (eds.). 1975. *Problemy Sistemnogo Izucheniia Derevni.* Novosibirsk: Nauka.

Zaslavsky, V. 1979. "The Problem of Legitimation in Soviet Society." In *Conflict and Control: Challenges to the Legitimacy of Modern Governments*, edited by A. Vidich and R. Glassman. Beverly Hills: Sage.

Zatsepin, V. 1981. *Shchast'ie kak Problema Sotsial'noi Psikhologii.* Lvov: Vysshaia Shkola.

Zdravomyslov, S. 1981. *Nravstvennaia Tsennost' Truda pri Sotsialisme.* Moscow: Politizdat.

Zhelezko, S. 1980. *Sotsiol'no-ekonomicheskie Problemy v Raione BAMa.* Moscow: Statistika.

Zhukhovitskii, C. 1986. "Tsena liubvi." *Novy Mir* 8:180–97.

Zhuravkov, M. 1974. *Sotsializm i Moral.* Moscow: Nauka.

Zinin, V., and I. Diskin. (eds.). 1985. *Kul'tura i Sredstva Massovoi Informatsii: Sotsial'no-ekonomicheskie Problemy.* Moscow: Ekonomika.

Zinoviev, A. 1978. *Svetloe Budushchee.* Lausanne: L'age d'homme.

Zuzin, D. 1978. *Kachestvo Podgotovki Spetsialistov Kak Sotsial'naia Problema.* Moscow: Nauka.

# Author Index

# Subject Index